THE BOOK OF WAGNER & GRISWOLD

MARTIN ◊ LODGE ◊ VOLLRATH ◊ EXCELSIOR

David G. Smith

Chuck Wafford

4880 Lower Valley Road, Atglen, PA 19310 USA

DEDICATION

We dedicate this book to our wives, Catherine Smith and Rita Wafford, in recognition of their tremendous support and sacrifices they made while we were working on this, and our previous book. We couldn't have done it without them.

Copyright © 2001 by David G. Smith and Chuck Wafford
Library of Congress Card Number: 00-105182

All rights reserved. No part of this work may be reproduced or used in any form or by any means—graphic, electronic, or mechanical, including photocopying or information storage and retrieval systems—without written permission from the copyright holder. "Schiffer," "Schiffer Publishung Ltd. & Design," and the "Design of pen and ink well" are registered trademarks of Schiffer Publishing, Ltd.

Designed by Bonnie M. Hensley
Typeset in Humanst521 BT/ Souvenir Lt BT

ISBN: 0-7643-1191-3
Printed in China
1 2 3 4

Published by Schiffer Publishing Ltd.
4880 Lower Valley Road
Atglen, PA 19310
Phone: (610) 593-1777; Fax: (610) 593-2002
E-mail: Schifferbk@aol.com
Please visit our web site catalog at
www.schifferbooks.com

In Europe, Schiffer books are distributed by Bushwood Books
6 Marksbury Avenue Kew Gardens
Surrey TW9 4JF England
Phone: 44 (0) 20-8392-8585; Fax: 44 (0) 20-8392-9876
E-mail: Bushwd@aol.com
Free postage in the UK. Europe: air mail at cost.

This book may be purchased from the publisher.
Include $3.95 for shipping. Please try your bookstore first.
We are always looking for people to write books on new and related subjects.
If you have an idea for a book please contact us at the above address.
You may write for a free catalog.

CONTENTS

ACKNOWLEDGMENTS 4

INTRODUCTION 5

How To Use This Book 5

PART 1 - THE WAGNER MANUFACTURING CO.

History 7
Skillets 9
Skillet Covers 31
Omelet & Sauce Pans 35
Griddles 42
Dutch Ovens & Oval Roasters 49
Kettles & Cookers 59
Tea Kettles, Coffee Pots & Pitchers 65
Waffle Irons 73
Display Stands 77
Baking Pans, Muffin/Gem Pans & Cake Molds ... 79
Toys, Miniatures & Child's Dishes 86
Scoops, Spoons, Ladles & Spades 91
Casseroles, Servers, Platters, Trays, Cups & Dishes .. 98
Molds & Forms 106
Miscellaneous 108
Color 113
Catalog Number List 120

PART 2 - THE GRISWOLD MANUFACTURING CO.

History 125
Skillets & Sauce Pans 128
Griddles 141
Dutch Ovens & Oval Roasters 147
Kettles 152
Tea Kettles, Coffee Pots, Tea Pots, & Pitchers ... 157
Waffle Irons 158
Muffin - Gem Pans 162
Toys & Miniatures 164
Serving Pieces, Casseroles & Patty Bowls 166
Food Choppers 170
Stove & Heaters 171
Stove Pipe Dampers & Slid Lifters 176
Miscellaneous 179
Color 184

Pattern Number List 192

PART 3 - THE KING STOVE & RANGE CO. & THE MARTIN STOVE & RANGE CO.

History 202
Skillets & Sauce Pans 203
Griddles 210
Dutch Ovens & Kettles 212
Gem Pans 214
Toys & Miniatures 215
Stoves & Miscellaneous 216

PART 4 - THE LODGE MANUFACTURING CO.

History 220
Skillets & Skillet Covers 222
Griddles & Long Pans 231
Dutch Ovens, Oval Roasters & Waffle Irons ... 232
Gem Pans, Muffin Pans & Cake Molds 234
Kettles & Tea Kettles 238
Sad Irons 239
Miscellaneous 239

PART 5 - THE VOLLRATH MANUFACTURING CO.

History 240
Skillets & Griddles 242
Dutch Ovens & Kettles 244

PART 6 - THE EXCELSIOR MANUFACTURING CO.

History 247
Gem Pans 249
Skillets 252
Dutch Ovens 252
Waffle Irons 253
Stoves 253
Toys 254

BIBLIOGRAPHY 255

INDEX 255

ACKNOWLEDGMENTS

We would like to thank our contributors who shared their knowledge, information and items to photograph:

Roger Auschenback-Canal Pattern, Doug Brown, Laura Griswold Clacino, Myfa Cirinna, Dennis Clayton, Michael Cook, Norbert DeMarge, William Dilbone, Gregory Draper, Raymond Fugene, Jim & Donna Gaylord, Janet Eshleman, Judy K. Fogt, Emma Grillio, Margaret Helmlinger, Dellmar & Dorothy Hess, Robert Karle, Steve King, Lynn Gearns, Leonard Lange, Doug Millhof, Don Mitchell, John & Donna Myers, Glenn Pehle, Paul Robinson, Patricia Sale, Joel Schiff, Howard Seifert, Ty Stewart, Julie Stueve, Jeff Tatro, Jerome Wagner Jr., Richard Wallace, Alex Wanner, Loren Watkins, Jan Weigandt, Diana Westerheide, Margarette Weihandt.

A Special thanks to Ken & Mary Burris, Larry & Sue Foxx, Debbie & Gary Franzen, Dan & Peg Sparks, Richard and Valera Slonkosky, and W. Dean and Patty Fitzwater, for their gracious hospitality, inviting us into their homes to photograph their collections. Also a special thanks to the Lodge Manufacturing Company, The Vollrath Company, and the Wagner Corporation for providing valuable information about their history and products.

INTRODUCTION

Collecting cast iron cookware and related items is steadily growing as more collectors are scouring antique shops, shows, and flea markets searching for treasures to add to their collections. In addition to adding pieces to their collections, collectors are seeking more information about the products and history of its manufacturers.

Five years ago, in response to that demand, the well researched, *The Book of Griswold & Wagner* was published. Immediately it was heralded as the most complete book available about this subject on the market. Because the subject was so enormous and complex, it was only a short time after that publication, that readers were asking, what about this piece or what about that? There were pieces that were not listed in the book. We also discovered that in our efforts to complete a collection of the finest pieces, we had overlooked many of the more common ones. Therefore, within a year after the publication of *The Book of Griswold & Wagner*, we began compiling data and taking pictures in preparation for a sequel.

This book continues from where *The Book of Griswold & Wagner* left off—illustrating hundreds of items not included in that book. Also, it should be stated very clearly, **this book contains less than five percent duplication** of *The Book of Griswold & Wagner*. This book has the same basic format as *The Book of Griswold & Wagner* therefore making it seem familiar and comfortable to use.

We had anticipated this compilation would take three years to complete. In our diligent search for more, it has now been five years. Even as we were completing this work, previously unseen pieces presented themselves. However, as the publisher stated to us, "You have to stop somewhere so we can get this book to print!"

Although this book will certainly stand alone, for those who want more complete information, particularly about Griswold or Wagner, should acquire *The Book of Griswold & Wagner*. Together, these books combine to complete, without question, the most thorough and complete reference for Griswold, Wagner, and the majority of the other major companies whose products are so sought after by collectors.

HOW TO USE THIS BOOK

VALUES

Values are for items in excellent condition, with no rust, chips or cracks. Values in this book are also based on current selling prices. Values are not based on auction, or asking prices, but are based on current retail sales. Values may vary however, in different geographical locations. Values indicated in this book are to be used as a guide; they are not intended to set prices. Neither the authors nor the publisher assumes responsibility for any losses that might be incurred as a result of consulting this text.

ABBREVIATIONS & EXPLANATIONS

p/n:	pattern number
c/n.:	Catalog Number
Circa or c.	time period of manufacture based on actual records, markings, or characteristics.
EPU	Erie, PA. U.S.A.
Logo	Trademark
TM	Trademark
Large Block:	3 1/4"+ diameter
Medium Logo:	2 1/4" - 2 1/2" diameter
Small Logo:	1 7/8" diameter
Value:	retail market value of items in EXCELLENT CONDITION, year 2000.
h, w, d, l.	high, wide, deep, long
dia.	diameter
pos.	position
struck	stamped by striking, verses cast in
Stylized Logo:	Single 'W' Wagner Ware trademark since 1915.

Where possible, the name used for the item is authentic to the period.

GRISWOLD FINISHES

IRON:
1) **Extra Finish Ware**—had a polished interior and in some cases they buffed the top of the handles.
2) **Plain iron**—unpolished.
3) **Hammered**
4) **Nickel-plated**—available from the late 1800s until about 1930.
5) **Chromium**—There were three chromium finishes introduced around 1932:
— *Chrome*: a highly polished finish.
— *Silverlike*: an unpolished, flat chromium finish.
— *Du Chro*: flat finish with polished highlights such as cover edges and handles.
6) **Porcelain**—There were three periods of enameling, or porcelainizing:
— 1930s, when they enameled skillets, skillet covers, and Dutch ovens. In this period the four colors were Mandarin Red, Canary Yellow, Jade Green, and Turquoise Blue;
— 1940s & 1950s, when a whole line of porcelain ware was introduced which included skillets, No. 3 Oval Roaster, Dutch ovens, and casserole sets. The most common colors were Flamingo Red with Cream, Buttercup Yellow with Dove Gray interiors, and plain iron with white porcelain interior, called Quaker Ware. There was also a black number 2598 hinged skillet and cover. The cover was black inside and outside, the skillet outside only. This was available in 1942. A few other color combinations have shown up from that time period.
— 1960s, when multi-colored and speckled design ashtrays were made. These pieces were marketed from Sidney, Ohio.

ALUMINUM:
1) **"ERIE"** line was introduced in the early 1890s.
2) **Polished**—highly polished outside with wood handles, 1940s.
3) **Hammercast**—hammered finish outside, 1940s.
4) **Aristocraft**—new modern artistic design, 1940s-1950s.

WAGNER FINISHES

IRON:
1) **Polished, Extra Finished, Delux**—polished interior, c.1884-1950s.
2) **Nickel-plated**, c. 1894-1920s.
3) **Chrome-plated**, c. 1940s-1950s.
3) **Porcelain**—Speckled, multi-colored ashtrays, c. 1960s.

ALUMINUM:
1) **Regular line**—introduced in the mid 1890s.
2) **Magnalite**—late 1930s-1970s. The logo then included GHC or General Housewares Corporation.

THE WAGNER MANUFACTURING COMPANY

Sidney, Ohio

Mathias Wagner was born in Stundweiller, Germany, on April 8, 1818. When Mathias was twelve years old, he and his parents immigrated to the United States and settled near Pittsburg, Pennsylvania, where Mathias worked in a tobacco factory. In 1837, at the age of nineteen, Mathias moved to Sidney, Ohio and began working on the construction of the Miami and Erie Canal. Around the same time he began a butchering business, selling the meat to canal workers. With his profits, he bought property around Sidney, which ultimately led him to become Sidney's wealthiest citizen.

In 1846 Mathias Wagner married Anna M. Rauth, who had immigrated from Bavaria with her parents. Their marriage produced eight children.

In 1891, their two sons Milton M. and Bernard P. Wagner organized a partnership, forming the Wagner Manufacturing Company in Sidney, Ohio on July 21. Another son, William H. Wagner, owned hardware stores in Columbus and Sidney, Ohio. William's store in Sidney was located adjacent to the Arcade department store, a family-owned business started by Mathias Wagner. William closed the Columbus store, allowing him to run the hardware store in Sidney while sharing management of the Arcade with his younger brother, Louis R. Wagner.

As the Wagner Manufacturing Company became more successful, William decided he wanted to join the company. To accommodate his move to the company (around 1897), Milton and Bernard decided to put out a second line of skillets to sell to jobbers and distributors. They purchased the Sidney Hollow Ware Foundry from Philip Smith, putting William H. Wagner in charge.

Around 1903, the family realized that the Sidney Hollow Ware Company (managed by William) was undercutting the sales of hollow wares produced by the Wagner parent company. Consequently, Milton and Bernard sold the Sidney Hollow Ware foundry back to Philip Smith, and brought William H. into the partnership of the Wagner Manufacturing Company. Because William was the oldest brother, he assumed the position of president. Shortly after, Louis "LR" Wagner left the Arcade (in which he had a 50% interest) to join the Wagner Manufacturing Company as Secretary and General Manager. Louis also became a director in the Wagner Hotel Company and the Wagner Realty Company.

In addition to hollow ware, the Wagner Manufacturing Company made brass castings, and installed nickel plating baths for the manufacture of the cash register and calculator they held patents for. Commercial small manufacture of these never materialized however, because they sold the patents to the Osgood Cash Register Company of Detroit, Michigan, a buying front for the National Cash Register Company.

The original Wagner shop was small, consisting of two buildings and employing twenty men. R.O. Bingham, who had been a molder and machinist, was hired as their superintendent and was responsible for designing and building the factory.

The company started with the production of cast iron hollow ware, and introduced nickel-plated hollow ware to their line in 1892. This was followed in 1894 by cast aluminum ware.

By 1913 the plant had grown to employ three hundred men. Eighty-three molders worked in the 110' x 450' foundry building, one of the many buildings in the rapidly expanding factory complex.

Wagner continued to produce cast iron items but their production was expanded to include aluminum utensils. The Wagner firm made a radical improvement in "aluminum cookware," as it was known, and braved the market with a line of seamless cast aluminum ware of heavier weight. Wagner's initiative was so successful that their aluminum line virtually exploded into the market during the first quarter of the twentieth century. They produced a huge line of aluminum ware, including cake and ice cream molds, spoons, scoops, coffee pots and percolators, tea pots, and pitchers. Wagner's aluminum won honors at the Chicago, Nashville, Paris, Buffalo, and St. Louis Expositions. At the San Francisco Exposition, Wagner Ware captured the Grand Prize, acknowledging it as the finest aluminum ware on the world market.

Bernard P. Wagner died in 1923, leaving his twenty-five percent of the Wagner stock to his wife. His son, Jerome Wagner, Sr., took his position as Vice President. Subsequently, Jerome's mother transferred what had been his father's stock to Jerome.

In 1929, William H. Wagner died at the age of 74. Milton Wagner moved from his position as Treasurer to President. Louis "LR" Wagner advanced from Secretary to Treasurer. Cable Wagner, William's son who had been hired as a teenager, replaced "LR" as Secretary.

Milton M. Wagner died at the age of 78 in 1940, leaving his quarter of the Wagner stock to his sons, Philip and Joseph. Philip Wagner was named as President, replacing his father.

Louis "LR" Wagner left the company in 1946, selling his stock to Philip and Joseph. Joseph Wagner joined his brother Philip in the company, replacing "LR" as Treasurer.

In 1953, Philip Wagner, then President, let it be known that he wanted to retire and sell off his stock in the company. He had been successful in other investments, and was tired of working. He liked Florida, and wanted to move there. Jerome Wagner did not want to invest any more in the company. Joseph wanted to stay but he also didn't want to invest. Cable decided to purchase the Wagner Hotel Company. After considerable financial negotiations, the Wagner Manufacturing Company was acquired by the Randall Company of Cincinnati, Ohio, a company connected with the automotive industry. Under the agreement, Jerome Wagner stayed on as an advisor for six months, and Joseph Wagner remained as General Manager.

Under Randall, in October of 1957 the Wagner Division purchased the Griswold Cookware Line from McGraw Edison, which had purchased all of the assets of the Griswold Manufacturing Company of Erie, Pennsylvania. In the purchase, Wagner acquired the patent and trademark rights, patterns, and existing inventory of the Griswold Cookware line.

In 1959, the Randall Company, including the Wagner Ware division, was acquired by Textron Incorporated of Providence, Rhode Island. Joe Wagner remained as General Manager until December 29, 1965, when he reached his sixty-fifth birthday and mandatory retirement age for Textron. He remained another three years, however, as a consultant.

Under Randall-Division of Textron, the Wagner Division acquired the Durham Manufacturing Company of Muncie, Indiana. They were a manufacturer of casual leisure furniture for household use, such as card tables and chairs, baby highchairs and playpens, and mailboxes.

In September of 1969, Textron Incorporated sold the household line to the General Housewares Corporation, a holding company. With the sale went all patent and trademark rights for both Wagner Ware and Griswold.

In the spring of 1997, the General Housewares Corporation sold the Wagner factory to a group of investors, incorporated as, The Wagner Corporation. Two years later, the factory closed for their July break and didn't reopen.

Wagner Ware factory workers; circa unknown. If you can identify any of these workers, contact the authors through Schiffer Publishing.

SKILLETS

Old King Cole Incorporated Canton, Ohio

"WAGNER"
c. 1891-1910

No. 6	$30
No. 7	$30
No. 8	$25
No. 9	$25
No. 10	$40
No. 11	$110-$140
No. 12	$95-$110

"WAGNER" (arc), SIDNEY, 0
c. 1900-1915

No. 5	$20-$30
No. 6	$20-$30
No. 6	$25-$30
No. 7	$25-$30
No. 8	$25-$30
No. 9	$35-$40
No. 10	$60-$75
No. 11	$100-$125
No. 12	$85-$125

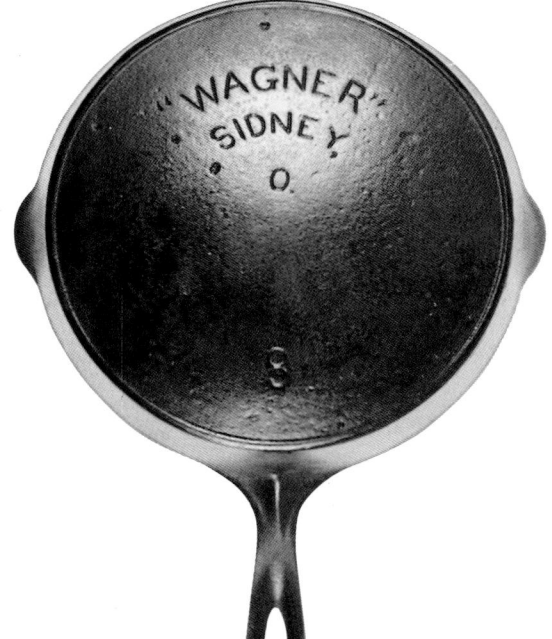

"WAGNER" (arc), SIDNEY, (arc), 0
c.1895-1915

No. 5	$20-$30
No. 6	$20-$30
No. 7	$25-$30
No. 8	$25-$30
No. 9	$35-$40
No. 10	$60-$75
No. 11	$100-$125
No. 12	$85-$100

"SIDNEY" (arc)
c.1905-1910

No. 6	$30-$45	
	No. 7	$30
	No. 8	$30
	No. 9	$40
	No. 10	$60-$75

SIDNEY (center)
c.1910-1929

No. 2	$150-$175		No. 5	$30-$40
No. 3	$30-$40		No. 6	$30-$40
No. 5	$30-$40		No. 7	$25-$35
			No. 8	$25-$35
			No. 9	$40-$50
			No. 10	$45-$60

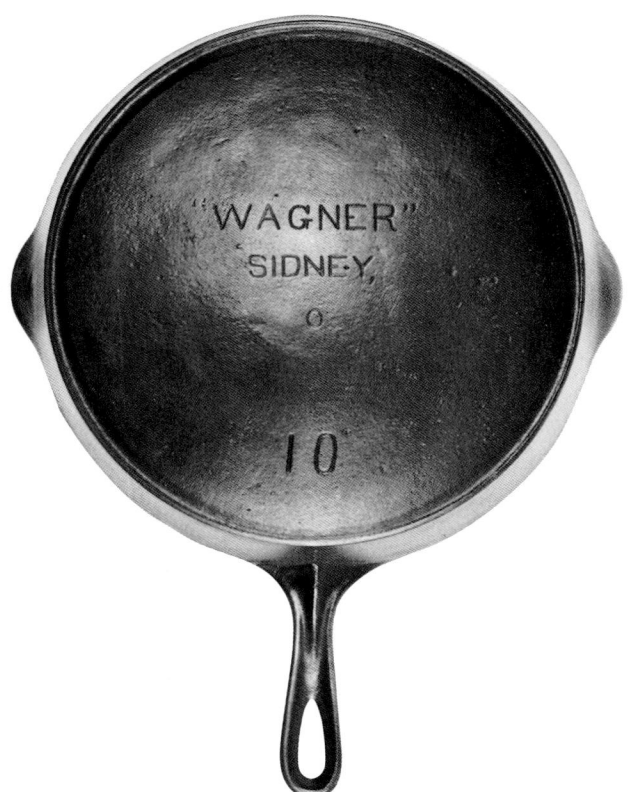

"WAGNER," SIDNEY, O
c. 1910-1915

No. 7	$30
No. 8	$25
No. 9	$35
No. 10	$45-$60

"WAGNER" (with star)
c.1910-1930s

No. 7	$40
No. 8	$40
No. 9	$40-$50

"WAGNER (arc), SIDNEY, O (high position.)
c. 1915-1920s

No. 5 $25
No. 6 $25
No. 7 $30
No. 8 $30
No. 9 $30-$40
No. 10 $60
No. 11 $110-$125
No. 12 $80-$100

Pie logo
c. 1915-1934

No. 2 $250-$300
No. 3 $10-$15
No. 4 $100-$125
No. 5 $20-$30
No. 6 $60-$70
No. 7 $50-$60
No. 8 $50-$60
No. 9 $60-$75
No. 10 $75-$100
No. 11 $200-$250
No. 12 $150-$200
No. 13 $500-$600
No. 14 $350-$450

Stylized logo, size no., Wood Handle c. 1914-1924

No. 3 $30-$40
No. 4 $75-$85
No. 5 $30-$40
No. 6 $35-$45
No. 7 $40-$50
No. 8 $50-$60
No. 9 $45-$60
No. 10 $60-$75

D, "SIDNEY" (also came with B)
c. 1920s

No. 7 $50-$50
No. 8 $40-$50
No. 9 $40-$50

"WAGNER" (arc), SIDNEY, O., with c/n
c.1923-1930s

No. 2	$100-$125	No. 8	$25-$30
No. 3	$20-$30	No. 9	$30-$40
No. 4	$60-$75	No. 10	$40-$60
No. 5	$24-$30	No. 11	$100-$150
No. 6	$25-$35	No. 12	$75-$100
No. 7	$25-$30		

Stylized logo (center position), with c/n.
c. 1920-1935

No. 2 $100-$125
No. 3 $10-$15
No. 4 $40-$60
No. 5 $15-$20
No. 6 $15-$20
No. 7 $20-$30
No. 8 $20-$25
No. 9 $25-$35
No. 10 $40-$50
No. 11 $125-$150
No. 12 $75-$100
No. 13 $200-$225
No. 14 $100-$125

Stylized logo (center position), with size no.
c. 1922-1930s

No. 11	$100-$125
No. 12	$75-$100
No. 13	$200-$250
No. 14	$125-$200

Stylized logo, with c/n, (OHR)
c. 1924

No. 2	$100-$125
No. 3	$10-$15
No. 4	$40-$60
No. 5	$15-$20
No. 6	$20-$30
No. 7	$20-$30
No. 8	$25-$30
No. 9	$25-$35
No. 10	$40-$50
No. 11	$100-$125
No. 12	$75-$100
No. 13	$225-$250
No. 14	$100-$125

Stylized logo, with size No.
c. 1925-1930

No. 2	$100-$125
No. 3	$10-$15
No. 4	$40-$60
No. 5	$20-$30
No. 6	$20-$30
No. 7	$25-$35
No. 8	$20-$30
No. 9	$30-$40
No. 10	$60-$75
No. 11	$100-$150
No. 12	$75-$100
No. 13	$200-$250
No. 14	$125-$150

Stylized logo, (smooth btm)
c. 1935-1959

No. 2	$125-$150
No. 3	$10
No. 4	$40-$60
No. 5	$15-$20
No. 6	$15-$20
No. 7	$50-$60
No. 8	$20-$25
No. 9	$100-$125
no. 10	$40-$50
No. 11	$75-$100
No. 12	$50-$60
No. 13	$200-$250
No. 14	$125-$150

NATIONAL (small letters) with size no.
c. 1914-1920

No. 7	$45-$60
No. 8	$45-$60
No. 9	$40-$50

NATIONAL with Star
c. 1914-1920s

No. 7	$50-$60
No. 8	$50-$60
No. 9	$50-$60s

NATIONAL (center arc) with size no.
c. 1914-1920s

No. 7 $45-$60
No. 8 $45-$60
No. 9 $40-$50

NATIONAL, Stylized logo with size no.
c. 1930s

No. 7 $40-$60
No. 8 $30-$40
No. 9 $40-$60

NATIONAL (upper arc), with size no.
c.1920s-1930s

No. 7 $40-$60
No. 8 $40-$60
No. 9 $40-$50

NATIONAL, Stylized logo with c/n
c. 1930-1940s

No. 6	$50-$65
No. 7	$45-$60
No. 8	$45-$60
No. 9	$50-$60

NATIONAL (small letter), stylized logo with c/n
c. 1930-1940s

No. 6	$50-$65
No. 7	$45-$60
No. 8	$45-$60
No. 9	$50-$60

WOOD HANDLE SKILLET-Size: No.7, 9 7/16" dia. x 2 1/8" deep; **c/n**: none; **Markings**: "WAGNER"; **Finish**: aluminum; **Circa**: 1897; **VALUE: $45-$50; No.8, $40-$50; No.9. $55-$65**.

REGULAR SKILLET-**Size**: No.7; **c/n**: none; **Markings**: "WAGNER" SIDNEY, 0; **Finish**: iron; **Circa**: 1924; **VALUE: $40-$50**. "A" at 3 o'clock position is an interesting variation. This variation is also seen in skillets marked "WAGNER" only.

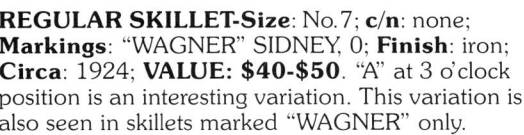

REGULAR SKILLET WITH COVER-**Size**: No.7; **c/n**: none, (cover) 1067; **Markings**: "WAGNER," SIDNEY O., 7B, (cover) DRIP DROP NO.7. SKILLET COVER, 1067; **Finish**: iron; **Circa**: 1920s; **VALUE: Skillet, $30; Cover, $50**. The nickel knob on a skillet cover is unusual. This knob was typical on Dutch ovens, circa. 1915.

WOOD HANDLE SKILLET-**Size**: No.3, 6 3/8" dia.; **c/n**: 503; **Markings**: stylized logo, 503, B; **Finish**: aluminum; **Circa**: 1915-1923; **VALUE: $20-$30**.

WOOD HANDLE SKILLET-**Size**: No.3; **c/n**: none; **Markings**: stylized logo, 3A; **Finish**: aluminum; **Circa**: 1920s; **VALUE: $30-$40**.

WOOD HANDLE SKILLET-Size: 10 inch; **c/n**: 578; **Markings**: stylized logo, NATIONAL ALUMINUM SKILLET, 578, PAT APL'D FOR, 10"H; **Finish**: aluminum; **Circa**: 1920s; **VALUE: $50-$60**.

FRYING PAN-Size: No.0, 6 1/4" dia; **c/n**: 520; **Markings**: stylized logo, FRYING PAN, 0; **Finish**: aluminum; **Circa**: 1920s; **VALUE: $55-$65**; No.1, 6 1/2", $35-$45; No.2, 7 1/2", $35-$45; No.3, 9 1/2", $35-$45; No.4, 11", $50-$60.

FRYING PAN-Size: No.1, 6 1/2" dia.; **c/n**: none; **Markings**: stylized logo, 1; **Finish**: aluminum; **Circa**: 1915; **VALUE: $35-$45**; No.2, $35-$45; No.3, $35-$45; No.4, $50-$60.

REGULAR SKILLET-Size: No.13; **c/n**: 1063; **Markings**: stylized logo; **Finish**: iron; **Circa**: 1920s; **VALUE: $250-$300**.

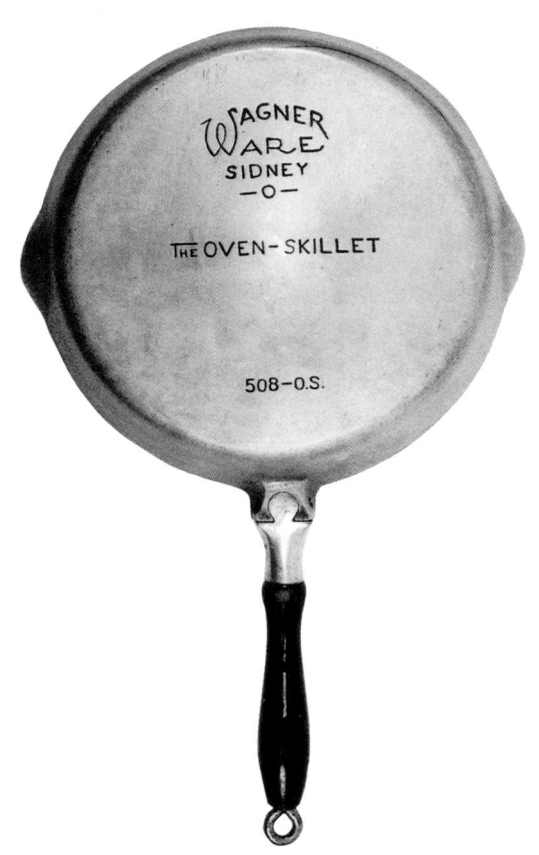

REGULAR SKILLET-Size: No.13; **c/n**: 1063; **Markings**: pie logo, 1063, CAST IRON SKILLET; **Finish**: iron; **Circa**: 1920s; **VALUE: $500-$600.**

OVEN SKILLET-Size: 10 3/8" dia. x 2" deep; **c/n**: 508 OS; **Markings**: stylized logo, THE OVEN SKILLET, 508-OS; **Finish**: aluminum; **Circa**: 1930s; **VALUE: $50-$60**. Note removable handle.

WOOD HANDLE SKILLET-Size: No.3; **c/n**: 3503; **Markings**: stylized logo, 3503; **Finish**: hammered aluminum; **Circa**: 1930s; **VALUE: $30-$40.**

REGULAR SKILLET-Size: No.3; **c/n**: H.S. 1053; **Markings**: stylized logo, H.A. 1053; **Finish**: hammered chrome; **Circa**: 1940s; **VALUE: $15**.

REGULAR SKILLET-Size: No.3; **c/n**: none; **Markings**: none; **Finish**: hammered iron; **Circa**: 1940s; **VALUE: $10**. Note dot on handle is the same as the marked skillet.

WARDS SKILLET-Size: No.4, 8 1/8" dia.; **c/n**: 1430; **Markings**: WARDS CAST IRON, MONTGOMERY WARD, 1430; **Finish**: iron; **Circa**: 1930s; **VALUE: $40-$50**; No.3, $20-$30; No.6, $20-$30; No.7, $25-$35; No.8, $20-$25.

SKILLET WITH HEAT REGULATOR-Size: No.13; **c/n**: 1063, (Heat Regulator) none; **Markings**: stylized logo, 1063, (Heat Regulator) not marked; **Finish**: iron; **Circa**: unknown; **VALUE: $200-$250; Heat Regulator, $100**. Raised edges of Heat Regulator fit the skillet heat ring perfectly.

CHEF SKILLET-Size: 11 1/4" dia.; **c/n**: 1389; **Markings**: stylized logo, 1389; **Finish**: iron; **Circa**: 1930s; **VALUE: $85-$100; 1386, $40-$60; 1384 $40-$40**. Note the regular skillet handle. These are much more difficult to find than the flared handle with thumb rest.

Advertisement for Chef Skillets, c. 1930s

CHEF SKILLET-Size: 10 inch; **c/n**: 1388; **Markings**: stylized logo, CHEF SKILLET, 10 INCH, 1388; **Finish**: iron; **Circa**: 1940-1050s; **VALUE: $40-$50; 9 inch, $30-$40; 11 inch, $50-$60**. Flared handle with thumb rest.

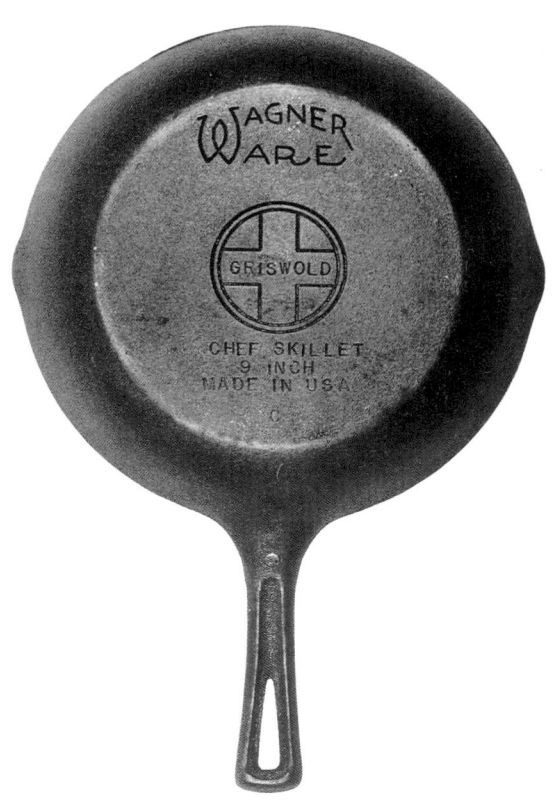

CORN BREAD SKILLET-Size: 9" dia.; **c/n**: none; **Markings**: double logo, MADE IN USA, B; **Finish**: iron; **Circa**: 1972; **VALUE: $20-$25**.

CHEF SKILLET-Size: 9 inch; **c/n**: none; **Markings**: double logo, CHEF SKILLET, 9 INCH, MADE IN U.S.A., C; **Finish**: iron; **Circa**: 1972; **VALUE: $15-$25**. Made by General House-wares Corp. According to a Wagner foundry foreman, the double logo was used for a year to phase out the Griswold logo.

SQUARE SKILLET-Size: 9 3/4" sq.; **c/n**: none; **Markings**: double logo, SQUARE SKILLET, MADE IN USA; **Finish**: iron; **Circa**: 1972; **VALUE: $15-$20**.

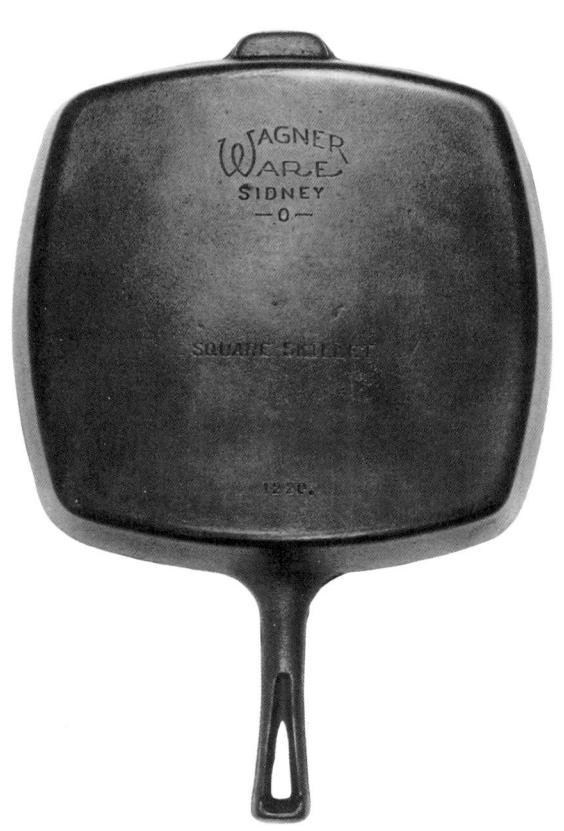

SQUARE SKILLET WITH COVER-Size: 9 5/8" sq.; **c/n**: 1218D, (cover) 1218; **Markings**: stylized logo, 1218D, (cover) 1218; **Finish**: iron; **Circa**: 1930s; **VALUE: $100-$125**; **Cover only $75**.

SQUARE SKILLET-Size: 11 1/4" sq. x 1 3/4" deep; **c/n**: 1220; **Markings**: stylized logo, SQUARE SKILLET, 1220; **Finish**: iron; **Circa**: 1960s; **VALUE: $45-$60; No.1218, $40-45**. The No.1218 does not have a tab opposite the handle.

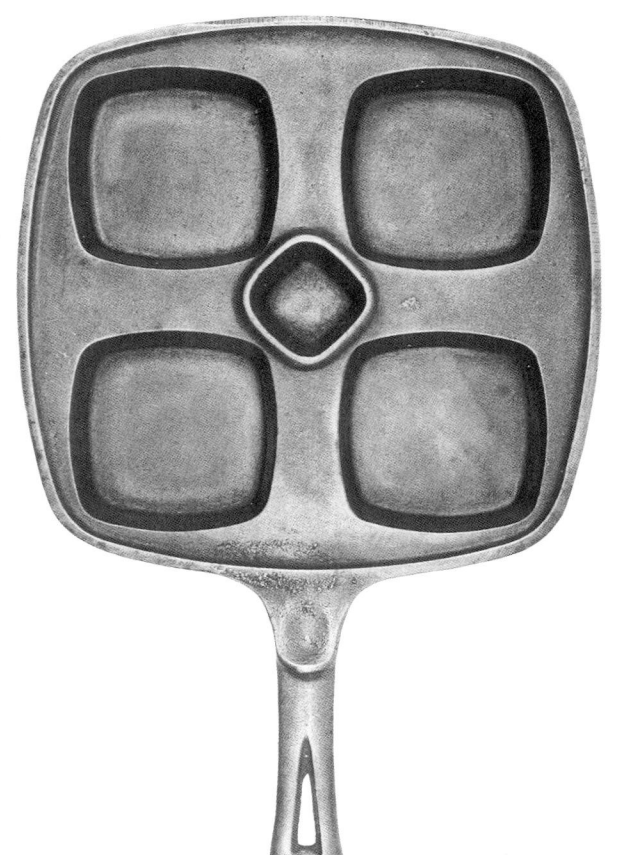

SQUARE SECTIONED SKILLET-SIZE: 9 5/8" sq.; **c/n**: none; **Markings**: none; **Finish**: iron; **Circa**: 1970s; **VALUE: $20-$25**. Sometimes called a Benedict pan. The center was used for basting.

BACON & EGG BREAKFAST SKILLET-Size: 9 1/8" x 9 5/16" x 1316" deep; **c/n**: 1101 A4; **Markings**: stylized logo, BACON & EGG BREAKFAST SKILLET 1101A4, PAT PENDING; **Finish**: iron; **Circa**: 1925; **VALUE: $30-$40 (skillet only)**.

BACON PRESS-Size: 4 3/16" x 7 11/16"; **c/n**: 1101A; **Markings**: WAGNER MFG. CO., SIDNEY O., 1101A; **Finish**: iron; **Circa**: 1925; **VALUE: $100-$150**.

SKILLET GRILL-Size: 9" dia.; **c/n**: 1126; **Markings**: stylized logo; **Finish**: iron; **Circa**: 1950s; **VALUE: $45-$60; No.1129, $60-$75**.

HOTEL SKILLET-Size: 18 1/4" dia. x 3 1/2" deep; **c/n**: 2166; **Markings**: stylized logo, 2166; **Finish**: aluminum; **Circa**: 1930s-1940s; **VALUE: $250-$300**.

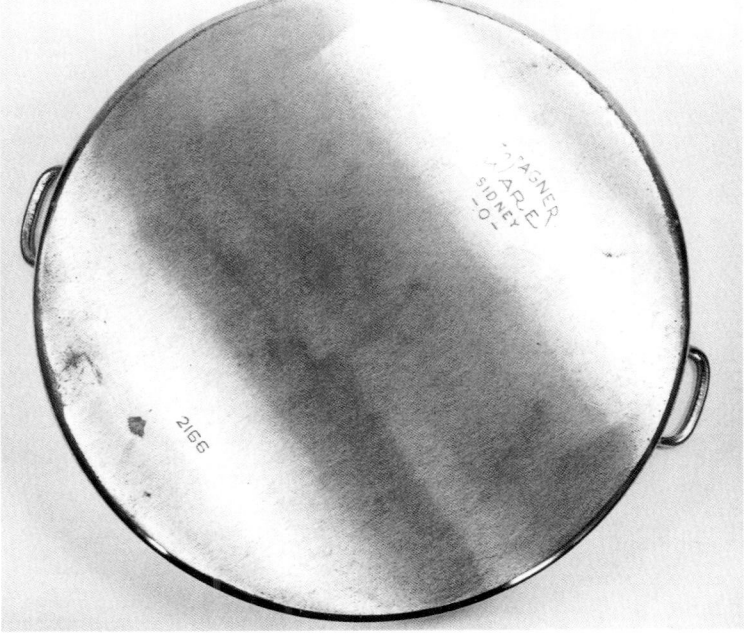

REGULAR SKILLET-Size: No.9, 11 3/4" dia.; **c/n**: none; **Markings**: stylized logo, GHC logo, GENERAL HOUSEWARES CORP., MADE IN USA; **Finish**: iron; **Circa**: 1990s; **VALUE**: $10-$20.

SIZZLE SERVER-Size: 7 3/8" x 15 1/2" including handle; **c/n**: 1095; **Markings**: stylized logo, SIZZLE SERVER 1095A; **Finish**: iron; **Circa**: 1960s; **VALUE**: $20-$25.s

REGULAR SKILLET-Size: 6 1/2" dia.; **c/n**: none; **Markings**: WAGNERS 1891 ORIGINAL, with seasoning instructions; **Finish**: iron; **Circa**: 1991-1995; **VALUE**: $10. This skillet and similar marked pieces were produced by the General House-wares Corp. to promote Wagner's 100th anniversary.

CHICKEN FRYER-Size: 19 1/2" dia. x 2 7/8" d.; **c/n:** 568; **Markings:** stylized logo, CHICKEN FRYER, 568M; **Finish:** aluminum; **Circa:** 1920s; **VALUE: $45-$55.** Round handle is earliest model.

COMMEMORATIVE SKILLET-Size: 8" dia. x 1 1/2" d.; **c/n**: none; **Markings:** WAGNER'S 1891 ORIGINAL, seasoning instructions, MAYFEST 93; **Finish:** iron; **Circa:** 1993; **VALUE: $20.** Mayfest is a celebration in Sidney, Ohio, home of Wagner.

COMMEMORATIVE SKILLET-Size: 8" dia.; **c/n**: none; **Markings:** stylized logo, MERRY CHRISTMAS 1995, GENERAL HOUSEWARES, 8 INCH SKILLET, MADE IN USA; **Finish:** iron; **Circa:** 1995; **VALUE: $75-$100.**

DEEP SKILLET-Size: 10 7/8" dia. x 3" d.; **c/n:** 1088; **Markings:** stylized logo, 1088; **Finish:** iron; **Circa:** 1950s; **VALUE: $25-$30;** (plated) $20-$25. Note tab opposite handle. The earlier version did not have this tab.

DEEP SKILLET-Size: 10 7/8" dia. x 3" d.; **c/n:** 1088; **Markings:** stylized logo, 1088; (cover) WAGNER DRIP DROP NO.8 SKILLET ROASTER; **Finish:** iron; **Circa:** 1920s-1930s; **VALUE: $100-$125** with cover; Cover only, $75-$100.

DEEP SKILLET WITH RINGED COVER-Size: No.8, 11 1/8" dia. x 3" deep; **c/n:** 1088; **Markings:** stylized logo, 1088A, 8, (cover) WAGNER WARE, SIDNEY -O-,1081A; **Finish:** iron; **Circa:** 1940s; **VALUE:** Skillet, **$35**, Cover, **$45**.

DEEP SKILLET-Size: 11" dia. x 2 7/8" deep; **c/n:** none; **Markings:** none, (cover) X; **Finish:** iron; **Circa:** 1920s-1930s; **VALUE: $60-$70**. Sold through outlet stores.

DOUBLE SKILLET-Size: 11 1/16" dia; **Finish:** nickel plated; **Circa:** 1930s; **VALUE: $85**; black iron, **$95-$125**.

DOUBLE SKILLET BOTTOM-Size: 11 1/16" dia. x 3" deep; **c/n:** 1401A; **Markings:** stylized logo, PAT NO 97022-1554360, 1401A; **Finish:** nickel plated; **Circa:** 1930s; **VALUE: $25-$30**; black iron, **$30-$40**.

DOUBLE SKILLET TOP-Size: 11 1/16" dia. x 1 3/4" deep; **c/n:** 1401B; **Markings:** stylized logo, 1411B; **Finish:** nickel plated; **Circa:** 1930s; **VALUE: $25-$30**; black iron, **$30-$40**.

DOUBLE SKILLET-Size: (bottom) 11" dia. x 3" deep, (top) 1 3/4" deep; **c/n:** none; **Markings:** 97022, 1554360; **Finish:** iron; **Circa:** 1940s; **VALUE: $75-$100**. Wagner identification can be made by the patent numbers and handle design.

SHALLOW SKILLET-Size: No.9; **c/n:** none; **Markings:** WAGNER WARE, SIDNEY, O, SHALLOW SKILLET, 9; **Finish:** iron; **Circa:** 1900-1920s; **VALUE: $100-$150**. Three hole handle.

SHALLOW SKILLET-Size: No.9; **c/n:** none; **Markings:** "WAGNER", 9; **Finish:** iron; **Circa:** 1891-1910; **VALUE: $100-$125**; No. 7, **$100-$125**; No. 8, **$75-$100**. Note three hole handle.

SHALLOW SKILLET-Size: No.7; **c/n:** none; **Markings:** WAGNER, SIDNEY, O, SHALLOW SKILLET; **Finish:** iron; **Circa:** 1894-1910; **VALUE: $125-$150**. Note three hole handle.

HALF SKILLET-Size: No.7; **c/n:** none; **Markings:** stylized logo, HALF SKILLET, 7A; **Finish:** iron; **Circa:** 1915; **VALUE: $125-$150**. Three hole handle.

SHALLOW SKILLET-Size: 9 5/8" dia x 3/4" deep; **c/n:** 1098; **Markings:** stylized logo, SHALLOW SKILLET, 1098A; **Finish:** iron; **Circa:** 1920-1930s; **VALUE: $75-$100**; No. 1099, **$75-$100**. Note single hole handle, and smooth bottom.

SKILLET COVERS

RAISED LETTER DRIP DROP COVER-Size: No.12, 13 1/2" dia.; **c/n:** 1072A; **Markings:** DRIP DROP, No 12, SKILLET COVER, PATENTED DEC.4-17, FEB. 10-20, MCH 8-21, MCH 14-22, 1072A; **Finish:** iron; **Circa:** 1920s **VALUE: $150-$200**; No. 8 **$30**; No. 9, **$30-$40**; No. 10, **$40-$60**.

RINGED SKILLET COVER-**Size:** No. 8; **c/n:** 1068; **Markings:** ringed top surface, WAGNER WARE, SIDNEY -0-, 1065B; **Finish:** iron; **Circa:** 1930s; **VALUE: $45-$55**; No.5, **$75-$100**; No.6, **$65-$90**; No.7, **$45-$65**; No.9, **$45-$65**; No. 10, **$65-$90**.

RINGED SKILLET COVERS DRIP RING STYLES-(left) zig zag; **Circa:** 1920-1949; (right) scalloped; **circa:** 1940-1960.

RAISED LETTER DRIP DROP COVER-**Size:** No.8; **c/n:** C-508; **Finish:** aluminum; **Circa:** 1917-1930s; **VALUE: $25**.

NATIONAL SKILLET COVER-**Size:** No.9; **c/n:** unknown; **Markings:** WAGNER DRIP DROP NATIONAL SKILLET COVER, No 9; **Finish:** iron; **Circa:** 1930s; **VALUE: $75-$100**; No.7, **$75-$100**; No.8, **$60-$75**.

SQUARE SKILLET COVERS-**Size:** (left) 9 3/4" sq. x 1 3/8" h.; (right) 10 1/4" sq. x 1 3/4" h.; **c/n:** (left) none; (right) 1400; **Markings:** (left) 1; (right) 1400; **Finish:** iron; **Circa:** 1930s; **VALUE:** (left) **$100-$125**; (right) **$75-$95**. Cover on the left fits the square skillet; Cover on the right fits the Chicken Fryer.

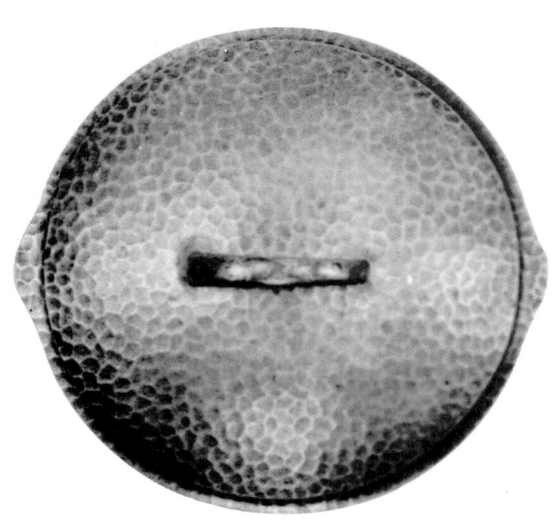

ALUMINUM SKILLET COVER-Size: No.8, 10 5/8" dia.; **c/n:** none; **Markings:** none; **Finish:** hammered aluminum; **Circa:** 1940s; **VALUE: $30**.

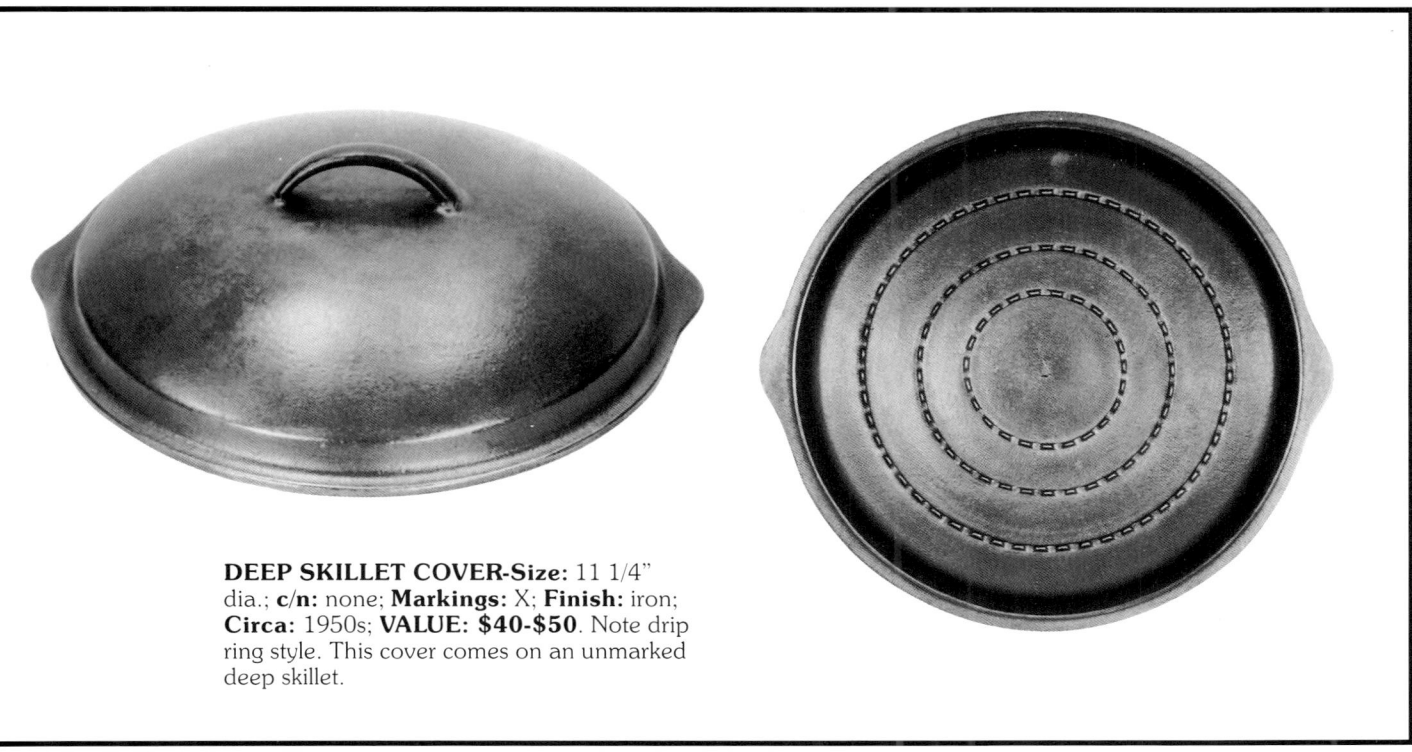

DEEP SKILLET COVER-Size: 11 1/4" dia.; **c/n:** none; **Markings:** X; **Finish:** iron; **Circa:** 1950s; **VALUE: $40-$50**. Note drip ring style. This cover comes on an unmarked deep skillet.

GLASS SKILLET COVER-Size: 11 3/4" dia.; **c/n:** none; **Markings:** stylized logo in oval; **Finish:** Pyrex; **Circa:** 1950s; **VALUE: $35-$50**. Fits No.10 skillet.

GLASS COVER-Size: 8" dia.; **c/n:** none; **Markings:** none; **Circa:** 1960s; **VALUE: $20-$30**. Fits 2 qt. Bean Pot, 1 1/2 qt. Sauce Pan, and HearthStone 7 3/4" skillet.

SQUARE GLASS COVER-Size: 9 13/16" square; **c/n:** none; **Markings:** stylized logo in oval; **Finish:** Pyrex; **Circa:** 1970s; **VALUE: $25-$35**. Used on skillets with thumb rest handle.

OMELET PANS AND SAUCE PANS

OMELET PAN-Size: (top) 9 1/2" dia. open; (btm.) 11 3/4" dia. open; **c/n:** (top) 820; (btm) 821; **Markings:** stylized logo; **Finish:** aluminum; **Circa:** 1920s; **VALUE:** No. 820, **$60-$75**; No. 821, **$40-$50**.

OMELET PAN-Size: 5 7/8" x 11 1/2", plus handles; **c/n:** 842; **Markings:** stylized logo, 842; **Finish:** aluminum; **Circa:** 1930s; **VALUE: $60-$80**.

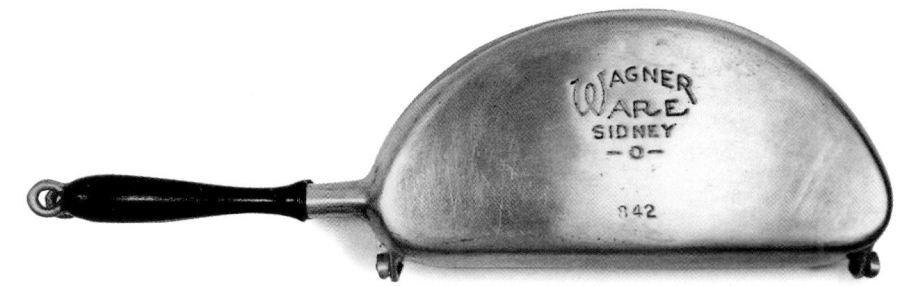

SAUCE PAN-Size: 5 7/8" dia. x 2 9/16" deep; **c/n:** 681; **Markings:** stylized logo, 681; **Finish:** aluminum, wood handle; **Circa:** 1920s; **VALUE: $35-$45**.

NURSERY SAUCE PANS-Size: 3 7/8" dia. x 2 1/2" d.; **c/n:** none; **Markings:** WAGNER WARE SIDNEY O. (in oval); (with pour lip) stylized logo; **Finish:** aluminum; **Circa:** 1915-1930; **VALUE: $45-$60**.

RICE BOILER OR COMBINATION PAN-Size: 2 qt., 7 1/8" dia. x 4 3/4" d.; **c/n:** none; **Markings:** WAGNER WARE SIDNEY, O., PAT'D FEB. 18, 1902; **Finish:** aluminum with spun aluminum cover; **Circa:** 1924; **VALUE: $50-$75; $75-$100** complete. This is the bottom of a double boiler. Also, note shape of the handle.

KITCHEN COOK-ALL SKILLET-c/n: 579; **Markings:** stylized logo, KITCHEN COOK-ALL, 579, M, (cover) 509M **Finish:** aluminum; **Circa:** 1930s; **VALUE: $75-$95.** Note removable handle.

KOOK-ALL-Size: 10 1/2" dia. c 4" deep; **c/n:** (kettle) 3254, (insert) 3254; **Markings:** (kettle) stylized logo, KOOK ALL, 3254, (insert) 3254, M, (cover) M; **Finish:** hammered aluminum; **Circa:** 1940s; **VALUE:** $100-$150 complete.

SHALLOW SAUCE PAN-Size: 7 1/2" dia. x 2 1/2" deep; **c/n:** 1832; **Markings:** stylized logo, 1832; **Finish:** aluminum with steel handle; **Circa:** 1930s; **VALUE: $75-$100**. This was from the commercial line.

DEEP SAUCE PAN-Size: 7" dia. x 3 1/2" deep; **c/n:** 1820; **Markings:** stylized logo, 1820; **Finish:** aluminum with steel handle; **Circa:** 1930s; **VALUE: $75-$100**. This was from the commercial line.

SAUCE PAN- c/n: 687; **Markings:** stylized logo, 687M; **Finish:** aluminum with wood handle; **Circa:** 1920s-1930s; **VALUE: $30-$40**.

THREE SECTION SAUCE PAN- Size: 9" dia. x 4 3/8" deep; **c/n:** 680; **Markings:** stylized logo, 680; **Finish:** aluminum with wood handle; **Circa:** 1930s; **VALUE: $100-$150**; (with cover), **$150-$175**.

SAUCE PAN-Size: 6 1/2' dia. x 3 1/4" deep;
c/n: 4681 1/2P; **Markings:** stylized logo,
Magnalite, 4681 1/2P, (cover) not marked;
Finish: aluminum; **Circa:** 1946-1950s;
VALUE: $45-$55.

GOURMET PAN-Size:; **c/n:** 4672P;
Markings: stylized logo, The Gourmet Pan,
Magnalite, 4672P; **Finish:** aluminum;
Circa: 1940s; **VALUE: $25-$35**.

SAUCE PAN-c/n: 4683M; **Markings:** stylized logo, Magnalite, 4683M; **Finish:** aluminum; **Circa:** 1950s; **VALUE: $30-$40**.

DEEP FAT FRYER-Size: 7 5/8" dia x 4 3/4" deep; **c/n:** 1265, (cover) 1265; **Markings:** stylized logo, 1265, (cover) 1265; **Finish:** iron; **Circa:** 1940s; **VALUE: $75-$100** with basket; **$50-$60** without basket; Cover, **$75-$100**.

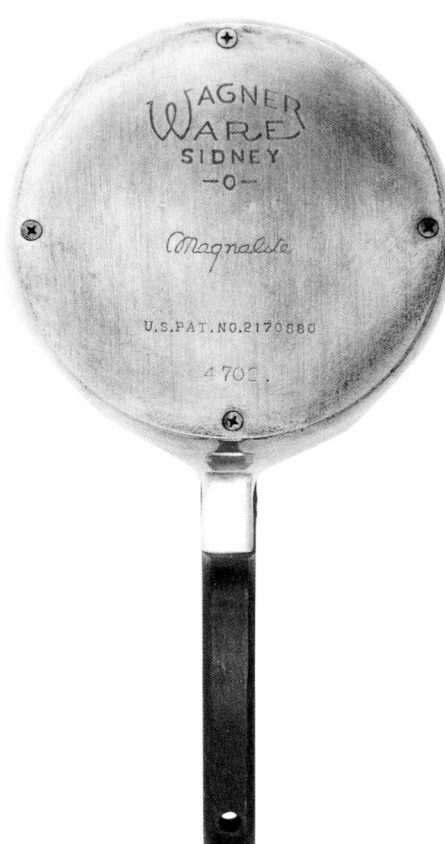

Sauce Pan-Size: 7" dia. x 3 5/8" deep; **c/n:** 4702; **Markings:** stylized logo, Magnalite, US PAT NO. 2170880, 4702, (cover) not marked; **Finish:** aluminum; **Circa:** 1950s; **VALUE: $65-$76**. Plate fastened to bottom acts as a heat regulator.

COVERED SKILLET-Size: 10 1/2" dia. x 3" deep; **c/n:** 4569; **Markings:** stylized logo, Magnalite, 4569P, (cover) not marked; **Finish:** aluminum; **Circa:** 1950s-1960s; **VALUE:** $45-$55. Note how bottom is ground, typical of later pieces.

TRIPLICATE SAUCE PANS-Size: 8 1/2" w. x 6 3/8" d. x 5 1/4" h.; **c/n:** 804; **Markings:** stylized logo, 804b; **Finish:** aluminum; **Circa:** 1920s; **VALUE:** $100-$150.

GRIDDLES

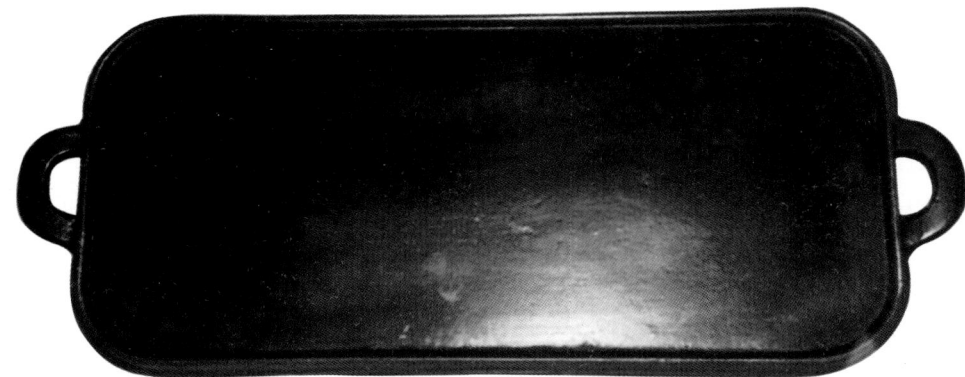

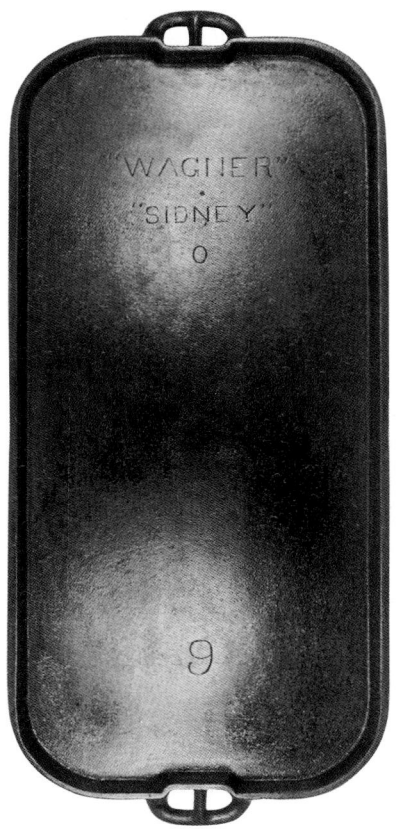

LONG GRIDDLE-Size: No.10, 12 1/2" x24 7/8"; **c/n**: none; **Markings**: WAGNER, SIDNEY O; **Finish**: iron; **Circa**: 1897- 1910; **VALUE: $75-$100**. Note the shape of the handle.

LONG GRIDDLE-Size: No.11, 13 3/8" x 25"; **c/n**: none; **Markings**: "WAGNER," SIDNEY, O., 11; **Finish**: iron; **Circa**: 1902-1915; **VALUE: $125-$150**; No. 7, $45; No. 8, $50-$60; No. 9, $50-$60; No. 10, $75.

LONG GRIDDLE-Size: No.9, 10 1/4" x 21 1/2"; **c/n**: none; **Markings**: "WAGNER", "SIDNEY", O, 9; **Finish**: iron; **Circa**: 1910; **VALUE: $40-$50**; No. 7, $40-$50; No. 8, $30-$35; No. 10, $75-$100.

LONG GRIDDLE-Size: No.8. 8 7/8" x 19 3/8"; **c/n**: none; **Markings**: "WAGNER", 8; **Finish**: iron; **Circa**: 1900-1915; **VALUE: $60-$70**. "WAGNER" appears to be upside down because there is a ghost mark of "WAGNER" on the opposite end which is in the same direction as the 8.

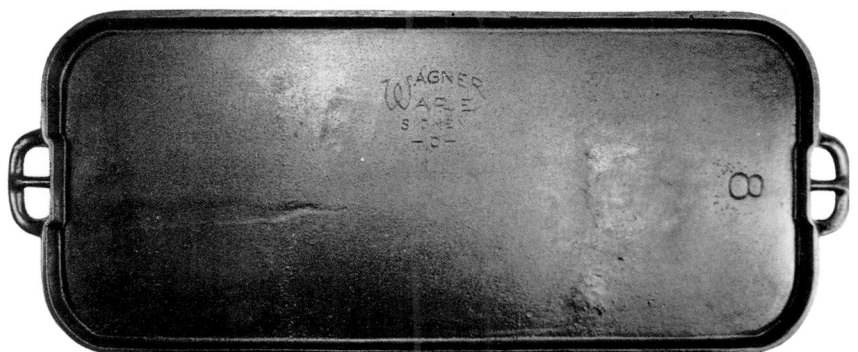

LONG GRIDDLE-Size: No.8, 8 7/8" x 19 3/8"; **c/n**: none; **Markings**: stylized logo, 8; **Finish**: iron; **Circa**: 1930s; **VALUE**: $30-$40; No. 7, $35-$40; No. 9, $40-$45; No. 10, $50-$60; No. 11, $65-$85.S

LONG GRIDDLE-Size: No.9, 10 1/2" x 21 1/2"; **c/n**: none; **Markings**: WAGNER", SIDNEY, 0., 9; **Finish**: iron; **Circa**: 1915; **VALUE**: $30-$40; No. 10, $50-$60; No. 11, $60-$75.

LONG GRIDDLE-Size: No.10, 12 1/2" x 25 1/8"; **c/n**: 1150; **Markings**: stylized logo, 1150A; **Finish**: iron; **Circa**: 1930s-1950s; **VALUE**: $75-$80; No. 8, $25-$30; No. 9, $35-$40.

LONG GRIDDLE-Size: 20 7/8" x 30 5/8"; **c/n**: none; **Markings**: U.S., 1942; **Finish**: iron; **Circa**: 1940s; **VALUE**: $100-$125; **if marked Wagner, $150-$200.**

SHALLOW LONG PAN OR SAD IRON HEATER-Size: No.8, 9 3/8" w x 21 3/16" l x 3/4" d; **c/n**: none; **Markings**: "WAGNER", 8; **Finish**: iron; **Circa**: 1897-1910; **VALUE: $100; No.7, $125; No.9, $125**.

SHALLOW LONG PAN OR SAD IRON HEATER-Size: No.8, 9 5/8" w x 21 3/16" l x 3/4" d; **c/n**: none; **Markings**: "WAGNER", SIDNEY O, 8; **Finish**: iron; **Circa**: 1900-1910; **VALUE: $100; No. 7, $125; No.9, $125**.

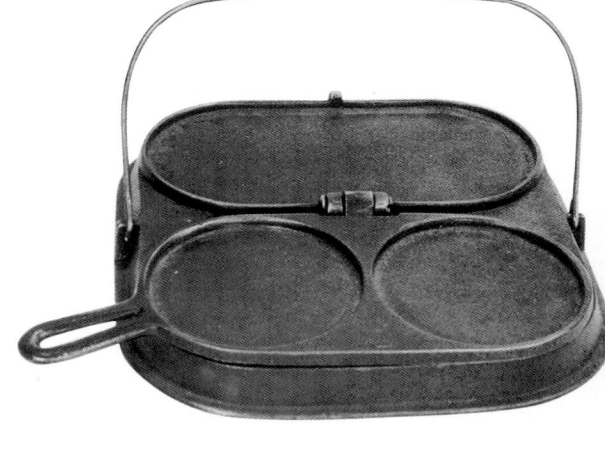

FLOP GRIDDLE-Size: 10 3/8" x 9 7/8"; **c/n**: none; **Markings**: WAGNER MFG CO., SIDNEY OHIO, No. 2; **Finish**: iron; **Circa**: 1894-1915; **VALUE: $250-$300**. Also came in a four section.

HANDLED GRIDDLE-Size: No.8, 9 3/4" dia.; **c/n**: none; **Markings**: "WAGNER" (high arc); **Finish**: iron; **Circa**: 1898; **VALUE: $50; No. 7, $30-$35; No.9, $40-$45**.

WOOD HANDLED GRIDDLE-Size: No.8; **c/n**: none; **Markings**: stylized logo, 8; **Finish**: aluminum; **Circa**: 1920s; **VALUE: $35-$45**.

WOOD HANDLED GRIDDLE-Size: No.9, 11" dia.; **c/n**: none; **Markings**: stylized logo; **Finish**: iron; **Circa**: 1920s-1930s; **VALUE: $45-$60**.

HANDLED GRIDDLE-Size: No.9; **c/n**: none; **Markings**: "SIDNEY", 9A; **Finish**: iron; **Circa**: 1915; **VALUE: $45-$55; No. 8, $35-$45**.

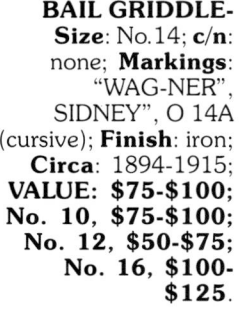

BAIL GRIDDLE-Size: No.14; **c/n**: none; **Markings**: "WAG-NER", SIDNEY", O 14A (cursive); **Finish**: iron; **Circa**: 1894-1915; **VALUE: $75-$100;** No. 10, $75-$100; No. 12, $50-$75; No. 16, $100-$125.

HANDLED GRIDDLE-Size: No.9; **c/n**: 1109; **Markings**: stylized logo, 1109A; **Finish**: iron; **Circa**: 1930s-1950s; **VALUE: $25-$30**; No. 7, $30-$35; No.8, $25-$30; No. 10, $45-$65.

BAIL GRIDDLE-Size: No.14; **c/n**: none; **Markings**: "WAG-NER", SIDNEY, O, 14; **Finish**: iron; **Circa**: 1910; **VALUE: $75-$100**; No.12, $50-$75; No.16, $100-$125.

BAIL GRIDDLE-Size: No.10, 10 5/8" dia.; **c/n**: none; **Markings**: stylized logo, 10B; **Finish**: iron; **Circa**: 1914-1923; **VALUE: $100-$125;** #12, $50-$75; No. 14, $75-$100.

HANDLED GRIDDLE-Size: No.6, 7 13/16" dia.; **c/n**: none; **Markings**: stylized logo, 6; **Finish**: iron; **Circa**: 1920s; **VALUE: $75-$100**; No. 7 $30-$35; No.8, $25-$30; No. 9, $25-$30.

BAIL GRIDDLE-Size: No.12, 12 3/4" dia.; **c/n**: 1122; **Markings**: stylized logo, 1122; **Finish**: iron; **Circa**: 1930s-1950s; **VALUE**: $50-$60; No. 14, $65-$75; No.16, $75-$95.

REVOLVING GRIDDLE-Size: about 12" dia.; **c/n**: none; **Markings**: WAGNER REVOLVING GRIDDLE, SIDNEY, O, PAT'D MARCH 2 1920, (base ring) not marked; **Finish**: iron; **Circa**: 1920s; **VALUE**: $400-$500.

**Wagner Revolving Griddle Brochure-
Size**: 3 1/2" x 6 1/4" bifold; **Circa**: 1920s;
VALUE: $60-$75.

FAT FREE FRYER-c/n: 1061; **Markings**: MADE IN USA, 1061; **Finish**: iron; **Circa**: 1970s; **VALUE: $40-$50**.

CREPE-ETTE PAN-Size: 8 1/2" dia.; **c/n**: none; **Markings**: CREPE-ETTE MASTER, U.S. PAT. PEND., WAGNER WARE; **Finish**: iron; **Circa**: 1970s; **VALUE**: $30.

DUTCH OVENS & OVAL ROASTERS

DUTCH OVEN-Size: No.9, 11 1/4" dia. x 4 3/8" deep; **c/n**: none; **Markings**: "WAGNER", SIDNEY, O., (cover), 9; **Finish**: iron; **Circa**: 1900-1930s; **VALUE**: $45-$60. The ring which is nickel plated brass, on the cover, is unusual. The cotter key holding it is vintage as is the washer. Is it original? The cover is commonly seen with a nickel plated knob.

ROUND ROASTER-Size: No.7, 9 1/4" dia. x 4" deep; **c/n**: 1267A, (cover) 1267; **Markings**: WAGNER WARE, SIDNEY, O., ROUND ROASTER, 1267A, (cover) stylized logo, 1267, and patent dates; **Finish**: iron; **Circa**: 1920s; **VALUE: $60-$70; No.8, $50-$60; No.9, $60-$75**.

ROUND ROASTER-Size: No.7; **c/n**: 247, (cover) 247; **Markings**: WAGNER WARE, SIDNEY O., ROUND ROASTER, 247, (cover) stylized logo, No 7, DROP DROP ROASTER; **Finish**: aluminum; **Circa**: 1920s; **VALUE: $45-$55; No.8, $35-$40; No.9, $45-$55**.

DUTCH OVEN-Size: No.8; **c/n**: none; **Markings**: 8, (cover) none, scalloped drip rings; **Finish**: hammered iron; **Circa**: 1940s; **VALUE: $45-$60; aluminum, $30-$40**.

DUTCH OVEN-Size: No.8; **c/n**: none; **Markings**: 82, (cover) 8; **Finish**: iron; **Circa**: 1940s; **VALUE: $75-$100**. Scalloped drip rings are typically Wagner as is the underlined 8. The vent is unusual.

DUTCH OVEN-Size: No.8; **c/n**: H.S.-1268; **Markings**: stylized logo, H.S.-1268, (cover) 8; **Finish**: hammered aluminum; **Circa**: 1940s; **VALUE: $40-$50**. The hammered finish is not common.

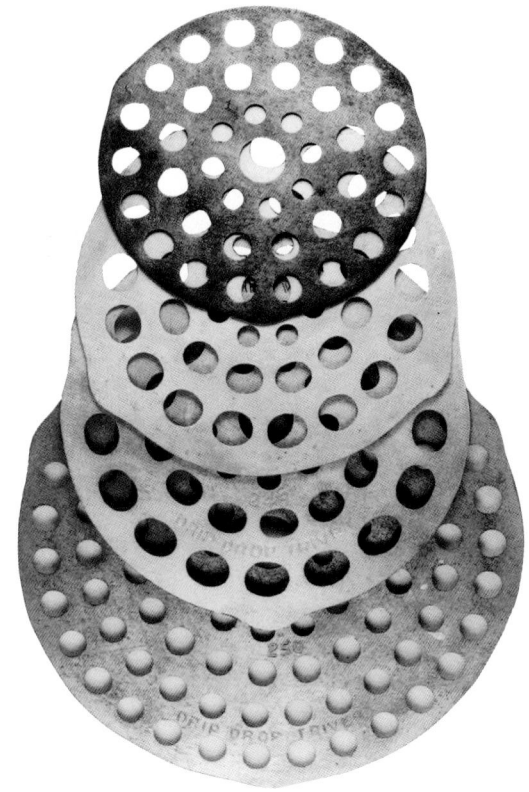

DUTCH OVEN TRIVETS-Size: (top to btm.) 6 1/2", 8", 8 5/8", 10 5/8"; **c/n**: (top) none, (next) 2M, (next) 248, (btm) 250; **Markings**: (top) stamped 1, (next) 2M, (next) WAGNER WARE DRIP DROP TRIVET, 248, (btm.) WAGNER WARE DRIP DROP TRIVET, 250; **Finish**: (top) iron, (rest) aluminum; **VALUE: (iron, by Dutch oven numbers) No.6, $75 -$100; No's 7, 8, & 9, $40-$60; No.10 $60-$75, No's 11 & 12, $75-$100**. Aluminum trivets were common with iron Dutch ovens, however, are valued 30% less.

MAGNALITE DUTCH OVEN-Size: 10" dia. x 4" deep; **c/n**: 4248M; **Markings**: stylized logo, Magnalite, 4248M, (cover) not marked; **Finish**: aluminum; **Circa**: 1945s-1950s; **VALUE: $45-$55**.s

No.1, & No.9 OVAL ROASTERS FOR SIZE COMPARISON.

OVAL ROASTER-Size: 2, 11 3/4" l. x 7 3/8" w. x 3 1/2" d.; **c/n**: none; **Markings**: "WAGNER", 2, (cover) 2; **Finish**: iron cover, nickel plated bottom; **Circa**: 1900; **VALUE: $200-$250**. Note early style handle.

OVAL ROASTER-Size: No. 4, 15 3/4" l. x 8 5/16" w. x 3 3/4" d.; **c/n**: none; **Markings**: "WAGNER" SIDNEY, O. 4, (cover) 4; **Finish**: iron; **Circa**: 1920s; **VALUE: $300-$350; No.3, $200-$250; No.5, $200-$250; No.6, $200-$250; No.7, $200-$250; No.8, $250-$300**. Nickel plated is 25% less.S

OVAL ROASTER-Size: No.1, 11 1/2" sl. x 6 5/8"w. x 3 1/8" d.; **c/n**: none; **Markings**: 'WAGNER"; **Finish**: iron with nickel knob; **Circa**: 1910; **VALUE: $200-$250**.

OVAL ROASTER-Size: No.3, 14 1/4" l. x 8" w. x 3 5/8" d.; **c/n**: none; **Markings**: "WAGNER" SIDNEY, O., 3, (cover) 3; **Finish**: iron cover, nickel plated bottom; **Circa**: 1910; **VALUE: $300-$250**. Gate mark inside the cover seems strange for this time period.

OVAL ROASTER-Size: No.1, 11 1/4" l. x 6 3/4" w, x 3" deep; **c/n**: none; **Markings**: "WAGNER", SIDNEY O, 1; **Finish**: aluminum with nickel knob; **Circa**: 1920s; **VALUE: $75-$100**.

OVAL ROASTER-Size; No.1, 13 1/16" l x 10" w. x 3 1/8" d. **c/n**: none; **Markings**: stylized logo, OVAL ROASTER, I, (cover) WAGNER DRIP DROP BASTER, (inside cover) full patent info.; **Finish**: iron (also available plated); **Circa**: 1920s; **VALUE: $250-$300; No.2, No.3, $200-$250, No.4 $300-$350, No.5, No.6, No.7, $200-$250**. Nickel plated is 25% less.

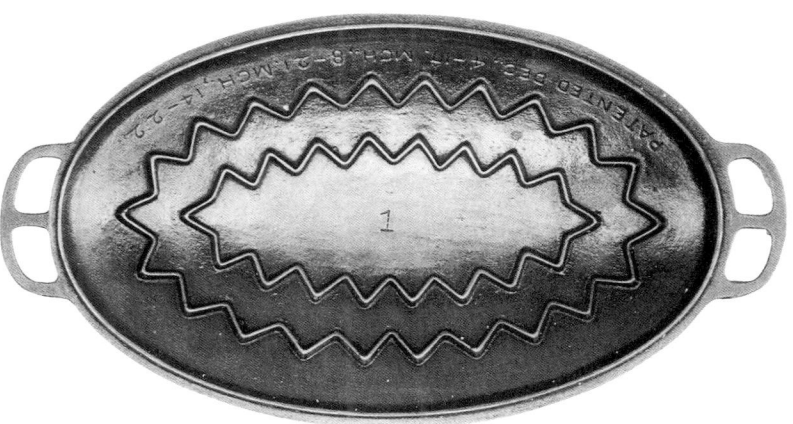

OVAL ROASTER-Size: No.1; **c/n**: none; **Markings**: stylized logo, OVAL ROASTER, 1, (cover) WAGNER DRIP DROP BASTER; **Finish**: aluminum; **Circa**: 1920-1940; **VALUE: $95-$125**: No.2, No.3, $75-$95; No.4, No.5, No.6, $65-$85; No.7, No.8, $75-$85.

OVAL ROASTER-Size: No.3, 14 1/2" l. x 8 3.8" w. x 3 3/8" d.; **c/n**: 1283, (cover) 1283; **Markings**: stylized logo, OVAL ROASTER, 1283, (cover) raised letter stylized logo, No. 3, DRIP DROP BASTER, 1283, (inside cover) patent information; **Finish**: iron; **Circa**: 1920s; **VALUE: $200-$250**; **No.1**, $300-$350; **No.2**, $300-$350; **No.4**, $300-$350; **No.5**, $200-$225; **No.6**, $200-$225; **No.7**, $275-$300; **No.8 & No.9**, $300-$350. Nickel plated is 25% less.

WARDWAY OVAL ROASTER-Size: 6, 15 3/4" l. x 11 3/8" w. x 4 1/2" d.; **c/n**: W-1416; **Markings**: Wardway, W-1416, (cover) SELF BASTING ROASTER; **Finish**: iron; **Circa**: 1940s; **VALUE: $200-$250**. The paper sticker on the bottom is seasoning instructions.

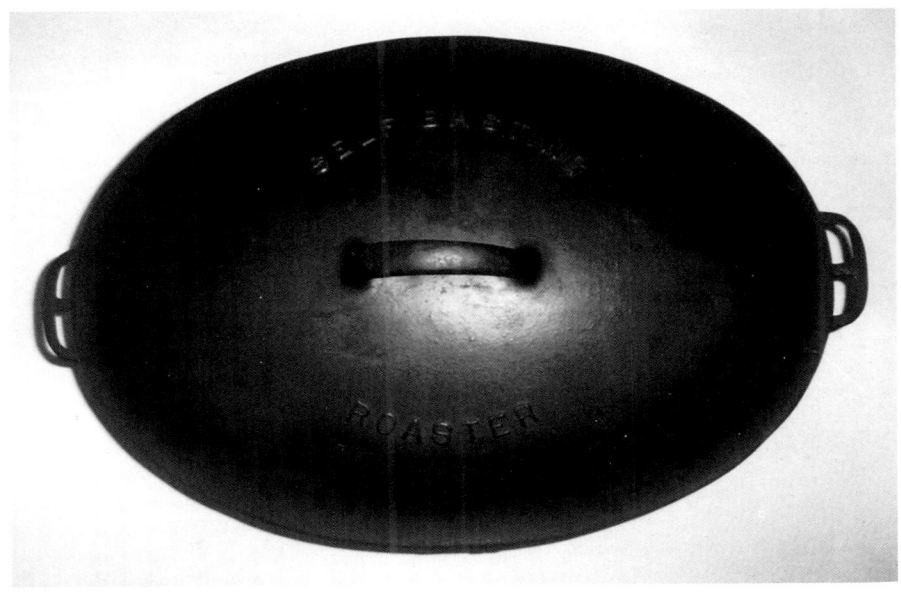

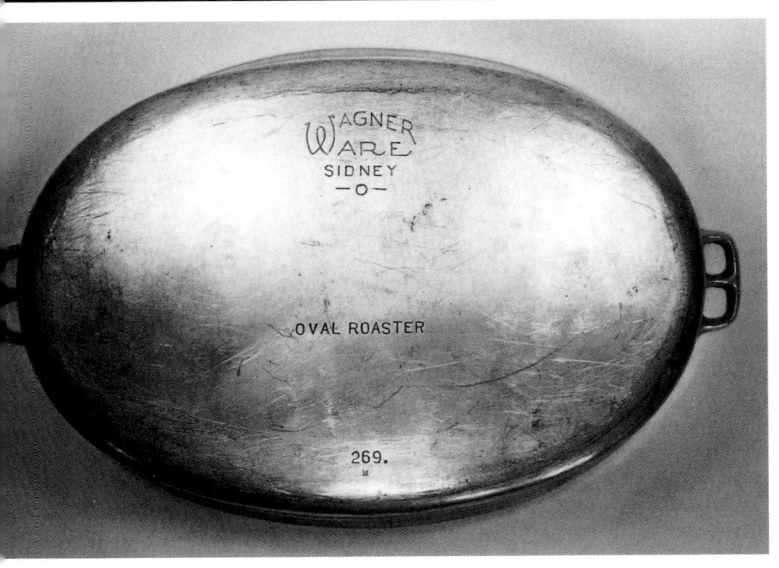

OVAL ROASTER-Size: no.9, 18 1/2" l. x 13 9/16" w.; **c/n**: 269; **Markings**: stylized logo, OVAL ROASTER, 259M, (cover) raised letter stylized logo, No.9, DRIP DROP ROASTER; **Finish**: aluminum; **Circa**: 1930s; **VALUE: $75-$125**.

OVAL ROASTER-Size: No.6, 12 7/8" l. x 9 1/2" w. x 4 3/4" d.; **c/n**: 3266, (cover) 3266M; **Markings**: stylized logo, 3266, (cover) 3266M; **Finish**: hammered aluminum; **Circa**: 1940s; **VALUE: $75-$100**. Note how large the hammered pattern is.

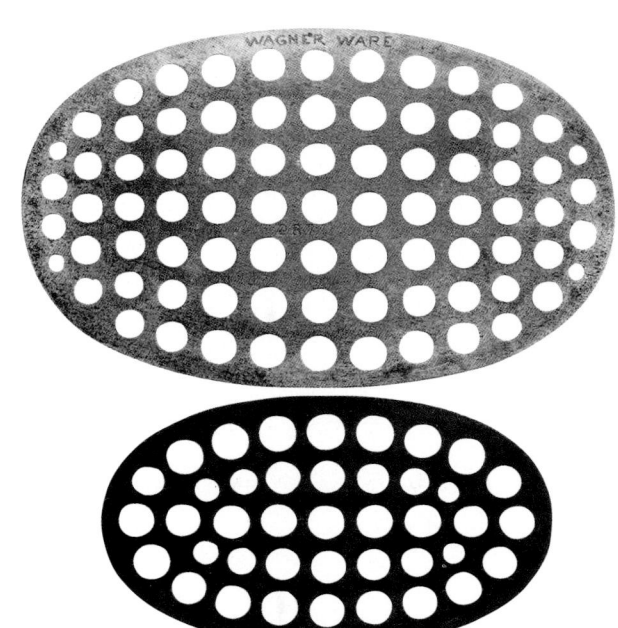

OVAL ROASTER TRIVETS-Size: 1 through 9; **Markings**: WAGNER WARE, (some are not marked); **Finish**: iron or aluminum; **Circa**: 1920s; **VALUE: No.1, $150; No.2, $125; No's 3,- 8, $85; No.9, $100**. Aluminum trivets are about 30% less.

MAGNALITE OVAL ROASTER-Size: 15 1/2" w. x 10" w. x 4 1/2" d.; **c/n**: 4265P; **Markings**: stylized logo, Magnalite, 4265P, (cover) not marked; **Finish**: aluminum; **Circa**: 1945-1950s; **VALUE: $50-$60**.

KETTLES & COOKERS

RIMMED POT-Size: No.8; **c/n**: none; **Markings**: 'WAGNER", RIMMED POT, 8; **Finish**: iron; **Circa**: 1890s - 1910; **VALUE**: $85.

FLAT BOTTOM KETTLE-Size: No.6, 8 1/8" dia. x 5 3/4" deep; **c/n**: none; **Markings**: "WAGNER", 6; **Finish**: nickel plated iron; **Circa**: 1890-1920; **VALUE**: $75-$100; No.7, $40-$60; No.8, $40-$60; No.9, $65-$85.

SCOTCH BOWL-Size: No.2, 9 1/8" dia. x 3 3/4" h.; **c/n**: none; **Markings**: "WAGNER", 2; **Finish**: iron; **Circa**: 1890s; **VALUE**: **$45-$60**. Note early kettle ears where bail attaches.

MIXING BOWL-Size: 11 1/4" dia.; **c/n**: none; **Markings**: WAGNER WARE SIDNEY O., 4; **Finish**: aluminum; **Circa**: 1915-1920s; **VALUE**: **$125**. Apparently converted from a Scotch bowl pattern.

MIXING BOWL-Size: 11 1/4" dia.; **c/n**: 434; **Markings**: "WAGNER", SIDNEY O., MIXING BOWL 434; **Finish**: aluminum; **Circa**: 1915-1930s; **VALUE**: **$125**. Pour ring acts as hanging ring.

SCOTCH BOWL-Size: No.3, 10 1/6" dia. x 4 1/4" h.; **c/n**: none; **Markings**: WAGNER" (arc), SIDNEY, O., 3; **Finish**: iron; **Circa**: 1900-1920s; **VALUE**: **$35-$45**; No.2, $45-$65; No.4, $35-$45; No.5, $45-$60.

YANKEE BOWL-Size: No.2, 9 1/4" dia. x 5 1/4" h.; **c/n**: none; **Markings**: "WAGNER" SIDNEY, O., 2; **Finish**: nickel plated; **Circa**: 1910-1920s; **VALUE: $60-$70**.

LOW KETTLE-Size: No.8, 9 7/8" dia. x 6 7/8" h.; **c/n**: none; **Markings**: WAGNER WARE, SIDNEY O, LOW KETTLE, 8, (cover) WAGNER WARE (single "W"), SIDNEY, O, 1228; **Finish**: iron; **Circa**: 1910-1920s, (cover) early 1920s; **VALUE: $75-$100** (kettle only), **(cover) $40-$50**.S

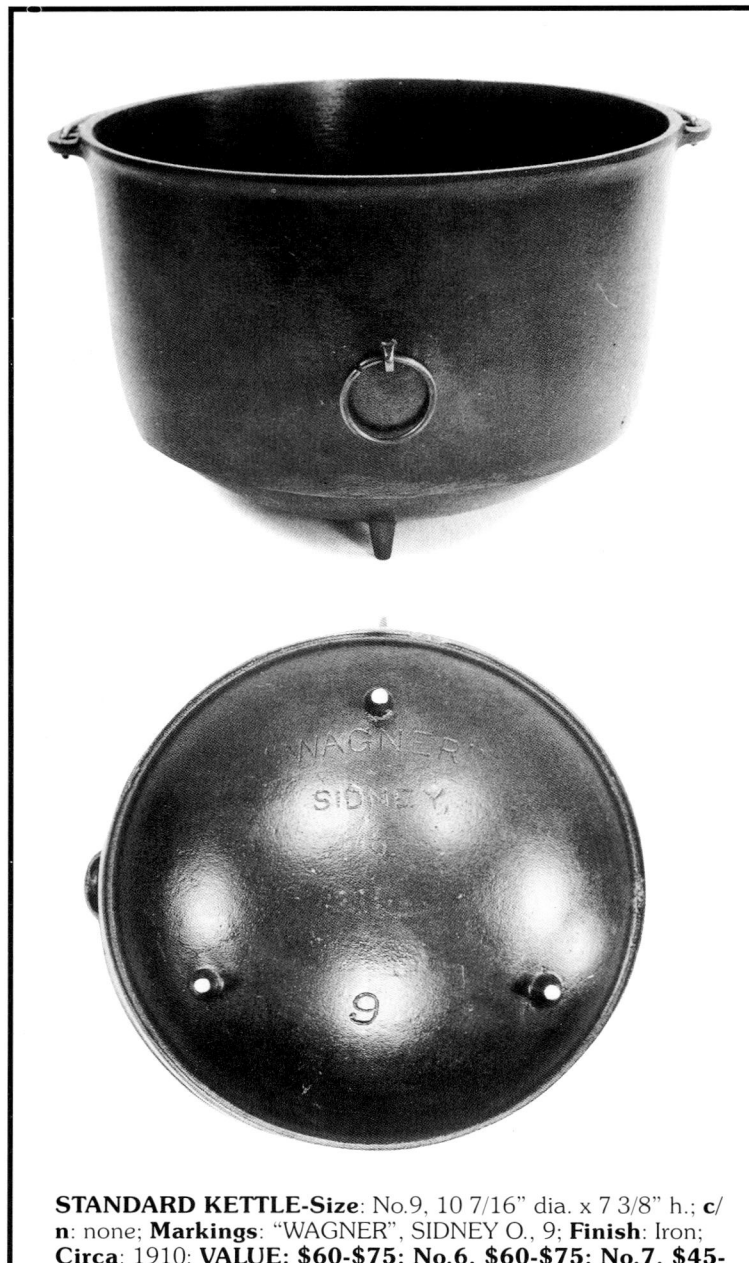

STANDARD KETTLE-Size: No.9, 10 7/16" dia. x 7 3/8" h.; **c/n**: none; **Markings**: "WAGNER", SIDNEY O., 9; **Finish**: Iron; **Circa**: 1910; **VALUE: $60-$75**; No.6, $60-$75; No.7, $45-$50, No.8, $45-$50.S

CONVEX KETTLE-Size: 6 3/4" dia. x 4 1/4" d.; **c/n**: none; **Markings**: WAGNER WARE, SIDNEY, O., CONVEX 1; **Finish**: aluminum; **Circa**: 1930s; **VALUE: $75-$100**. Loop handles, rather than bail.

KOOK ALL-Size: 10 1/2" dia. x 4" deep; **c/n**: (kettle) 3254, (skillet) 3254; **Markings**: (kettle) stylized logo, KOOK ALL, 3254, (skillet) 3254, (cover) not marked; **Finish**: aluminum; **Circa**: 1940s; **VALUE: $100-$150**. Skillet stacks in kettle to form double boiler.S

STEAM PRESSURE COOKER-Size: 20 qts, 12" h. x 11 1/2" top dia.; **c/n**: (cover) 118; **Markings**: WAGNER M'F'G' CO, SIDNEY OHIO, WAGNERS STEAM PRESSURE COOKER, stylized logo on bottom, (cover) DRIP DROP BASTER, PAT'D DEC 4, 1917; **Finish**: galvanized iron; **Circa**: 1927-1930s; **VALUE: $100-$150**. This came in four sizes: 10, 15, 20, & 25 quarts.

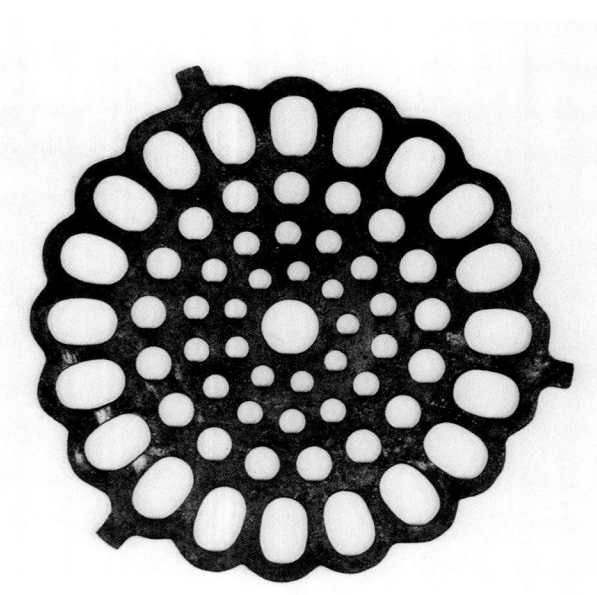

Trivet

TEA KETTLES, COFFEE POTS & PITCHERS

TEA KETTLE-Size: 9" dia. x 8 1/2" h.; **c/n**: none; **Markings**: (cover) WAGNER, SIDNEY O.; **Finish**: iron; **Circa**: 1890s-1910; **VALUE: $75**.S

TEA KETTLE-Size: No.7, 8" dia. x 6" h.; **c/n**: none; **Markings**: (cover) "WAGNER" SIDNEY O, (bottom) 7; **Finish**: aluminum; **Circa**: 1897-1910; **VALUE: $45-$65**.

REPRODUCTION TEA KETTLE-Size: 7 1/2" dia. x 6" h.; **c/n**: none; **Markings**: stylized logo, MADE IN USA; **Finish**: iron with chromed handle; **Circa**: 1970s-1990s; **VALUE: $25**.

COLONIAL TEA KETTLE-Size: No.6, 7 1/2" dia. x 5 7/8" h.; **c/n**: none; **Markings**: WAGNER, PAT'D FEB. 18, 1890, 6; **Finish**: aluminum; **Circa**: 1902-1910; **VALUE: $65-$75**. This style handle is very early, c. 1900. Also note the grove worn in the handle from the cover lever and years of use. What a story this piece could tell.

COLONIAL TEA KETTLE-Size: 5 qt.; **c/n**: 107; **Markings**: stylized logo, COLONIAL TEA KETTLE, 5 QTS, 107; **Finish**: aluminum; **Circa**: 1915-1920s; **VALUE: $30-$45**.

GRAND PRIZE TEA KETTLE-Size: No.6, 7 pts.; **c/n**: 156; **Markings**: stylized logo, GRAND PRIZE TEA KETTLE, PATENTED SEPT. 26, 1916, 6; **Finish**: aluminum; **Circa**: 1917- 1920s; **VALUE: $125-$150**. Also made sizes 7 and 8.

Brochure Cover-Size: **Circa**: 1920s; **VALUE $35**.

PURITAN TEA KETTLE-Size: No.7, 9" dia. x 6" h.; **c/n**: none; **Markings**: stylized logo, Puritan, PATENT APL'D FOR, 7A; **Finish**: aluminum; **Circa**: 1920s-1930s; **VALUE: $65—$75**.

TEA KETTLE-Size: 5 qt.; **c/n**: 3127M; **Markings**: stylized logo, 5 QT, 3127M; **Finish**: hammered aluminum; **Circa**: 1940s; **VALUE: $60-$65**.

COFFEE POT-Size: 3 qt.; **c/n**: none; **Markings**: WAGNER WARE, SIDNEY, O., SIDNEY COFFEE POT, 3 QT.; **Finish**: aluminum; **Circa**: 1915-1920s; **VALUE: $75-$100**.

MAGNALITE TEA KETTLE-Size: 8 3/4" dia. x 4 1/4" h.; **c/n**: 4133M; **Markings**: stylized logo, Magnalite, 4133M; **Finish**: aluminum; **Circa**: 1945-1960s; **VALUE: $60-$75**.

TWO WAY COFFEE POT - Colonial Design-Size: **c/n**: none; **Markings**: "WAGNER", SIDNEY, O., PAT'D FEB. 18, 1920s; **Finish**: aluminum with ebonized handle; **Circa**: 1920s; **VALUE: $60-$70**. This pot could be used as a percolator, or by removing the interior parts could be used as a regular coffee pot for boiled coffee.

LOW COLONIAL PATTERN PERCOLATOR-Size: 3 qt., 8"h x 6 1/2" dia.; **c/n**: none; **Markings**: WAGNER WARE, SIDNEY O., PAT'D FEB. 18, 1902, COLONIAL COFFEE POT, 3 QT.; **Finish**: aluminum; **Circa**: 1915-1920s; **VALUE: $60-$75**.

LOW COLONIAL PATTERN PERCOLATOR-Size: 2 qt.; **c/n**: 192; **Markings**: stylized logo, COLONIAL COFFEE POT, 2 QT, 192; **Finish**: aluminum; **Circa**: 1916-1940s; **VALUE: $60-$70**.

COLONIAL COFFEE POT-Size: 6 qt.; **c/n**: 196; **Markings**: WAGNER WARE, SIDNEY O., 196, COLONIAL COFFEE POT, SECOND TO NONE; **Finish**: aluminum; **Circa**: 1920s-1930s; **VALUE: $125-$150**. Wire handle was an ordering option.

LOW PERCOLATOR-Size: 6 qt.; **c/n**: none; **Markings**: "WAGNER", LOW PERCOLATOR, PAT'D JULY 2-18, MAR 14-22 6 QT, 22 CUPS, SIDNEY, O.; **Finish**: aluminum; **Circa**: 1918-1920s; **VALUE: $100-$150**. Note feet which protrude 1/4" to balance center which protrudes to accommodate base of riser tube for percolator. Bail handle was an ordering option.

COFFEE POT-Size: unknown; **c/n**: 3192; **Markings**: stylized logo, 3192; **Finish**: aluminum; **Circa**: 1940s; **VALUE: $50-$60**.

COFFEE POT-Size: 8" h. x 6 1/2" dia. with 1 1/2" high stand; **c/n**: 228; **Markings**: stylized logo, 228; **Finish**: aluminum; **Circa**: 1930s; **VALUE: $75-$100**.

"SIDNEY" PATTERN TEA POT-Size: 1 pint, 3 3/4" dia. x 4 1/2" h.; **c/n**: 211; **Markings**: WAGNER WARE, SIDNEY O., 21 1PT; **Finish**: aluminum; **Circa**: 1910-1930; **VALUE: $65-$85**.

MAGNALITE COFFEE POT-Size: 12" h. x 4 3/4" dia.; **c/n**: 4192; **Markings**: stylized logo, 4192, Magnalite; **Finish**: aluminum; **Circa**: 1945-1950s; **VALUE: $75-$100**.

TEA POT-Size: 8" h. x 5 3/4" dia.; **c/n**: 230; **Markings**: stylized logo, 230; **Finish**: aluminum; **Circa**: 1930s; **VALUE: $75-$100**.

INDIVIDUAL COFFEE OR TEA POT-Size: 1/2 pint, 3 1/2" h. x 3 3/16" dia.; **c/n**: 212; **Markings**: Stylized logo, 212; **Finish**: aluminum; **Circa**: 1930s; **VALUE: $65-$75**.

PITCHER-Size: 2 1/2 quarts; **c/n**: 409; **Markings**: stylized logo, 409; **Finish**: aluminum; **Circa**: 1930s; **VALUE: $65-$75**.

WATER PITCHER-Size: 7 1/2" h; **c/n**; **Markings**: "WAGNER" SIDNEY O; **Finish**: aluminum; **Circa**: 1910-1920s; **VALUE: $100-$125**.

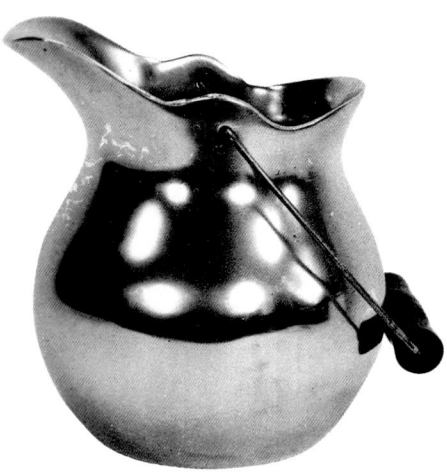

BELL BOYS PITCHER-Size: 8" h. x 6" dia.; **c/n**: none; **Markings**: none; **Finish**: aluminum; **Circa**: 1930s; **VALUE: $100-$125**.

1 PINT & 1 QUART MEASURES-Size: (left), 4 3/4" h. x 3 1/2" dia.; (right) 6 1/4" h. x 4 1/4" dia.; **c/n**: none; **Markings**: "WAGNER", SIDNEY O., LIQUID; **Finish**: aluminum; **Circa**: 1910- 1925; **VALUE: $60-$75**.

MEASURE-Size: 1 quart, 5 3/4" h. x 4 1/2" dia.; **c/n**: none; **Markings**: "WAGNER", SIDNEY O., LIQUID 1 QT; **Finish**: aluminum; **Circa**: 1910; **VALUE: $60-$75**.

Water Pitcher-Size: 9 1/2" h. x 6 3/4" dia.; **c/n**: 410; **Markings**: stylized logo, SECOND TO NONE; **Finish**: aluminum; **Circa**: 1930s; **VALUE: $85-$100**.

MEASURE-Size: 4 quarts, 10 1/4" h. x 6 1/2" dia.; **c/n**: none; **Markings**: stylized logo, LIQUID, 4 QT., 1 GAL (on front); **Finish**: aluminum; **Circa**: 1914-1924; **VALUE: $100-$125**.

MEASURE-Size: 1 qt., 6 1/4" high; **c/n**: 985; **Markings**: stylized logo, LIQUID, 1 QT. 985; **Finish**: aluminum; **Circa**: 1930s; **VALUE**: $75-$100.

WAFFLE IRONS

WAGNER WAFFLES BROCHURE-Size: 3 1/2" x 6 1/4", 10 pages; **Circa**: 1920s; **VALUE: $75-80**.

WAFFLE IRON-Size: No.8, 7 1/2" dia.; **c/n**: none; **Markings**: THE WAGNER, No.8, 8 & 9, (reverse) WAGNER MFG CO. SIDNEY O, PAT'D JULY 26, 1899; **Finish**: iron with screw-on wood handles; **Circa**: 1900; **VALUE: $75-$100**. Unusual handles. Also note stops at 3 and 9 O'clock.

BROCHURE-Size: 3 7/8" x 2 7/8", 8 pages; **Markings**: DELICIOUS WAFFLES; **Circa**: 1915; **VALUE**: $45-65.

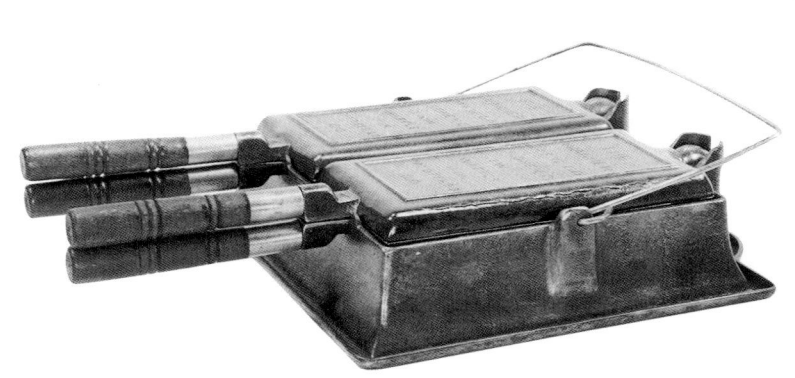

TWIN WAFFLE IRON-Size: (paddles) 4 1/2" x 8 3/8", (base) 11 5/8" x 11"; **c/n**: none; **Markings**: THE WAGNER MFG CO, SIDNEY, O., TWIN WAFFLE IRON, PAT'D FEB. 22, 1910; **Finish**; **Circa**; **VALUE**: $350-$400.ss

TWIN WAFFLE IRON-Size: approx. 10 3/4" x 11"; **c/n**: none; **Markings**: WAGNER M'F'G CO., SIDNEY, OHIO, PATD JULY 26 1892; **Finish**: iron; **Circa**: 1890s-1910; **VALUE**: $250-$300.

ROUND WAFFLE IRON-**Size**: No.8; **c/n**: 1408; **Markings**: stylized logo, 1408, PAT'D SEPT. 15, 1925, E, (reverse) D, (base) A, CH; **Finish**: iron with Alaskan handles; **Circa**: 1930s; **VALUE: $40-$50**.s

ROUND WAFFLE IRON-**Size**: No.8, 7 9/16" dia; **c/n**: none; **Markings**: stylized logo, 8, pat'd Feb. 22, 1910 (base) CHC; **Finish**: iron with Alaskan handles; **Circa**: 1920s; **VALUE: $40-$45**.

ELECTRIC WAFFLE IRON-Size: plate dia. 6 7/8" dia.; **c/n**: none; **Markings**: WAGNERS WAFFLE IRON, WATTS 580, VOLTS 110, THE WAGNER MFG CO. SIDNEY OH, MADE IN USA; **Finish**: steel with aluminum; **Circa**: 1920s; **VALUE: $75-$125**.

DISPLAY STANDS

SKILLET DISPLAY STAND-Size: 24 3/4" l. x 5 3/4" w.; **c/n**: none; **Markings**: stylized logo plate; **Finish**: wood with steel wire and cast iron, nickeled plate; **Circa**: 1914-1930s; **VALUE: $250-$300**.

SKILLET DISPLAY STAND-Size: 24 1/2" long; **c/n**: none; **Markings**: stylized logo plate; **Finish**: wood with steel wires, and cast iron nickeled plate; **Circa**: 1920s-1930s; **VALUE: $200-$250**.

UTENSIL DISPLAY STAND-Size: 25" l. x 7 3/4" h.; **c/n**: none; **Markings**: tin plate on front; **Finish**: steel wire; **Circa**: 1950s; **VALUE: $200-$250**. This unit folds for shipping.

GLASS COVER DISPLAY STAND- **Markings**: enameled plate; **Finish**: steel wire with tin plate; **Circa**: 1950s-1960s; **VALUE: $125-$150**. Holds four glass covers.

UTENSIL DISPLAY RACK- **Size**: 53" high; **c/n**: none; **Markings**: WAGNER HOLLOW WARE on arms; **Finish**: nickel plated; **Circa**: 1902-1920; **VALUE: $1,800-$2,000 with good nickel finish**. This stand was made available to promote nickel plated ware, and given to merchants purchasing the required package. It was also available for sale at $2.50 each.

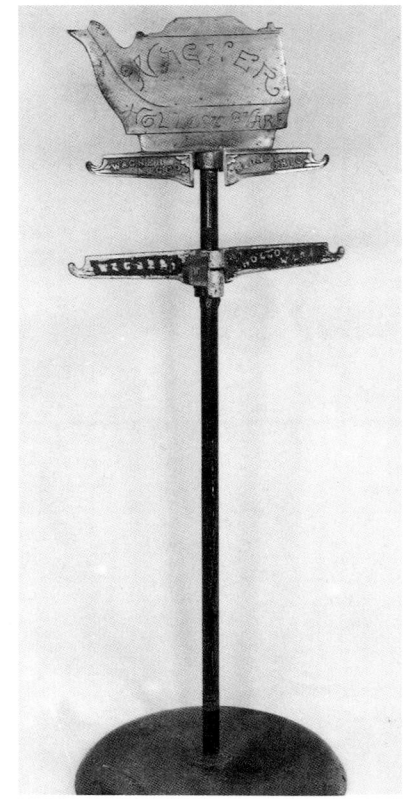

DUTCH OVEN DISPLAY STAND-Size: 32 1/2" high; **c/n**: none; **Markings**: stylized logo plate, (shelf) WAGNER; **Finish**: iron; **Circa**: 1920s-1930s; **VALUE: $450-$550**.

UTENSIL DISPLAY RACK-Size: 53" high; **c/n**: none; **Markings**: (top plaque) WAGNER HOLLOW WARE, WAGNER MFG. CO, SIDNEY OHIO, (arms) WAGNER HOLLOW WARE; **Finish**: nickel; **Circa**: 1890s-1902; **VALUE: $1,800-$2,000 complete with all arms and with good nickel finish**. This unit is not complete; arms are missing.

BAKING PANS, MUFFIN/GEM PANS, & CAKE MOLDS

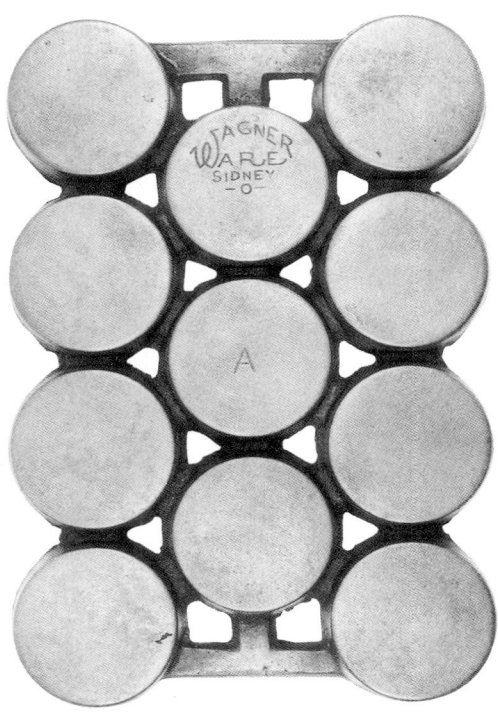

STYLE B POPOVER PAN-Size: 7 3/4" x 11 1/4", (cups) 1 3/4" d.; **c/n**: none; **Markings**: WAGNER WARE, B; **Finish**: iron; **Circa**: 1900-1924; **VALUE: $35-$50**.

STYLE A GEM PAN-Size: 7 5/8" x 11 1/4", (cups) 7/8" deep; **c/n**: none; **Markings**: stylized logo, A; **Finish**: iron; **Circa**: 1913-1925; **VALUE: $45-$60**.

STYLE A GEM PAN-Size: 11 1/2" x 7 9/16", (cups) 2 1/2" dia. x 7/8" d.; **c/n**: 1322; **Markings**: stylized logo, 1322; **Finish**: iron; **Circa**: 1940s; **VALUE: $100-$150**. Solid frame is less common.

STYLE C SHELL GEM PAN-Size: 7 1/16" x 10 5/16"; **c/n**: 1324; **Markings**: 1324, C; **Finish**: iron; **Circa**: 1920s; **VALUE: $75-$100**. Solid frame is less common.

STYLE EE BREAD FINGERS PAN-c/n: 460M; **Markings**: "EE" BREAD FINGERS, WAGNER WARE, SIDNEY OHIO, 460M, PAT PENDING; **Finish**: aluminum; **Circa**: 1930; **VALUE: $40-$50; (iron) $50-$65**.

STYLE F GEM PAN-Size: 9 7/8" x 6 5/8"; **c/n**: 1328; **Markings**: WAGNER WARE, F, 1328; **Finish**: iron; **Circa**: 1920s; **VALUE: $75-$100**. Solid frame less common.

STYLE D GEM PAN-Size: 12 3/4" x 6 9/16"; **c/n**: 1325; **Markings**: stylized logo, D Gem Pan, 1325A; **Finish**: iron; **Circa**: 1920s; **VALUE: $75-$100**.

STYLE F GEM PAN-Size: **c/n**: none; **Markings**: F, 9; **Finish**: iron; **Circa**: 1902-1910; **VALUE: $35-$45**.

STYLE G GEM PAN-Size: 7 1/2" x 11 3/8"; **c/n**: none; **Markings**: G. 7; **Finish**: iron; **Circa**: 1902-1915; **VALUE: $35-$45**.

STYLE F GEM PAN-Size: 10" l. X 6 9/16" w; **c/n**: 1328; **Markings**: WAGNER WARE, F 1328; **Finish**: iron; **Circa**: 1920s; **VALUE: $75-$100**. Different shaped handles than the other solid example.

STYLE G GEM PAN-Size: 7 7/16" x 11 15/16"; **c/n**: 1329; **Markings**: stylized logo, 1329; **Finish**: iron; **Circa**: 1920s-1930s; **VALUE: $60-$75**. Solid frame is less common. Hanging hole appears to be drilled, but is actually cast in.

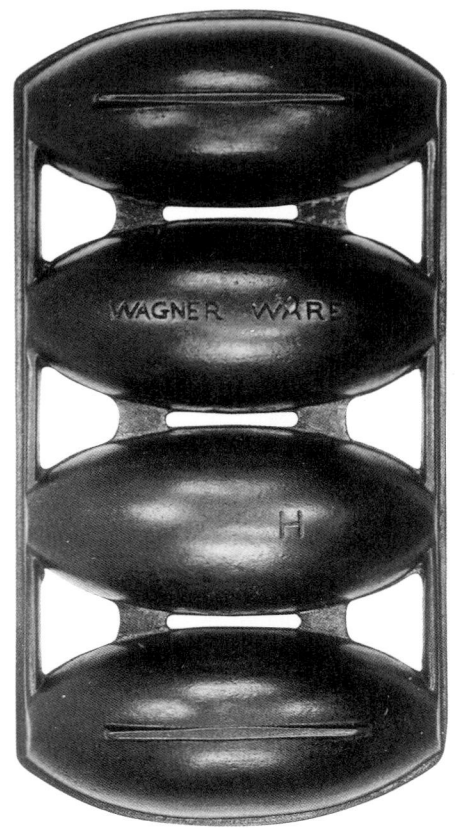

VIENNA BREAD PAN-Size: 12 7/16" l. x 6 3/8" w. x 1 1/4" d.; **c/n**: none; **Markings**: WAGNER WARE, H; **Finish**: iron; **Circa**: 1902-1920; **VALUE: $400-$450**.

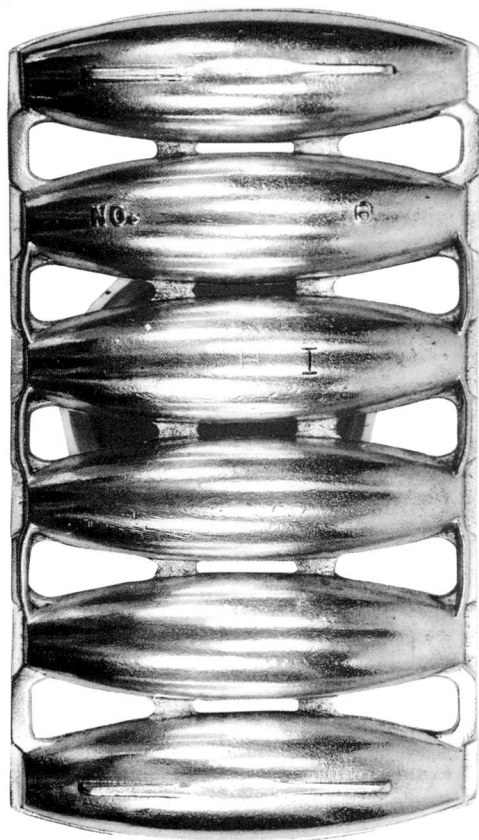

STYLE M GEM PAN-Size: 3 9/16" w. x 9 3/16" l. x 3/4" h.; **c/n**: none; **Markings**: none; **Finish**: iron; **Circa**: 1915; **VALUE: $350-$400**.

VIENNA ROLL PAN-Size: 12 1/4" l. x 6 5/8" w.; **c/n**: none; **Markings**: No.6, I, ghost of H; **Finish**: aluminum; **Circa**: 1930s; **VALUE: $30-$45**. The H ghost mark is strange. H was the designation for the four section pan.

STYLE R GEM PAN-Size: 7 7? 16" x 8 3/16" l. x 1 1/2" d.; **c/n**: none; **Markings**: WAGNER WARE, R; **Finish**: iron; **Circa**: 1920s; **VALUE: $60-$75**. This pan, with cut outs, is more difficult to find than the solid frame.

STYLE T GEM PAN-Size: 9" w. x 11 3/4" l.; **c/n**: 1338; **Markings**: WAGNER WARE, T, 1238; **Finish**: iron; **Circa**: 1920s; **VALUE: $250-$300**. Solid frame is very unusual.

STYLE U GEM PAN-Size: 7 3/4" x 11 1/8" plus handles; **c/n:** 1339; **Markings:** WAGNER WARE, 1339; **Finish:** iron; **Circa:** 1920s-1930s; **VALUE: $75-$100.**

LITTLE GEM PAN-Size: 7" x 9 5/8", (cups) 1 3/4" dia. x 3/4" d.; **c/n:** 466; **Markings:** LITTLE GEM, WAGNER WARE, PAT PENDING, 12 CUPS, 466; **Finish:** iron; **Circa:** 1920s-1940; **VALUE: $100-$125;** aluminum **$75.** Note star - upper left.

LITTEL GEM PAN-Size: 7 1/8" sq.; **c/n:** none; **Markings:** LITTLE GEM, WAGNER WARE, 9 CUPS, PATENT PENDING; **Finish:** iron; **Circa:** 1930s; **VALUE: $125-$150.**

KRUSTY KORN KOB MOULD-Size: Junior; **c/n:** unknown; **Finish:** iron; **Circa:** 1930s; **VALUE: $35-$45** in original sleeve.

POPOVER PAN-c/n: none; **Markings:** Double logo, MADE IN USA, B; **Finish:** iron; **Circa:** 1972; **VALUE: $20-$30**.

BUNDT PAN-Size: 10" dia. x 4" d.; **c/n:** none; **Markings:** WAGNER WARE, B; **Finish:** aluminum; **Circa:** 1914-1930s; **VALUE: $75-$100**.

BREAD PAN-Size: 7" l. x 3 9/16" w. x 2 7/8" h.; **c/n:** none; **Markings:** WAGNER WARE, 6; **Finish:** iron; **Circa:** 1915; **VALUE: $250-$300**. Also made in aluminum. **VALUE: $150-$200**.

BREAD OR LOAF PAN-Size: 8 1/8" l. x 4 5/8" w. x 2 7/8" d.; **c/n:** none; **Markings:** "WAGNER", 1; **Finish:** aluminum; **Circa:** 1915-1924; **VALUE: $75-$100**. Also made in sizes 2 & 3.

MAGNALITE ROAST & BAKE PAN-Size: 15 3/8" l. x 12 3/4" w. x 1 3/4" d.; **c/n:** unknown; **Markings:** Magnalite, ROAST BAKE PAN, stylized logo, OM; **Finish:** aluminum; **Circa:** 1940s-1950s; **VALUE: $100-$150**.

PIE PAN-Size: 10 1/2" dia.; **c/n:** 364; **Markings:** stylized logo, PIE PAN, 364; **Finish:** aluminum; **Circa:** 1920s; **VALUE: $75-$100**. No. 363 is the same value.

JELLY CAKE PAN-Size: 9 1/4" dia. x 1" d.; **c/n:** none; **Markings:** (Pie logo) WAGNER SIDNEY O.; **Finish:** aluminum; **Circa:** 1915-1920; **VALUE: $100-$125**.

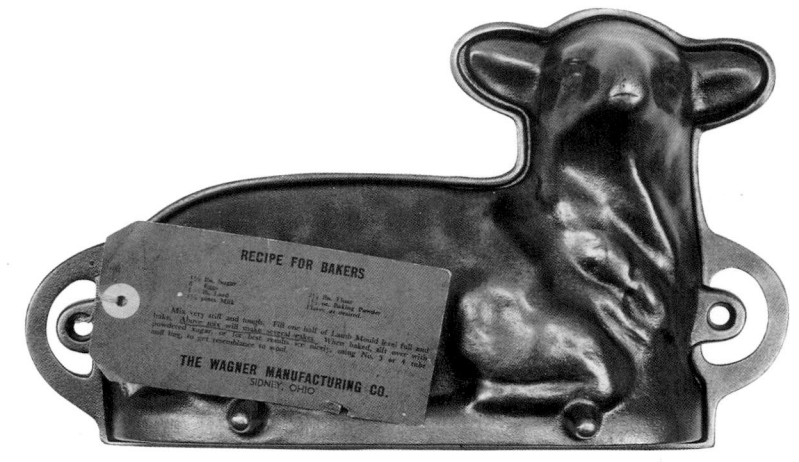

PIE TIN-Size: 8: or 9: dia.; **c/n:** none; **Markings:** MRS. WAG-NER'S PIES; **Finish:** tin; **Circa:** 1960s; **VALUE: $15-$20**. Although sometimes acquired by Wagner collectors, this piece has no connection with the Wagner Mfg. Co. of Sidney Ohio.

LAMB CAKE MOLD-Size: 13 7/8" l. x 8 1/4" h.; **c/n:** none; **Markings:** none; **Finish:** iron; **Circa:** 1930s; **VALUE: $200**; plated **$150**; aluminum **$100**. The Wagner Lamb is larger than the 866 Griswold Lamb.

Note the facial detail, and the very smooth finish.

MINIATURES, TOYS & CHILD'S DISHES

TOY SKILLETS-Size: '0'; **Clockwise: 1) Markings:** stylized logo; **Finish:** nickel; **Circa:** 1924; **VALUE: $45-$60**. **2) Markings:** "WAGNER", SIDNEY, O.; **Finish:** IRON; **Circa:** 1920; **VALUE: $50-$65**. **3) Markings:** SIDNEY; **Finish:** iron; **Circa:** 1910; **VALUE: $75-$100**. **4) Markings:** stylized logo, 1365; **Finish:** iron; **Circa:** 1924; **VALUE: $50-$60**. **5) Markings:** "WAGNER"; **Finish:** nickel; **Circa:** 1898; **VALUE: $75-$85**.

TOY SKILLET-Size: "0", 4 1/2" dia.; **c/n**: none; **Markings**: WAGNER MFG. CO, SIDNEY, O.; **Finish**: iron; **Circa**: 1910; **VALUE: $100-$125**.

COMMERATIVE TOY SKILLET-Size: 4 1/2" dia.; **c/n**: none; **Markings**: PAN AMERICAN EXPOSITION, BUFFALO; **Finish**: iron; **Circa**: 1901-1903; **VALUE: $300-$350, (finished inside) $450**.

COMMERATIVE TOY SKILLET-Size: 4 1/2" dia; **c/n**: none; **Markings**: WAGNER MFG. CO. TENN. CENTENNIAL EXPOSITION 1897; **Finish**: nickel plated iron; **Circa**: 1897; **VALUE: $450-$500**.

TOY SKILLET-Size: (left) 4 1/2" dia., (right) 3 5/16" dia.; **c/n**: (left) 1365, (right) 1367; **Markings**: stylized logo; **Finish**: iron; **Circa**: 1930s; **VALUE: (left) $50-$60, (right) $150-$200**.

TOY BAIL GRIDDLES-Size: No. 0, 4 13/16" dia.; **c/n**: none; **Markings**: (left) "WAGNER", (right) stylized logo; **Finish**: iron; **Circa**: (left) 1920s, (right) 1940s **VALUE: (left) $150-$200, (right) $100-$150**.

TOY KETTLE-Size: 4 1/8" dia. x 2 7/8" h.; **c/n**: none; **Markings**: WAGNER WARE, SIDNEY O; **Finish**: iron; **Circa**: 1920s; **VALUE: $65-$75**.

TOY TEA KETTLES-Size: (left) 4 3/8" dia. x 3 1/2" h., (right) 4 7/8" dia. x 3 1/2" h.; **c/n**: none; **Finish**: (left) aluminum, (right) iron; **Circa**: 1924-1940; **VALUE: (left) $75-$125, (right) $100-$150**.

TOY SET BOX-Size: 10 1/2" x 5" d.; **c/n**: none; **Markings**: cardboard; **Circa**: 1924; **VALUE: $100-$150**.

BAILED GRIDDLE-Size: 4 3/4" dia.; **c/n**: none; **Markings**: stylized logo; **VALUE: $75-$100**.

ALUMINUM TOY SET-Size: "0"; **Circa**: 1920s; **VALUE: $500-$550**.

TEA KETTLE-Size: 4 3/8" dia. x 3 1/2" h.; **c/n**: none; **Markings**: stylized logo, B; **VALUE: $100-$150**.

SKILLET-Size: "0"; **c/n**: none; **Markings**: stylized logo; **Finish**: aluminum; **VALUE**: $50-$75.

TOY HANDLE & BAIL GRIDDLE-Size: "0"; **c/n**: (left) 855, (right) none; **Markings**: stylized logo; **Finish**: aluminum; **Circa**: 1920s; **VALUE**: (handle) $150-$200, (bail) $75-$100.

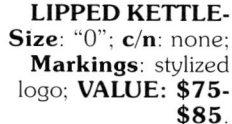

LIPPED KETTLE-Size: "0"; **c/n**: none; **Markings**: stylized logo; **VALUE**: $75-$85.

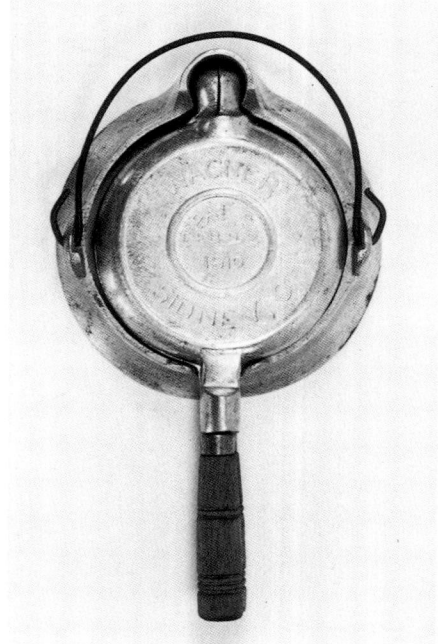

WAFFLE IRON-Size: (Paddles) 3 1/4" dia.; **c/n**: none; **Markings**: "WAGNER", PAT'D FEB. 22, 1910; **VALUE**: $200-$250.

CHILDS WARM PLATE- Markings: MANY HAPPY BIRTHDAYS FROM THE WAGNER MFG. CO. SIDNEY O; **Finish**: aluminum; **Circa**: unknown; **VALUE**: $100-$150. See other examples in the color section.

SCOOPS

Scoops

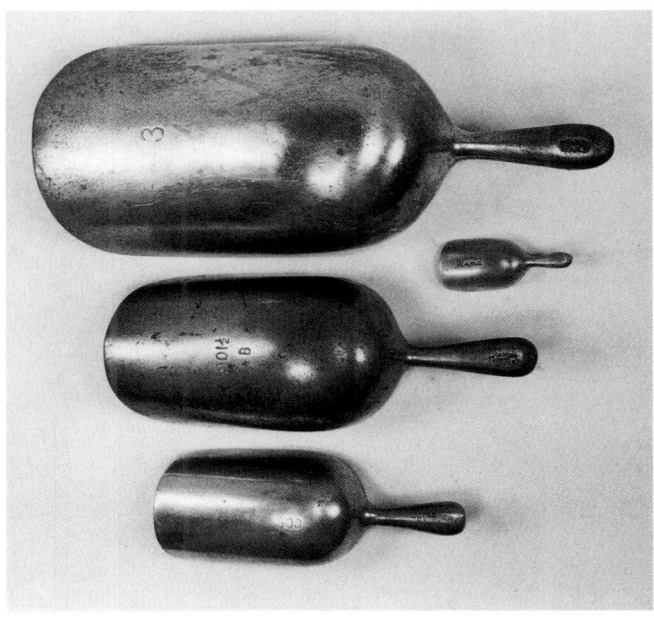

SUGAR SCOOPS-Size: 15 1/4" x 5 7/8" to 3 5/8" x 1 1/2"; **c/n**: (middle) 901 1/2, (bottom) 900; **Markings**: stylized logo; **Finish**: aluminum; **Circa**: 1920s-1940s; **VALUE: (top) $40, (mini) $20-$30, (middle) $30, (bottom) $25**.

SUGAR SCOOP-Size: No. 01, 10 1/2" x 4"; **c/n**: 01; **Markings**: stylized logo, 01E; **Finish**: aluminum; **Circa**: 1920s; **VALUE: $25-$30**.

SUGAR SCOOP- Size: 10 3/4" x 4 1/8"; **c/n**: 901; **Markings**: stylized logo, 910D; **Finish**: iron; **Circa**: 1930s; **VALUE: $35-$45**. Iron is unusual. The decorative design appears to be aluminum.

ADVERTISING SUGAR SCOOP- Size: 10 3/8" x 3 7/8"; **c/n**: none; **Markings**: 00B, WAGNER MFG. CO., SIDNEY O. (in oval), ORANGE BLOSSOM GLYCERINE SOAP, QUEEN REGENT TOILET SOAP; **Finish**: aluminum; **Circa**: 1940s; **VALUE: $45-$60**.

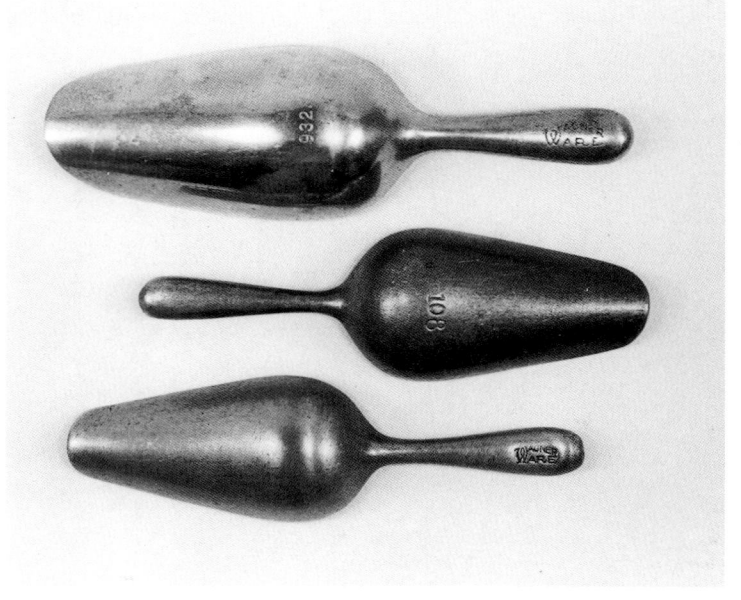

ICE SCOOP (TOP) & NARROW SCOOPS- Size: (Ice Scoop) 10" x 3 1/8", (narrow Scoops) 9' x 2 3/4"; **c/n**: (top) 932, (center) 108, (btm.) none; **Markings**: (top and btm.) stylized logo; **Finish**: aluminum; **Circa**: 1920s; **VALUE: $30-$50**. Ice scoops are difficult to find.

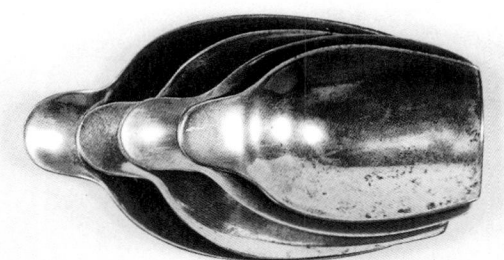

DRUG SCOOPS-Size: 5 5/8" x 3 9/16 to 4 1/4" x 2 1/2"; **c/n**: unknown; **Markings**: stylized logo; **Finish**: aluminum; **Circa**: 1920s -1930s; **VALUE: $25-$35 each**.

THUMB SCOOP-Size: 7 7/8" x 3"; **c/n**: 930; **Markings**: stylized logo, 930; **Finish**: aluminum; **Circa**: 1920s; **VALUE: $25-$35**.

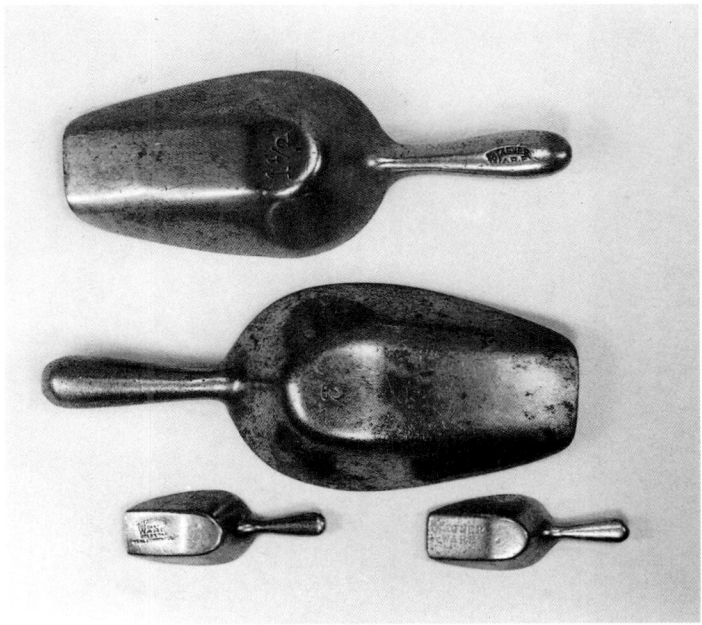

COFFEE SCOOPS-Size: 9 1/2" x 3 7/8" to 3 5/8 x 1 3/8"; **c/n**: none; **Markings**: stylized logo; **Finish**: aluminum; **Circa**: 1920s -1940s; **VALUE: $25-$60**.

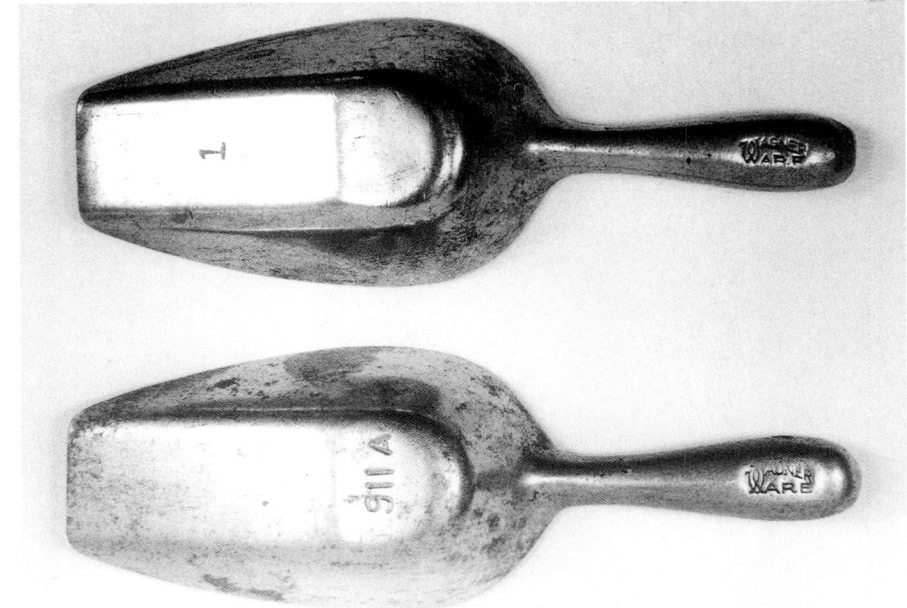

COFFEE SCOOPS-Size: 8 1/2" x 3"; **c/n**: (btm) 911; **Markings**: (top) stylized logo, 1, (btm) stylized logo, 911A; **Finish**: aluminum; **Circa**: (top) 1915-1920s, (btm) 1920s; **VALUE: $15-$20; No.2, $20-$25; No.3, $15-$20; No.4, $20-$25; No.5, $25-$30**.

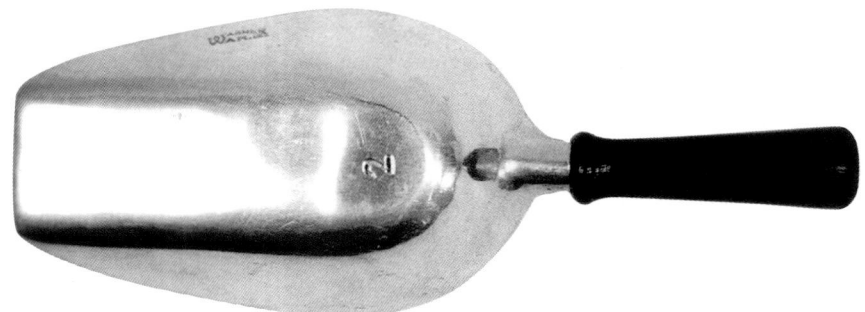

WOOD HANDLED COFFEE SCOOP-Size: No.2, 10" l.; **c/n**: none; **Markings**: 2, stylized logo (no Sidney O) on side; **Finish**: aluminum; **Circa**: 1920s; **VALUE: $30-$35**.

ADVERTISING COFFEE SCOOP-Size: 9" x 3 1/2"; **c/n**: none; **Markings**: 1 1/2, stylized logo, ELLIS & HELFER CO, LOG CABIN CANDIES; **Finish**: aluminum; **Circa**: 1930s; **VALUE: $60-$75**.

WOOD HANDLED CONFECTIONERY SCOOP-Size: 8 3/4" l. x 2 11/16" w.; **c/n**: none; **Markings**: stylized logo, BRECHT, DENVER (inside); **Finish**: aluminum; **Circa**: 1920; **VALUE: $45-$60**.

SPOONS-Top to Bottom: 1) BASTING SPOON WITH HOOK-Size: 13 3/4"; **c/n**: none; **Markings**: (stamped) WAGNER MFG; **Finish**: aluminum; **Circa**: 1915; **VALUE: $35-$40; 2) FLAT SPOON- Size**: 15 3/4"; **c/n**: 711; **Markings**: 711, stylized logo; **Finish**: aluminum; **Circa**: 1915-1940s; **VALUE: $40-$60; 3) EGG WHIP-Size**: 11 1/4"; **c/n**: none; **Markings**: stylized logo; **Finish**: aluminum; **Circa**: 1915-1940s; **VALUE: $30-$40; 4) FLAT SPOON-Size**: 10 7/8"; **c/n**: 709; **Markings**: stylized logo; **Finish**: aluminum; **Circa**: 1915-1940s; **VALUE: $20-$25; 5) SPOON WITH HOOK-Size**: 10 5/8"; **c/n**: none; **Markings**: 5, stylized logo; **Finish**: aluminum; **Circa**: 1915-1925; **VALUE: $25-$30**.

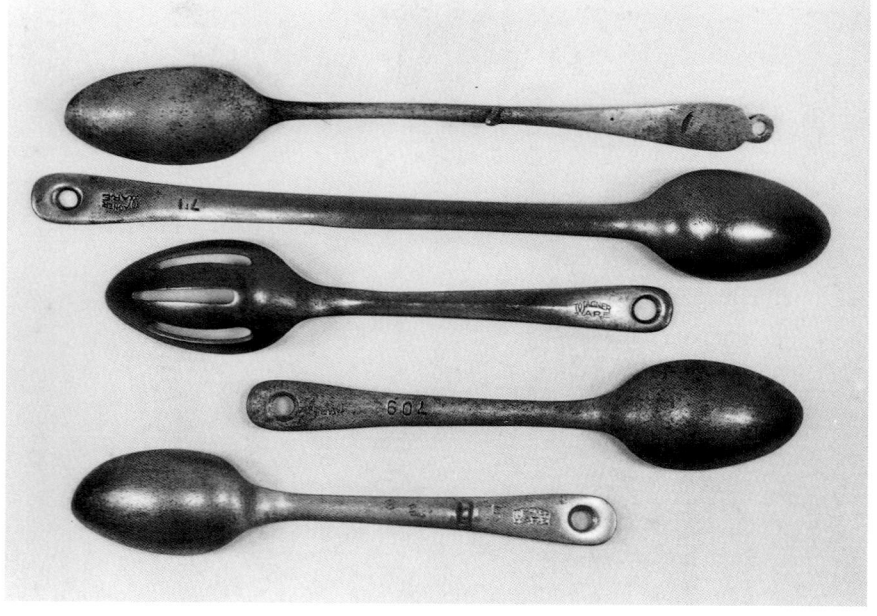

SPOONS-Size: 10 1/2"; **c/n**: 718; **Markings**: WAGNER WARE, (top) 718, (btm) 718B; **Finish**: aluminum; **Circa**: unknown; **VALUE: $30-$40**. Author could not find reference to this spoon in any catalog.

CAKE OR EGG BEATER-Size: 9 3/4"; **c/n**: 719; **Markings**: WAGNER WARE, 719; **Finish**: aluminum; **Circa**: 1920s-1930s; **VALUE: $50-$60**.

SOLID ICE CREAM SPADE-Size: 11 3/4"; **c/n**: 940; **Markings**: none; **Finish**: aluminum; **Circa**: 1920s-1930s; **VALUE: $30-$40**.

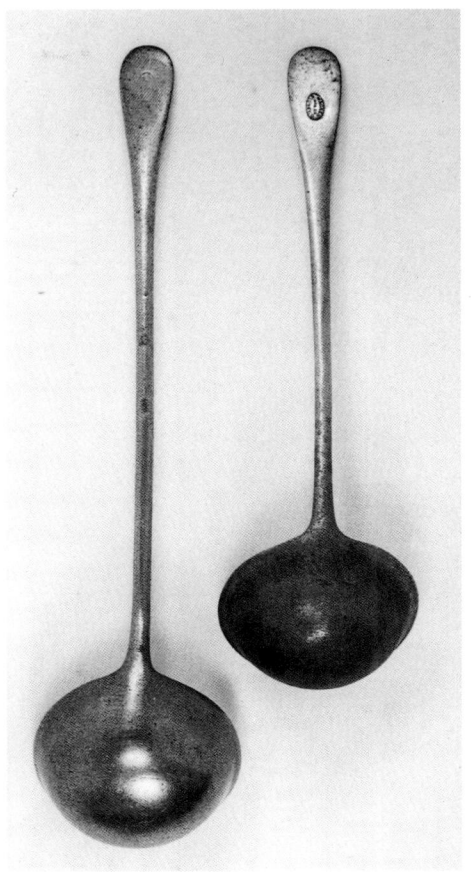

LONG HANDLED LADLES-Size: (left) 14 7/8", (right) 11 3/4"; **c/n**: none; **Markings**: WAGNER MFG CO. (in oval); **Finish**: aluminum; **Circa**: 1900-1915; **VALUE: $30-$50**.

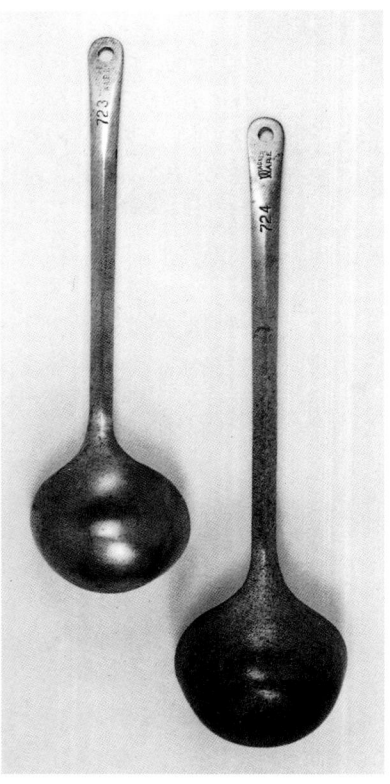

LONG HANDLED LADLES-
Size: (left) 13 1/2", (right) 15";
c/n: Left) 723, (right) 724;
Markings: stylized logo, (left) 723, (right 724; **Finish**: aluminum; **Circa**: 1920s;
VALUE: $40-$50.

SOUP LADLE (top), and **Fruit Ladle with Hook**, (bottom)-
Size: (top) 9 1/2", (btm) 6 3/4"; **c/n**: (top) 708, (btm.) none;
Markings: (top) stylized logo, 708, (btm) WAGNER MFG. CO, SIDNEY O. (inside circle); **Finish**: aluminum; **Circa**: 1915-1930s; **VALUE: $40-$50**.

SOUP LADLE-Size: 9 3/4";
c/n: none; **Markings**: stylized logo, SOUP; **Finish**: aluminum; **Circa**: 1918-1930;
VALUE: $40-$50.

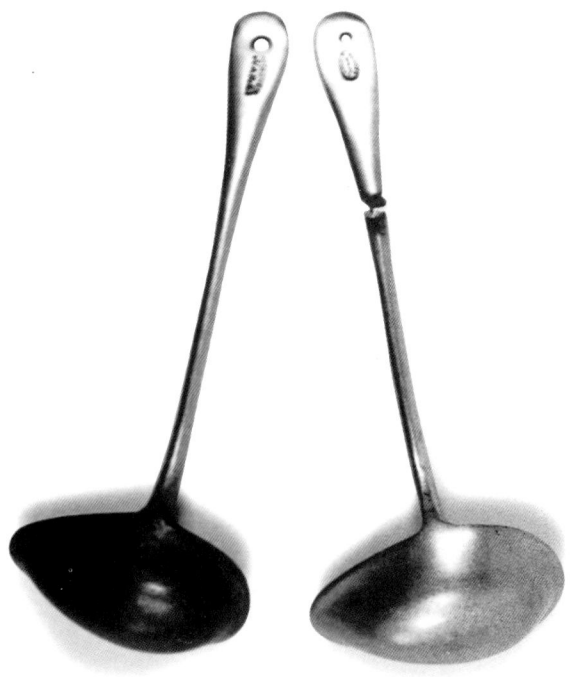

TOM & JERRY LADLES-Size: (left) 9 1/2", (right) 9 1/4"; **c/n**: none; **Markings**: (left) stylized logo, (right) WAGNER MFG. SIDNEY O. (in oval); **Finish**: aluminum; **Circa**: 1915-1920s; **VALUE: $20-$30**.

SMALL DIPPER-Size: 1 Pint, 9 1/2" handle, (cup) 4 5/16" dia x 2 3/4" d.; **c/n**: none; **Markings**: stylized logo, 1 PT; **Finish**: aluminum; **Circa**: 1913-1930s; **VALUE: $50-$60**.

DIPPER-Size: 1 Pint, 13 5/16" long, (cup) 4 3/8" dia. x 2 3/4" d.; **c/n**: none; **Markings**: stylized logo, SECOND TO NONE (in oval); **Finish**: aluminum; **Circa**: 1913-1920; **VALUE: $75-$100**; (1 Quart) **$75-$100**.

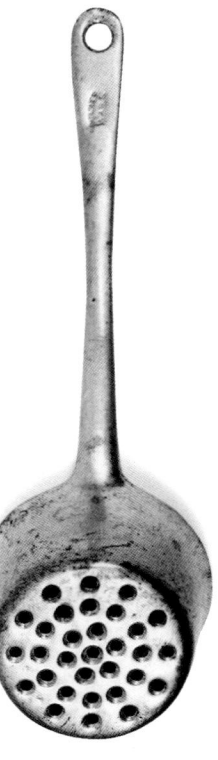

PICKLE DIPPER-Size: 13 3/4" long (cup) 4 3/4" dia. x 3" d.; **c/n**: none; **Markings**: stylized logo; **Finish**: aluminum; **Circa**: 1920s; **VALUE: $60-$70**.

LARD OR TRANSFER LADLE-Size: 10" x 6 1/2" w.; **c/n**: none; **Markings**: stylized logo; **Finish**: aluminum; **Circa**: 1920s; **VALUE: $35-$40**.

LARD LADLE-Size: 4" w. x 9 1/2" l.; **c/n**: 976; **Markings**: 976, stylized logo; **Finish**: aluminum; **Circa**: 1915-1920s; **VALUE: $20-$30**.

LARD LADLE-Size: 8 1/2" x 3 1/16"; **c/n**: 975; **Markings**: stylized logo, 975; **Finish**: aluminum; **Circa**: 1920s-1930s; **VALUE: $25-$30**.

Left: LARD LADLE-Size: 8 3/4" x 3 1/8"; **c/n**: 975; **Markings**: stylized logo, PACKERS & BUTCHERS SUPPLY, TAMPA FL., 975; **Finish**: aluminum; **Circa**: 1920s-1950; **VALUE: $25-$35**.

Center: LARD LADLE-c/n: none; **Markings**: stylized logo, OTTENHEIMER BROS., BALT., MD, F.R.M.; **Finish**: aluminum; **Circa**: 1930; **VALUE: $40-$50**.

Right: LARD SPADE-Size: 10 1/2" x 3 5/16"; **c/n**: none; **Markings**: WAGNER MFG. CO., SIDNEY O. (in oval); **Finish**: aluminum; **Circa**: 1915; **VALUE: $25-$30**.

CASSEROLES, SERVERS, PLATTERS, TRAYS, CUPS & DISHES

OVAL CASSEROLE-Size: 8 5/8" l. x 6 1/8" w. x 3 7/8" d.; **c/n**: none; **Markings**: "WAGNER", SIDNEY, O. 1, (cover) 1; **Finish**: aluminum; **Circa**: 1915; **VALUE: $75-$100**. Made in three sizes.

ROUND CASSEROLE-Markings: stylized logo (stamped), (cover) unmarked; **Finish**: aluminum; **Circa**: 1920s; **VALUE: $30-$50 with cover**.

OVAL CASSEROLE-Size: 11 1/4" l. x 6 3/4" l. x 3 1/2" d.; **c/n**: 282; **Markings**: stylized logo, CASSEROLE, 282; **Finish**: aluminum; **Circa**: 1920s-1930s; **VALUE: $60-$75**.

ROUND CASSEROLE-Size: 4 5/8" dia. x 2 1/2" d.; **c/n**: none; **Markings**: WAGNER WARE SIDNEY, O., ROUND CASSEROLE, 2; **Finish**: aluminum; **Circa**: 1915; **VALUE: $45-$65**. Made in four sizes

CASSEROLE PAN & SHIRRED EGG PAN-Size: (left) 6 7/16" dia. x 1 3/8" d., (right) 5 9/16" x 7/16"; **c/n**: (left) 331, (right) 312; **Markings**: Stylized logo, (left) CASSEROLE PAN, 331, (right) SHIRRED EGG PAN, 312; **Finish**: aluminum; **Circa**: 1915-1940s; **VALUE: $40-$60**. Both of these were made in two sizes.

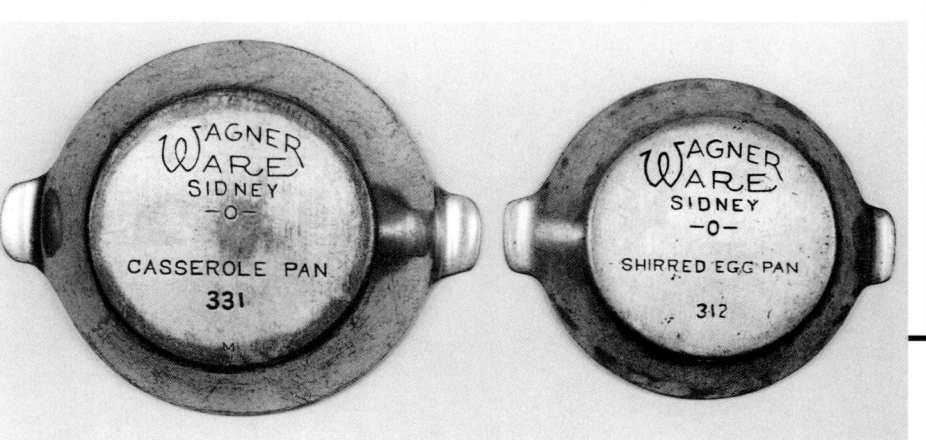

BAKER DISH-Size: 4 5/16" l. x 3" w. x 7/8" d.; **c/n**: none; **Markings**: stylized logo; **Finish**: aluminum; **Circa**: 1915-1920s; **VALUE: $30-$40**.

BUN WARMER-Size: 8 7/8" dia.; **c/n**: 4052; **Markings**: stylized logo (in oval), Magnalite; **Finish**: aluminum; **Circa**: 1940s-1950s; **VALUE: $100-$125**.

HANDLED RAMEQUINS-Size: 3 3/16" dia. x 1 1/16" d.; **c/n**: none; **Markings**: stylized logo; **Finish**: aluminum; **Circa**: 1915-1920s; **VALUE: $30-$50 each**.

CUSTARD CUP-Size: 3 1/4" dia. x 1 7/8" d.; **c/n**: 322; **Markings**: stylized logo, 2; **Finish**: aluminum; **Circa**: 1920s; **VALUE: $30-$40**.

AL CARDERS SIZZLING STEAK PLATTER-Size: 13 3/4" x 9 1/4"; **c/n**: 335 1/2M; **Markings**: stylized logo, AL CARDERS SIZZLING STEAK PLATTER, TRADE MARK REG., 335 1/2M; **Finish**: aluminum; **Circa**: 1950s **VALUE: $40-$60**. Also made in sizes 333, 10" x 7", and 334, 11 1/2" x 8", at same value.

SIZZLING STEAK PLATTER-Size: 14 1/8" x 9 1/2"; **c/n**: 3341; **Markings**: stylized logo, THE ORIGINAL SIZZLING STEAK PLATTER, TRADE MARK REG., U.S. PAT. OFF.; **Finish**: hammered aluminum; **Circa**: 1940s; **VALUE: $45-$50**: No. 3340, $60-$75; No. 3342, $60-$75.

ROUND SIZZLING PLATTER-Size: 7 5/8" dia.; **c/n**: 332 1/2B; **Markings**: stylized logo, 332 1/2B, a star in circle, CARDERS SIZZLING PLATTER; **Finish**: aluminum; **Circa**: 1950s; **VALUE: $30-$40**.

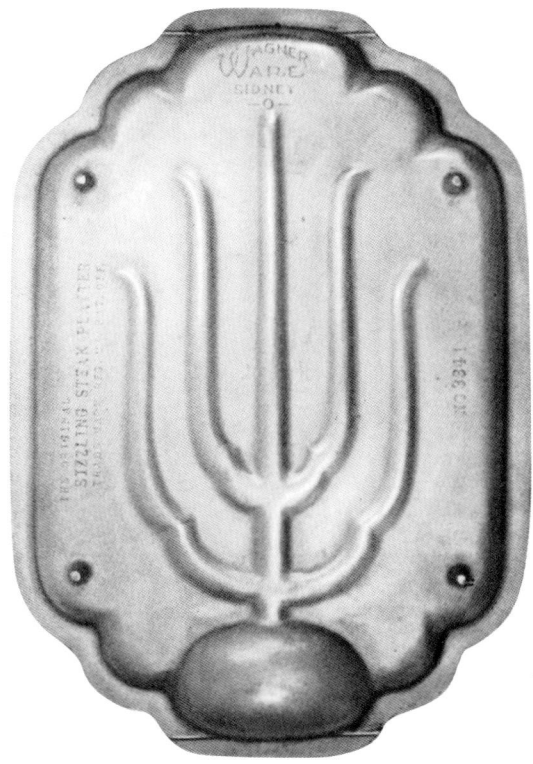

MAGNALITE SIZZLING HOST PLATTER- Size: 17 3/8" x 12 5/8"; **c/n**: 4343; **Markings**: stylized logo, Magnalite, SIZZLING HOST PLATTER, TRADE MARK, REG. US PATENT OFC, DESIGN PATENT 101399; **Finish**: aluminum; **Circa**: 1940s; **VALUE: $40-$50 with wood handles**.

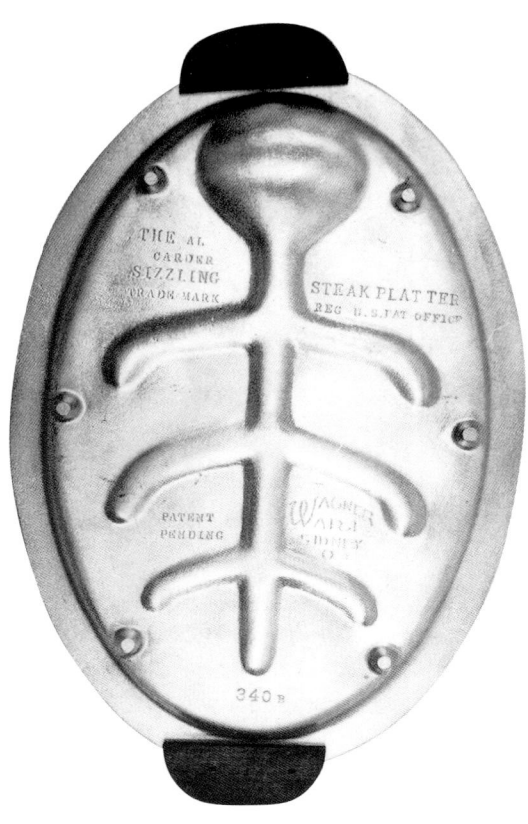

AL CARDERS STEAK PLATTER-Size: 12 7/8" x 9"; **c/n**: 340; **Markings**: THE AL CARDER STEAK PLATTER, TRADE MARK, REG. U.S. PATENT OFFICE, PATENT PENDING, stylized logo, 340E; **Finish**: aluminum; **Circa**: 1940s-1950s; **VALUE: $75-$100**. The removable wood handles are slotted and fit over the ends.

MAGNALITE SIZZLING PLATTER-Size: 15 1/4" x 11 1/4"; **c/n**: 4341; **Markings**: stylized logo, 4341, Magnalite SIZZLING PLATTER, TRADE MARK, REG. US PATENT OFC; **Finish**: aluminum; **Circa**: 1940s; **VALUE: $40-$50**.

SIZZLING VEGETABLE PLATTER-Size: 15 1/4" x 11 1/4"; **c/n**: 4344; **Markings**: stylized logo, 4344, Magnalite, SIZZLING VEGETABLE PLATTER, TRADE MARK, REG. US PAT. OFFICE; **Finish**: aluminum; **Circa**: 1940s; **VALUE: $60-$75**.

MAGNALITE SIZZLING PLATTER-Size: 15 1/4" x 11 1/4"; **c/n**: 4341; **Markings**: stylized logo, Magnalite SIZZLING PLATTER, 4341; **Finish**: aluminum; **Circa**: 1950s-1960s; **VALUE: $40-$60**. No notches for handles.

MAGNALITE PLATTER-Size: 17 3/4" x 11 5/8"; **c/n**: none; **Markings**: MAGNALITE COUNTRY COLLECTION; **Finish**: aluminum; **Circa**: 1960s; **VALUE: $75-$100**.

ROUND TRAY-Size: 12" dia. x 3/4" d.; **c/n**: none; **Markings**: "WAGNER" SIDNEY, O., 12; **Finish**: aluminum; **Circa**: 1910; **VALUE: $95-$125**.

DISH OR PIE PAN-Size: 6 5/8" dia. x 1" d.; **c/n**: none; **Markings**: WAGNER MFG. CO., SIDNEY (in oval); **Finish**: aluminum; **Circa**: unknown; **VALUE: $30-$50**.

OVAL PLATTER-Size: 16" x 13 1/4"; **c/n**: none; **Markings**: stylized logo, 16; **Finish**: aluminum; **Circa**: 1915; **VALUE: $125-$150**.

MAGNALITE BAKING PAN-Size: 10" square x 1 1/2" d.; **c/n**: 4510; **Markings**: stylized logo, Magnalite, 4510; **Finish**: aluminum; **Circa**: 1940s-1970s; **VALUE: $75-$100**.

CANDY TRAY-Size: 13" x 7 3/4"; **c/n**: 964; **Markings**: stylized logo, 964; **Finish**: aluminum; **Circa**: 1915-1920s; **VALUE: $100-$150**. Available in 9 sizes, No.'s 962, 7 3/4" x 9" to 968-2, 8" x 20". Sized to fit in candy display cases.

SMALL CUP-Size: 2 3/4" dia. x 2" d.; **c/n**: none; **Markings**: WAGNER MFG. CO. SIDNEY O. (in oval); **Finish**: aluminum; **Circa**: 1915; **VALUE: $20-$30**.

LARGE CUPS-Size: 3 3/4" dia. x 2 1/2" d.; **c/n**: 404; **Markings**: (left) stylized logo, (center) WAGNER MFG. CO, SIDNEY O., (right) stylized logo, 404, SECOND TO NONE; **Finish**: aluminum; **Circa**: 1915-1920s; **VALUE: (left) $20-$30; (center) $25-$35; (right) $30-$40**.

TALL CUP-Size: 3 3/4" h. x 3" d.; **c/n**: none; **Markings**: stylized logo; **Finish**: aluminum; **Circa**: 1915 - 1920s; **VALUE: $30-$40**.

HEAVY DUTY PRISON PAN-Size: 7 7/8" dia. 2" d.; **c/n**: 1954; **Markings**: stylized logo, 1954M; **Finish**: aluminum; **Circa**: 1930s; **VALUE: $100-$125**.

MIXING CUP-Size: 6 7/8" h. x 4" d., 1 1/2 pint; **c/n**: 960; **Markings**: stylized logo, 960; **Finish**: aluminum; **Circa**: 1920s; **VALUE: $30-$40**.

INDIVIDUAL BUTTER DISH-Size: 2 13/16" dia.; **c/n**: none; **Markings**: stylized logo; **Finish**: alum; **Circa**: 1915 - 1920s; **VALUE: $25-$35**.

MOLDS & FORMS

JELLY MOULD-Size: 7 7/8" l. x 5 3/4" w. x 2 3/16" d.; **c/n**: 424; **Markings**: stylized logo, 424; **Finish**: aluminum; **Circa**: 1915-1920s; **VALUE: $60-$75**.

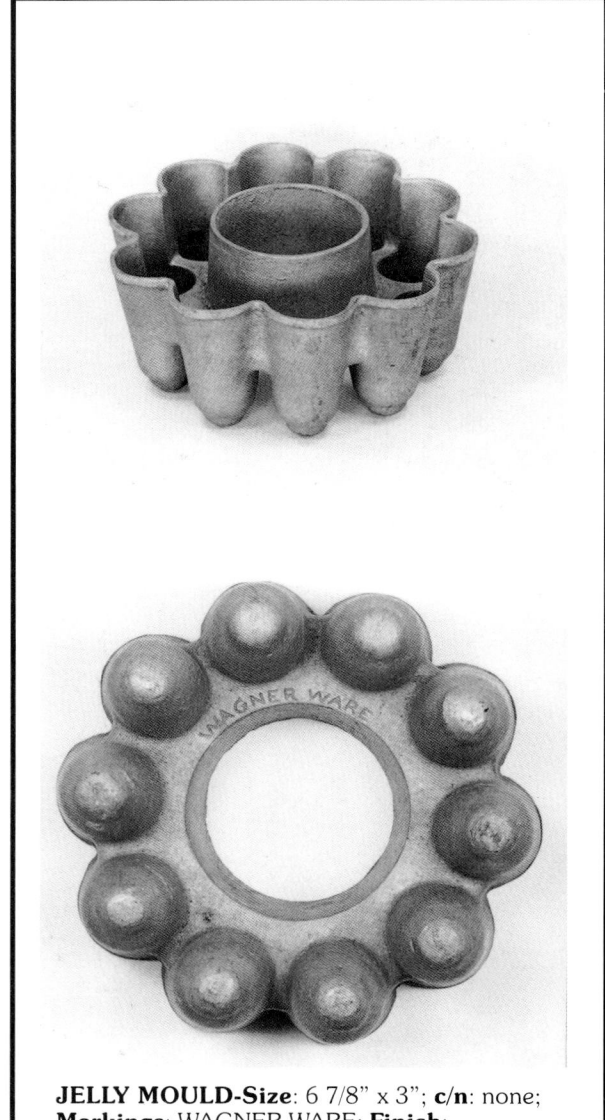

JELLY MOULD-Size: 6 7/8" x 3"; **c/n**: none; **Markings**: WAGNER WARE; **Finish**: aluminum; **Circa**: 1915-1920s; **VALUE: $75-$100**.

PATTY MOULD SET-**Finish**: aluminum; **Circa**: 1924; **VALUE**: $30-$35. Patented 1907. Date of this set determined by graphics on the box.

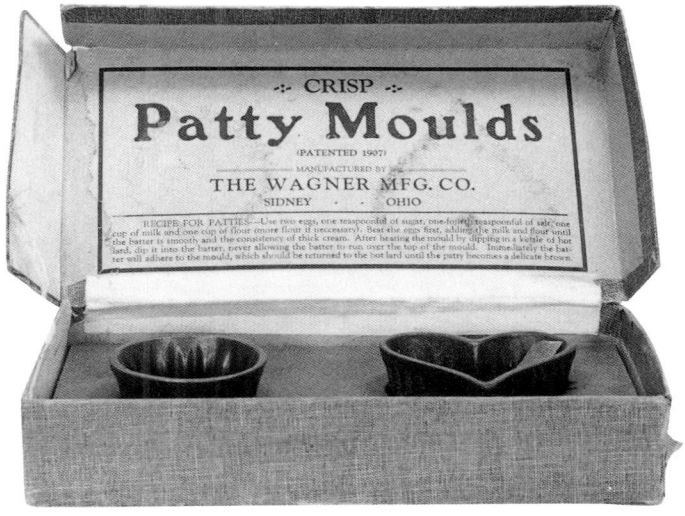

PATTY MOULD SET-**Finish**: Iron; **Circa**: 1920s-1930s; **VALUE**: $30-$35.

ICE CREAM PAIL MOLDS-**Size**: 1 Pint and 1 Quart in different forms; **c/n**: none; **Markings**: WAGNER CAST WARE, or stylized logo; **Finish**: aluminum; **Circa**: 1915-1930s; **VALUE**: $40-$60. Used to hold ice cream cartons while packing from bulk.

MISCELLANEOUS

PICNIC GRILL-Size: 12 1/4" square; **c/n**: 1000; **Markings**: stylized logo, THE PICNICKER, PAT PEND; **Finish**: aluminum with tin tray; **Circa**: 1938; **VALUE**: $150-$200.

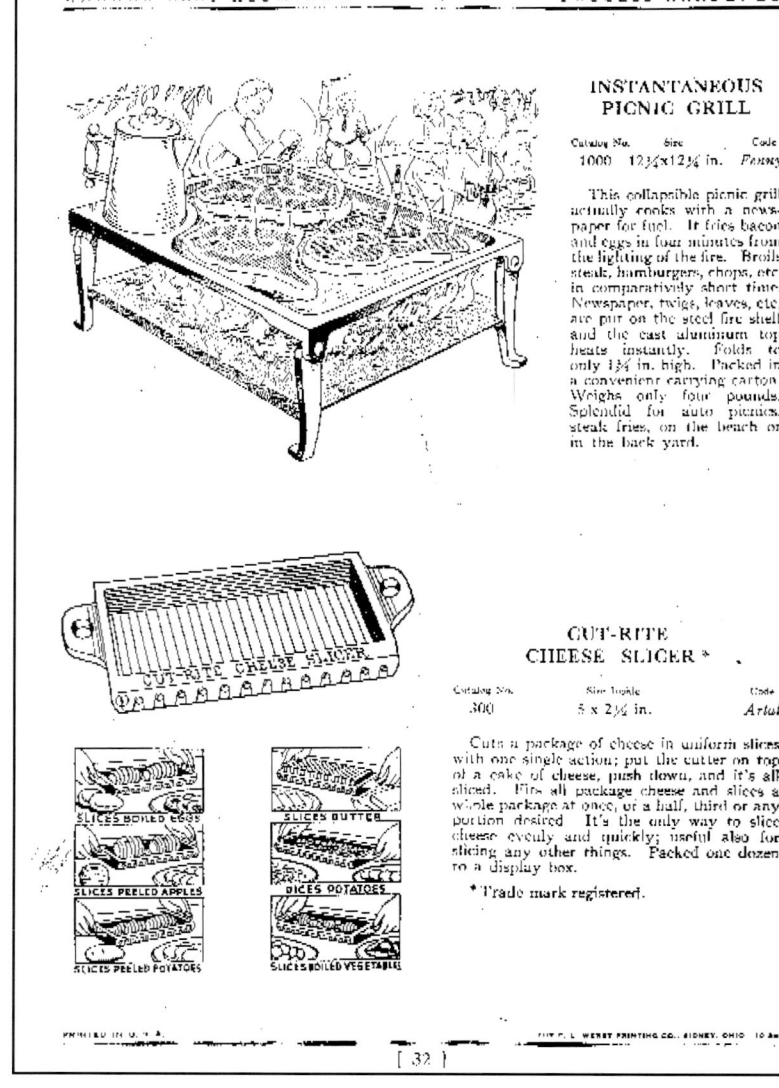

Page from a 1938 Wagner catalog.

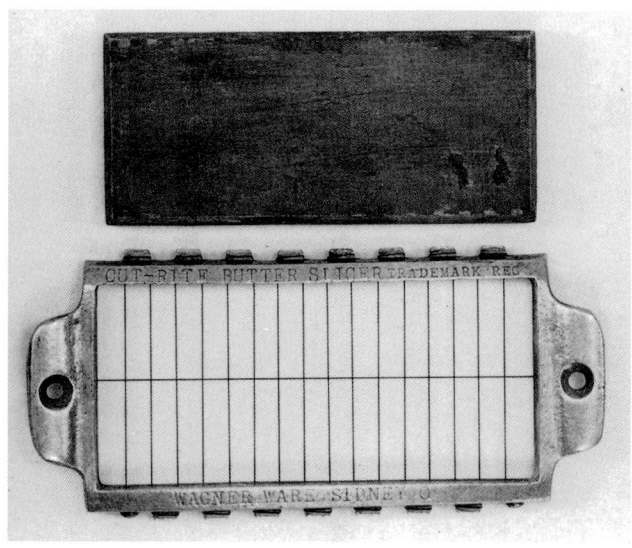

BUTTER SLICER-Size: 8 1/2" x 4"; **c/n**: 298; **Markings**: CUT-RITE BUTTER SLICER, TRADEMARK REG., WAGNER WARE, SIDNEY O; **Finish**: aluminum with steel wire; **Circa**: 1930s; **VALUE: $125-150**. Wood block was used to push the butter through.

CHEESE SLICER-Size: 7" x 3 1/8"; **c/n**: 300; **Markings**: WAGNER WARE, SIDNEY O., CUT-RITE CHEESE SLICER, 300, PAT. PEND.; **Finish**: aluminum with steel wire; **Circa**: 1930s; **VALUE: $75**.

LEMON JUICE EXTRACTORS-Size: (left) 6 1/4" dia, (right) 3 1/2" dia.; **c/n**: (left) 453, (right) none; **Markings**: (Left) stylized logo, 453, CAST ALUMINUM, B.M, (right) none; **Finish**: aluminum; **Circa**: 1915-1920s; **VALUE: (left) $30-$45; (right) $45-$55**.

LEMON JUICE EXTRACTOR-Size: 3 5/8" dia.; **c/n**: 450; **Markings**: 450; **Finish**: aluminum; **Circa**: 1910-1920s; **VALUE: $30-$40**.

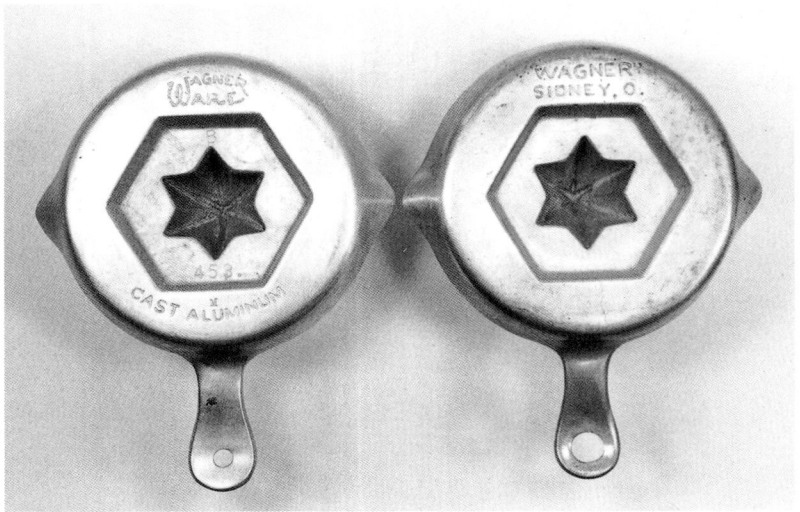

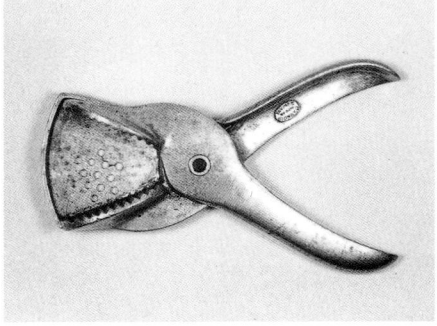

LEMON JUICE EXTRACTORS-Size: 6 1/4" dia.; **c/n**: (left) 453, (right) none; **Markings**: (left) stylized logo, CAST ALUMINUM, 453, (right) WAGNER SIDNEY O.; **Finish**: aluminum; **Circa**: 1915-1930s; **VALUE: (left) $30-$45; (right) $40-$50**. Note different handle styles.

LIME SQUEEZER-Size: 7 1/4"; **c/n**: none; **Markings**: WAGNER MFG CO. SIDNEY O. (in oval); **Finish**: aluminum; **Circa**: 1915; **VALUE: $40-$50**.

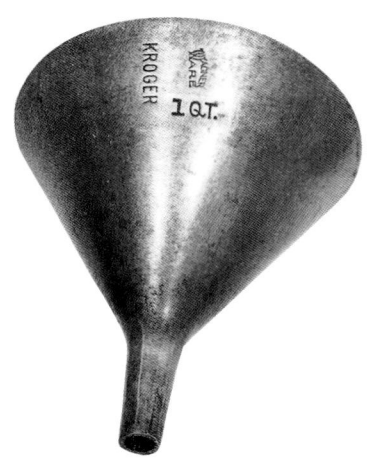

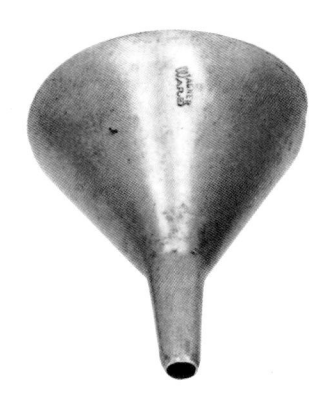

FUNNELS-Size: (left) 7", (right) 6"; **c/n**: none; **Markings**: (left) stylized logo, 1 QT, KROGER, (right) stylized logo; **Finish**: aluminum; **Circa**: **(left) $50-$60; (right) $40-$50; VALUE**.

FRUIT PRESS-Size: 12" h. x 7" dia.; **c/n**: none; **Markings**: WAGNER, 2 QT (on handle), PATENTED AUGUST__ (on press plate); **Finish**: iron and tin; **Circa**: 1915; **VALUE: $125-$150**.

FONDUE POT-Size: 9" plus knob x 6 1/8" dia.; **c/n**: none; **Markings**: none; **Finish**: iron; **Circa**: unknown; **VALUE: Rare**. It is said that only five of these were made and that they never went into production.

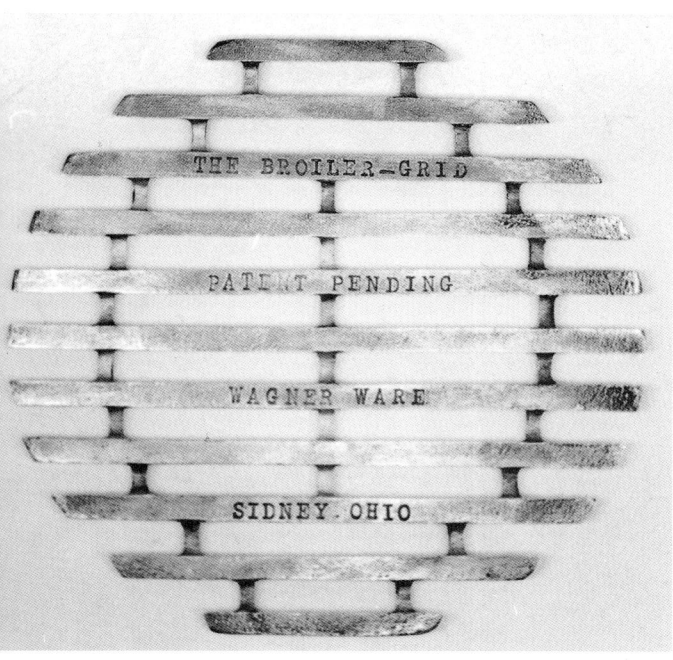

BROILER GRID-Size: 8 7/16" dia.; **c/n**: none; **Markings**: THE BROILER GRID, PATENT PENDING, WAGNER WARE, SIDNEY OHIO; **Finish**: aluminum; **Circa**: 1930s; **VALUE: $75-$100; iron, $100-$150**.

SAD IRON HEATER-Size: 10 1/2" dia.; **c/n**: none; **Markings**: WAGNER MFG CO, SIDNEY O, SAD IRON HEATER; **Finish**: iron; **Circa**: 1914-1920s; **VALUE: $125-$150**.

SEALING WAX LADLE-Size: 6" l. x 3 3/16" dia. x 2" d.; **c/n**: 1514; **Markings** 1514; **Finish**: iron; **Circa**: 1920s; **VALUE: $50-$60**.

HEAT REGULATOR-Size: 7 3/4" dia.; **c/n**: 1309; **Markings**: PROTECTIVE HOT PLATE, stylized logo, (reverse) 1309, PAT APPLIED FOR; **Finish**: iron; **Circa**: 1930s; **VALUE: $125-$150**.

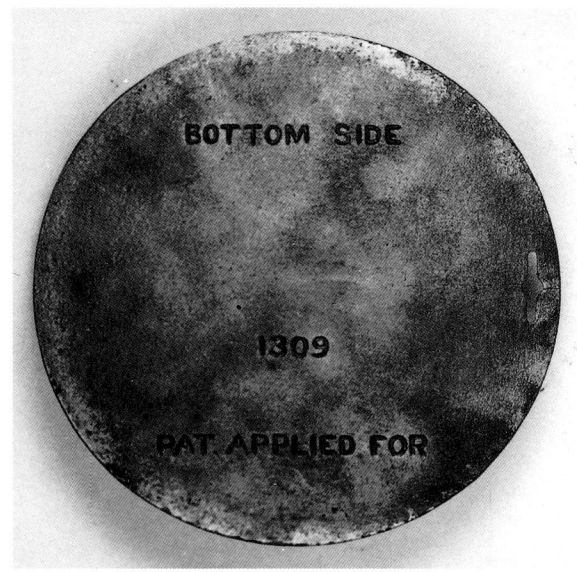

MILK PAIL-Size: 11 1/2" dia. x 9" h.; **c/n**: none; **Markings**: stylized logo; **Finish**: heavy aluminum; **Circa**: 1920s; **VALUE: $125-$150**.

DECORATIVE TRIVET-Size: 5 3/8" dia. x 7 7/8" l.; **c/n**: none; **Markings**: stylized logo; **Finish**: flat black; **Circa**: 1990s; **VALUE: $15**.

DOOR FOR BOILER & FEED COOKER-Size: 14 3/4" x 11 1/2"; **c/n**: none; **Markings**: WAGNER M'F'G CO, SIDNEY O; **Finish**: iron; **Circa**: 1897-1920s; **VALUE: $45-$65**.

CIGARETTE LIGHTER-Size: **c/n**: none; **Markings**: stylized logo (in oval), (bottom) ATL, Super Delux, JAPAN; **Finish**: plated; **Circa**: 1960s; **VALUE: $100-125**.

STOVE LID LIFTER-Size: 9"; **c/n**: none; **Markings**: WAG-NER MFG CO; **Finish**: iron; **Circa**: 1902-1920; **VALUE: $150-$200**.

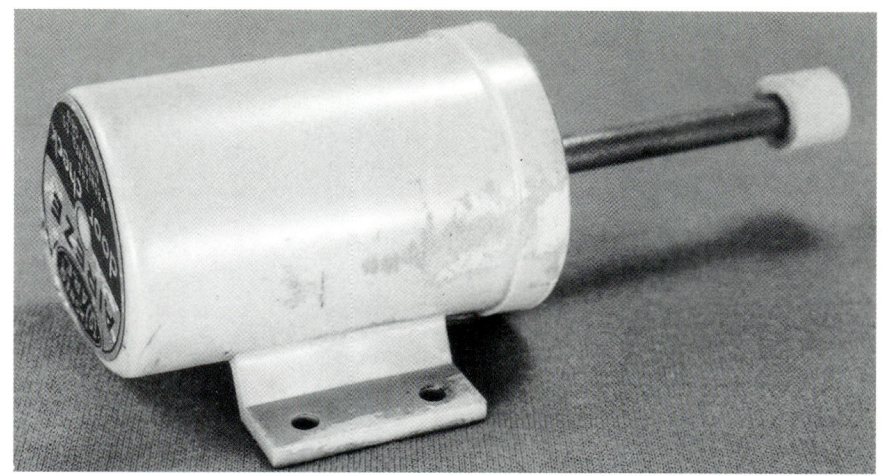

DOOR CHECK-Size: (cylinder) 1 5/8" dia. x 2 1/2", (total length) 4 7/8"; **c/n**: none **Markings**: (sticker) stylized logo, AIREZE door check, THE WAGNER MFG. CO., SIDNEY OHIO; **Finish**: plastic with steel plunger; **Circa**: 1960s; **VALUE: $150-$200**. Made during Randall era.

MAILBOX-Size: 10" h. x 7" w. x 2" d.; **c/n**: none; **Markings**: stylized logo; **Finish**: enameled steel; **Circa**: 1960; **VALUE: $40-$50**. Made during Randall era.

Wagner Color

BANNER-Size: 61" 31"; **Circa**: 1991; **VALUE: $150-$250**.

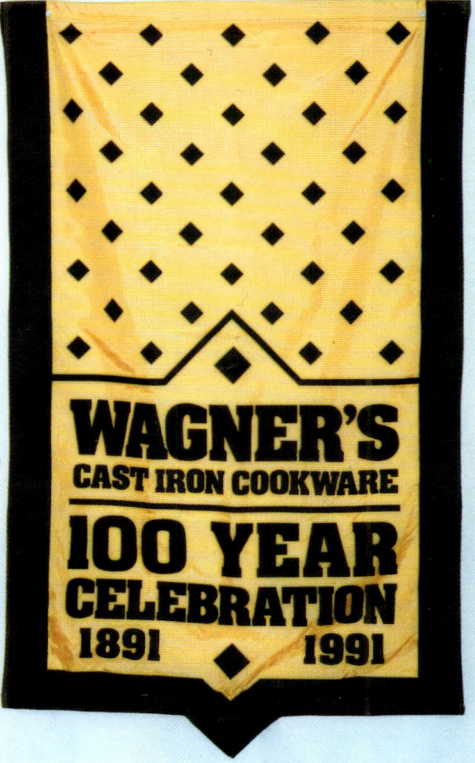

SKILLET PATTERN-Size: 8 1/2" dia.; **c/n**: none; **Markings**: none; **Finish**: wood with epoxy handle; **Circa**: 1990; **VALUE: $200-$250**. The first step in making a master pattern is creating it from wood. This original pattern was modified to the later style by adding a handle of epoxy. The next step in creating the final master would be to duplicate this pattern from aluminum.

CALCULATOR-Size: 14" l. x 8" h. x 3/4" cylinder dia.; **c/n**: none; **Markings**: Wagner Calculator (as part of the scroll work), WAGNER MFG. CO., SIDNEY OHIO; **Finish**: brass with paper dial; **Circa**: 1892; **VALUE: RARE**. This item never went into commercial production.

Co-author, David Smith, photographing the Wagner Calculator.

BEAN POT PATTERN-Size: 8 1/4" dia. x 3 1/2" d.; **c/n**: none; **Markings**: Wagners 1891 Original...; **Finish**: wood; **Circa**: 1990; **VALUE: $200-$250**. Wood pattern done by Canal Pattern for General Housewares Corp. The kettle ears would be added prior to finishing the master pattern.

CHEF SKILLET and Fat Free Fryer-Finish: Pink Porcelain; **Circa**: 1964.

CHEF SKILLET-Size: 10 inch; **c/n**: 1388; **Markings**: stylized logo, CHEF SKILLET, 10 INCH, 1388; **VALUE: $75-$100**.

FAT FREE FRYER-Size: 11 3/16" dia.; **c/n**: 1102; **Markings**: stylized logo, FAT FREE FRYER, PAT PENDING, 1102A; **VALUE: $100-$150**. Also made a No. 8 Dutch oven to be sold as a 3 piece set.

ASHTRAYS-Size: 3 3/4" dia.; **c/n**: 1050; **Markings**: stylized logo, 1050; **Finish**: black porcelain with (left to right): green, red, blue speckles; **Circa**: 1980s; **VALUE: $10-$20**.

REGULAR SKILLET-Size: No.3; **c/n**: 1053; **Markings**: Pie logo, CAST IRON SKILLET, 1053; **Finish**: appears and feels to be Teflon coated; **Circa**: 1980s; **VALUE: $30-$45**.

DECORATIVE TRIVET, DECORATIVE TRIVET HOOK- Finish: painted iron; **Circa**: 1990s; **VALUE: $15 each**.

FRUIT & LARD PRESS-Size: 32" h. x 13" dia.; **c/n**: none; **Markings**: stylized logo (on press plate); **Finish**: iron with tin cylinder; wood legs; **Circa**: 1915-1930s; **VALUE: $250-$300**.

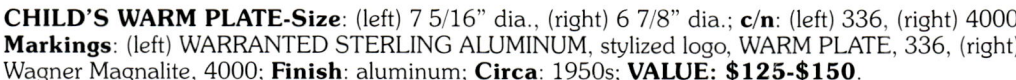

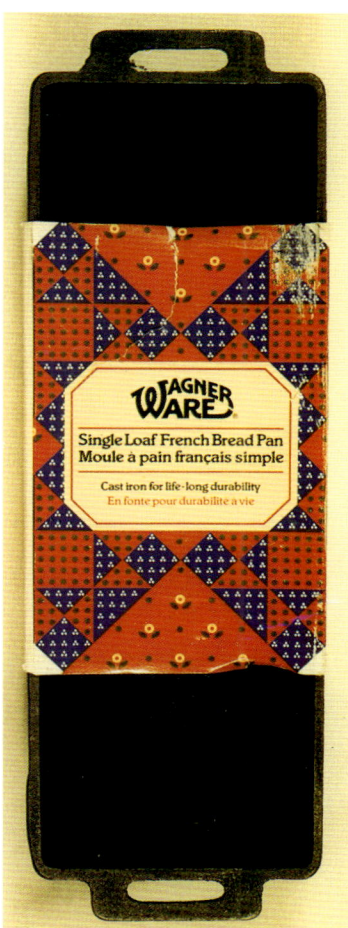

SINGLE LOAF PAN-Size: 13 1/2" l x 4 3/8" w. x 2 1/4" d.; **c/n**: none; **Markings**: WAGNER WARE, MADE IN USA; **Finish**: iron; **Circa**: 1990s; **VALUE**: $30-$40.

CHILD'S WARM PLATE-Size: (left) 7 5/16" dia., (right) 6 7/8" dia.; **c/n**: (left) 336, (right) 4000; **Markings**: (left) WARRANTED STERLING ALUMINUM, stylized logo, WARM PLATE, 336, (right) Wagner Magnalite, 4000; **Finish**: aluminum; **Circa**: 1950s; **VALUE**: $125-$150.

RECIPE BOOK-Size: 2 1/2" x 4" (unfolds to 20"); **Circa**: 1930s; **VALUE**: $75-$100.

BROCHURE-Size: 3 1/2" 6 1/4" (tri-fold, opens to 9 3/4"); **Circa**: 1930s; **VALUE: $50-$60**.

EMPLOYEE MANUAL-Circa: unknown; **VALUE: $75-$100**.

CATALOG-Size: 4 1/2" x 8 3/4", 92 pages; **Circa**: 1905-1910; **VALUE: $250-$300**.

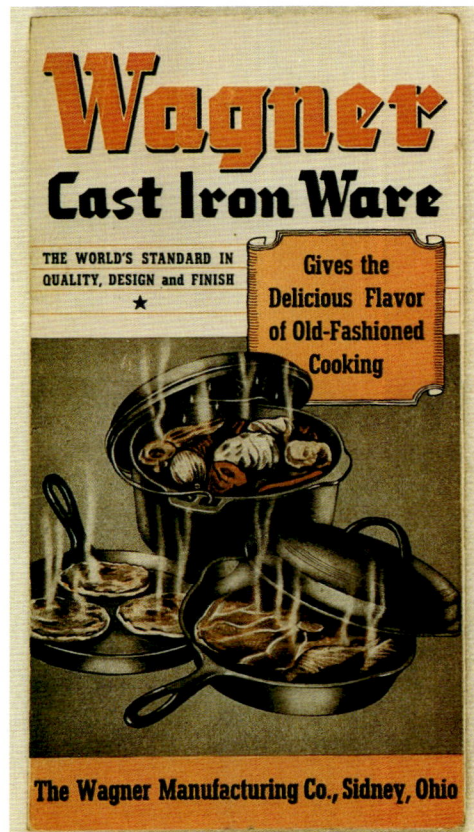

BROCHURE-Size: 3 1/4" x 6 3/8" (opens to 13"); **Circa**: 1940s; **VALUE: $75-$100**.

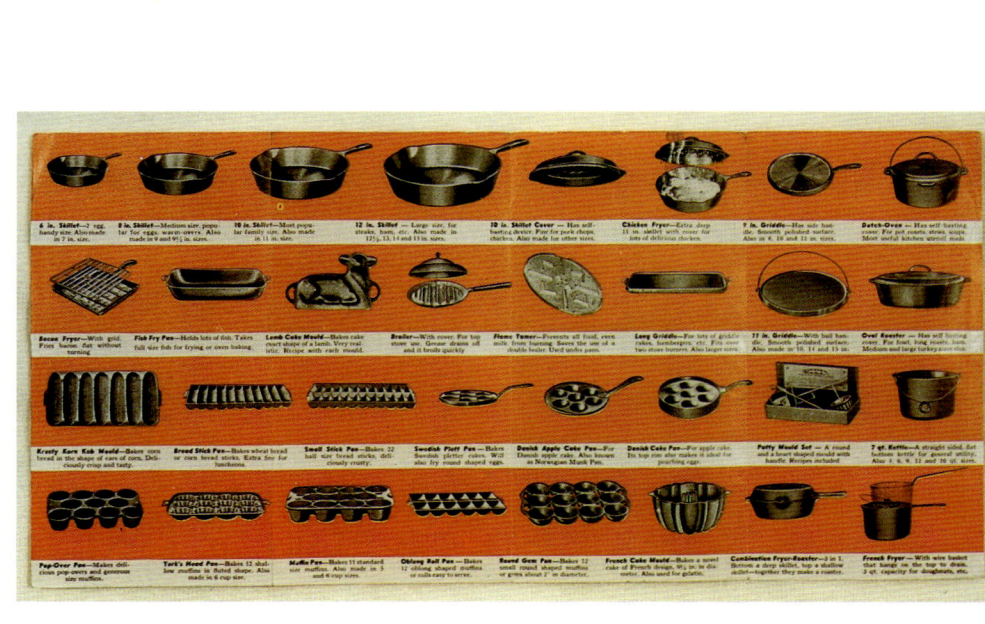

CATALOG-Size: 6 1/2" x 4", 62 pages; **Circa**: 1893; **VALUE: $250-$350**.

BROCHURE-Size: 3 1/2" X6 1/4". 10 pages; **Circa**: 1920s; **VALUE: $40-$50**.

BROCHURE-Size: 3 1/2" x 6 1/4", bifold; **Circa**: 1930s; **VALUE: $60-$75**.

CATALOG No.48-Size: 7 1/2" x10 1/8", 96 pages; **Circa**: 1927; **VALUE: $350**.

Wagner Catalog Numbers

CAST IRON

118	Pressure Cooker Cover
466	Little Gem Pan
1050	Skillet Ashtray
1051	Kettle, Cigarette Holder
1052	Regular Skillet (2)
1053	Regular Skillet (3)
1054	Regular Skillet (4)
1055	Regular Skillet (5)
1056	Regular Skillet (6)
1057	Regular Skillet (7)
1058	Regular Skillet (8)
1059	Regular Skillet (9)
1060	Regular Skillet (10)
1061	Regular Skillet (11)
1061	Fat Free Fryer
1062	Regular Skillet (12)
1063	Regular Skillet (13)
1064	Regular Skillet (14)
1065	Skillet Cover, (5)
1067	Skillet Cover, (7)
1068	Skillet Cover, (8)
1069	Skillet Cover, (9)
1070	Skillet Cover, (10)
1071	Skillet Cover, (11)
1072	Skillet Cover, (12)
1073	Skillet Cover, (14)
1075	Skillet, Wood Handle (5)
1076	Skillet, Wood Handle (6)
1077	Skillet, Wood Handle (7)
1078	Skillet, Wood Handle (8)
1079	Skillet, Wood Handle (9)
1080	Skillet, Wood Handle (10)
1081	Skillet Cover, Drip Drop (8) (fits skillet 1088)
1081	Skillet Cover, Ringed (8)
1082	Skillet Cover, Drip Drop (9) (fits skillet 1089)
1088	Skillet, Extra Deep (8)
1088-C	Skillet Roaster (8)
1089	Skillet, Extra Deep (9)
1089-C	Skillet Roaster (9)
1090	Skillet, Extra Deep (10)
1095	Sizzle Server
1097	Skillet Griddle (7)
1098	Skillet Griddle (8)
1099	Skillet Griddle (9)
1100	Skillet Griddle (10)
1101	Bacon and Egg Skillet
1101A	Bacon Press
1102	Greaseless Frying Skillet
1106	Handled Griddle (6)
1107	Handled Griddle (7)
1108	Handled Griddle (8)
1109	Handled Griddle (9)
1110	Handled Griddle (10)
1120	Bailed Griddle (10)
1122	Bailed Griddle (12)
1124	Bailed Griddle (14)
1126	Bailed Griddle (16)
1126-V	Skillet Grill 9" dia. (6)
1129-V	Skillet Grill 10 1/2" dia. (9)
1137	Griddle, Wood Handle (7)
1138	Griddle, Wood Handle (8)
1139	Griddle, Wood Handle (9)
1140	Griddle, Wood Handle (10)
1147	Long Griddle, (7)
1148	Long Griddle, (8)
1149	Long Griddle, (9)
1150	Long Griddle, (10)
1151	Long Griddle, (11)
1157	Long Griddle with bail (7)
1158	Long Griddle with bail (8)
1159	Long Griddle with bail (9)
1160	Long Griddle with bail (10)
1168	Long Griddle, (flat bottom) (8)
1169	Long Griddle, (flat bottom) (9)
1172	Scotch Bowl 3 qt. (2)
1173	Scotch Bowl 4 qt. (3)
1174	Scotch Bowl 5 qt. (4)
1175	Scotch Bowl 6 qt. (5)
1182	Yankee Bowl 4 qt. (2)
1183	Yankee Bowl 6 qt. (3)
1184	Yankee Bowl 7 qt. (4)
1185	Yankee Bowl 9 qt. (5)
1194	Maslin Kettle 4 qt. (4)
1196	Maslin Kettle 6 qt. (6)
1198	Maslin Kettle 8 qt. (8)
1202	Maslin Kettle, 12 qt. (12)
1206	Regular Kettle, 4 qt. (6)
1207	Regular Kettle, 6 qt. (7)
1208	Regular Kettle, 8 qt. (8)
1209	Regular Kettle, 10 qt. (9)
1217	Low Kettle, 5 qt. (7)
1218	Low Kettle, 6 qt. (8)
1218	Late Square Skillet
1218	Square Skillet Cover
1218D	Square Skillet
1219	Low Kettle, 8 qt. (9)
1219	Late Square Warm Over Pan, 9 5/8"
1220	Square Skillet, 11 1/4"
1226	Flat Bottom Kettle, 4 qt. (6)
1227	Flat Bottom Kettle, 6 qt. (7)
1228	Flat Bottom Kettle, 7 qt. (8)
1229	Flat Bottom Kettle, 9
1230	Flat Bottom Kettle, 10
1232	Flat Bottom Kettle, 12
1237	Flat Bottom Bulged Pot, 7
1238	Flat Bottom Bulged Pot, 8
1239	Flat Bottom Bulged Pot, 9
1247	Regular Bulged Pot, 7
1248	Regular Bulged Pot, 8
1249	Regular Bulged Pot, 9
1257	Eccentric Pot, (New England Style), 7
1258	Eccentric Pot, (New England Style), 8
1259	Eccentric Pot, (New England Style), 9
1265	Deep Fat Fryer
1265	Cover for Deep Fat Fryer
1266	Round Roaster, Drip Drop 2 1/2 qt. (6)
1267	Round Roaster, Drip Drop 3 1/2 qt. (7)
1268	Round Roaster, Drip Drop 5 qt. (8)
1269	Round Roaster, Drip Drop 6 qt. (9)
1270	Round Roaster, Drip Drop 8 qt. (10)
1271	Round Roaster, Drip Drop 12 qt. (11)

Cast aluminum trivets were furnished with the Iron Round Roasters. Lids were match numbered to the pot section of the roasters. Cast iron trivets were provided later.

1275-1	Skillet Oven (top)
1275-2	Skillet Oven (bottom)
1276-1	Skillet Oven (top)
1276-2	Skillet Oven (bottom)
1281	Oval Roaster, Drip Drop 6 5/8" x 11 1/8", 2 7/8 qts. (1)
1283	Oval Roaster, Drip Drop 8" x 12 1/4", 4 qts. (3)
1285	Oval Roaster, Drip Drop 9 1/4" x 14 1/4", 5 1/3 qts. (5)
1287	Oval Roaster, Drip Drop 10 7/8" x 15 3/4", 9 qts. (7)
1289	Oval Roaster, Drip Drop 12 3/8" x 18 1/2", 14 1/2 qts. (9)

Cast aluminum trivets were furnished with the Iron Oval Roasters. Lids were match numbered to the pot section of the roasters. Cast iron trivets were provided later.

1298	Dutch Oven, with Legs 5 qts. (8)
1299	Dutch Oven, with Legs 6 qts. (9)
1300	Dutch Oven, with Legs 8 qts. (10)
1301	Dutch Oven, with Legs 12 qts. (11)
1305	Square Iron Heater (polished or plain) 11" x 11"
1308	Round Iron Heater (polished or plain) 10 1/2"
1309	Flame Tamer
1310	Cake Mould (bundt) 10" dia.
1312	Danish Cake Pan (aebleskiver) 9" (no rim)
1314	Danish Cake Pan (aebleskiver) 9 3/8" (rimed)
1316	Swedish Plett Pan (swedish pancake pan) 9 1/4"
1317	Krusty Korn Kob (tea size)
1318	Krusty Korn Kob (senior size)
1319	Krusty Korn Kob (junior size)
1320	Little Gem Pan (9 cups)
1320	Little Gem Pan (12 cups)
1321	Little Gem Pan (9 cups)
1322	Gem Pan (Style A) (11 cup flat)
1323	Gem Pan (Style B) (11 cup pop-over)
1324	Gem Pan (Style C) (11 cup turk head without rim)
1325	Gem Pan (Style D) (12 cup french roll)
1326	Gem Pan (Style E) (11 cup bread stick)
1327	Gem Pan (Style EE) (22 cup bread stick)
1328	Gem Pan (Style F) (12 cup golfball)
1329	Gem Pan (Style G) (8 cup rectangular)
1330	Gem Pan (Style H) (4 cup french bread)

1331	Gem Pan (Style I) (6 cup vienna roll)		1557	Sugar Kettle, New Style (35 gal.)
1334	Gem Pan (Style O) (5 cup large french roll)		1558	Sugar Kettle, New Style (40 gal.)

1331   Gem Pan (Style I) (6 cup vienna roll)
1334   Gem Pan (Style O) (5 cup large french roll)
1335   Gem Pan (Style Q) (5 cup pop-over with lid lifter handle)
1336   Gem Pan (Style R) (8 cup pop-over with lid lifter handle)
133   Gem Pan (Style S) (11 cup pop-over with lid lifter handle)
1338   Gem Pan (Style T) (12 cup turk head with rim)
1339   Gem Pan (Style U) (6 cup turk head with rim)
1340   Little Slam Gem Pan
      With the exception of the 1326, 1327, 1334, and 1340 all pans came with and without cut-outs.
1350   Broiler, Improved with tin lid 10 1/2" dia.
1357   Skillet, National (7)
1358   Skillet, National (8)
1359   Skillet, National (9)
      National Skillet Covers are match numbered to the skillets.
1362   Lipped Pot (bailed)
1363   Hot Pot with lid, 4 1/4" dia.
1364   Hot Pot with lid, 3 1/2" dia.
1365   Skillet (toy)
1366   Griddle, bailed (toy)
1366   Toy Skillet Cover
1367   Waffle Iron (toy)
1367   Toy Skillet, (small, 3 1/2" dia.)
1368   Kettle (toy)
1368   Toy Lipped Kettle [smooth bottom]
1369   Tea Kettle (toy)
1370   Handled Griddle (toy All toys are 4 1/2 in. dia.
1374   Patty Mould Set (round, rosette)
1375   Patty Mould Set (heart, hexagon, round)
1376   Patty Mould Set (heart, hexagon)
1377   Patty Mould Set (hexagon, round)
1378   Patty Mould Set (heart, spade, club, diamond)
1379   Patty Mould Set (deep heart, deep round)
1380   Timbale Iron, (patty iron), plain round
1381   Timbale Iron, (patty iron), fluted round
1382   Timbale Iron, (patty iron), fluted oval
1383   Timbale Iron, (patty iron), fluted heart
1384   Timbale Iron, (patty iron), fluted club
1384   Chef Skillet (7 1/2" dia.)
1385   Timbale Iron, (patty iron) fluted diamond
1386   Timbale Iron, (patty iron) fluted spade
1386   Chef Skillet, 9" dia.
1388   Chef Skillet 10" dia.
1389   Chef Skillet, 11 inch
1390   Lamb Cake Mold (11 3/4" x 7 3/4" x 7 1/2")
1400   Square Chicken Fryer with cover
1401   Double Skillet
1402-T   Combination Fryer - Roaster (double skillet)
1407   Waffle Iron, 6 5/8" pans, low base (7)
1408   Waffle Iron, 7 9/16", pans, low base (8)
1409   Waffle Iron, 8 5/8" pans, low base (9)
      Pans available with either wood or wire handles.
1417   Waffle Iron, 6 5/8" pans (high base) (7)
1418   Waffle Iron, 7 9/16" pans (high base) (8)
1419   Waffle Iron, 8 5/8" pans (high base) (9)
1420   Waffle Iron, square pans 6 3/4" x 6 3/4", high base
1421   Waffle Iron, twin pattern, square pans, high base
1422   Waffle Iron, double twin pattern, square pans, high base
1423   Waffle Iron, Hotel with gas stove, double twin pattern
1425   Griddle, Hotel with gas stove, 12" x 22 1/2"
1426   Krusty Korn Kob corn dog maker (domestic size)
1427   Krusty Korn Kob corn dog maker, 2 pans (restaurant size)
1430   Krusty Korn Kob corn dog and sandwich maker (2 corn dog pans, 1 sandwich fryer pan, restaurant size)
1430   Wards Skillet, No.4
1431   Same as 1430 with gas stove included.
1431   No.3 Wardway Skillet
1450   Wafer Iron with Wood Handles, 5 1/4" pans, (No.1)
1451   Wafer Iron with Long Steel Handles, 5 1/4" pans, (No.2)
1455   Minute Sandwich Toaster 6" x 6" pans
1458   Cake and Omelet Baker, 7 9/16" pans
1508   Ham Boiler, 12" x 22" x 10 3/4"
1512   Wax Ladle with Wooden Handle
1514   Wax Ladle, with Iron Handle
1522   Fruit and Lard Press, 2 qts.
1523   Fruit and Lard Press, 3 qts.
1524   Fruit and Lard Press, 4 qts.
1526   Fruit and Lard Press, 6 qts.
1528   Fruit and Lard Press, 8 qts.
1530   Fruit and Lard Press, 10 qts.
1532   Fruit and Lard Press, 12 qts.
1541   Lard Press, 2 3/4 gal.
1542   Lard Press, 5 3/4 gal.
      Lard press 1541 was available with or without a sausage stuffer attachment.
1551   Sugar Kettle, New Style (10 gal.)
1552   Sugar Kettle, New Style (15 gal.)
1553   Sugar Kettle, New Style (20 gal.)
1554   Sugar Kettle, New Style (22 gal.)
1555   Sugar Kettle, New Style (25 gal.)
1556   Sugar Kettle, New Style (30 gal.)
1557   Sugar Kettle, New Style (35 gal.)
1558   Sugar Kettle, New Style (40 gal.)
      New style sugar kettles have three short legs.
1561   Sugar Kettle, Old Style (35 gal.) (Furnace Kettle)
1562   Sugar Kettle, Old Style (48 gal.) (Furnace Kettle)
1563   Sugar Kettle, Old Style (55 gal.) (Furnace Kettle)
1564   Sugar Kettle, Old Style (60 gal.) (Furnace Kettle)
1565   Sugar Kettle, Old Style (70 gal.) (Furnace Kettle)
1566   Sugar Kettle, Old Style (85 gal.) (Furnace Kettle)
      Old style sugar kettles have no legs.
1581   Boiler and Feed Cooker (15 gal.)
1582   Boiler and Feed Cooker (25 gal.)
1583   Boiler and Feed Cooker (30 gal.)
1584   Boiler and Feed Cooker (35 gal.)
1585   Boiler and Feed Cooker (40 gal.)
1586   Boiler and Feed Cooker (50 gal.)
1587   Boiler and Feed Cooker (55 gal.)
1590   Fire Pot for Cookers
1600   Tamper 7" x 7"
1601   Tamper 8" x 8"
1602   Tamper 9" x 9"
1603   Tamper 10" x 10"
1605   Maul with wooden block 8 lb.
1606   Maul with wooden block 10 lb.
1607   Maul with wooden block 12 lb.
1608   Maul with wooden block 14 lb.
1609   Maul with wooden block 16 lb.
1610   Maul, Solid 8 lb.
1611   Maul, Solid 10 lb.
1612   Maul, Solid 12 lb.
1613   Maul, Solid 14 lb.
1614   Maul, Solid 16 lb.
1965
1709   Long Life Handle Griddle (9)
1753   Long Life Skillet (3)
1757   Long Life Skillet (7)
W-1416   Wardway Oval Roaster

NICKEL PLATED CAST IRON

1012   Regular Skillet (2)
1013   Regular Skillet (3)
1014   Regular Skillet (4)
1015   Regular Skillet (5)
1016   Regular Skillet (6)
1017   Regular Skillet (7)
1018   Regular Skillet (8)
1019   Regular Skillet (9)
1020   Regular Skillet (10)
1021   Regular Skillet (11)
1022   Regular Skillet (12)
1025   Skillet, Wood handle (5)
1026   Skillet, Wood Handle (6)
1027   Skillet, Wood Handle (7)
1028   Skillet, Wood Handle (8)
1029   Skillet, Wood Handle (9)
1030   Skillet, Wood Handle (10)
1036   Handled Griddle (6)
1037   Handled Griddle (7)
1038   Handled Griddle (8)
1039   Handled Griddle (9)
1040   Handled Griddle (10)
1058   Hammered Finish Skillet (8)
1401A   Double Skillet Bottom
1401B   Double Skillet Bottom

CHROME PLATED CAST IRON (SILVERLITE)

S-1053   Regular Skillet (3)
S-1054   Regular Skillet (4)
S-1055   Regular Skillet (5)
S-1056   Regular Skillet (6)
S-1057   Regular Skillet (7)
S-1058   Regular Skillet (8)
S-1059   Regular Skillet (9)
S-1060   Regular Skillet (10)
S-1061   Regular Skillet (11)
S-1062   Regular Skillet (12)
S-1063   Regular Skillet (13)
S-1064   Regular Skillet (14)
S-1065   Skillet Cover (5)
S-1067   Skillet Cover (7)
S-1068   Skillet Cover (8)
S-1069   Skillet Cover (9)
S-1070   Skillet Cover (10)
S-1071   Skillet Cover (11)
S-1072   Skillet Cover (12)
S-1073   Skillet Cover (14)
S-1074   Wood Handled Skillet (4)
S-1075   Wood Handled Skillet (5)

S-1076	Wood Handled Skillet (6)		203	3 pt. Colonial Tea Pot
S-1077	Wood Handled Skillet (7)		204	4 pt. Colonial Tea Pot
S-1078	Wood Handled Skillet (8)		211	1 pt. Sidney Tea Pot
S-1079	Wood Handled Skillet (9)		212	1/2 pt. Sidney Tea Pot
S-1080	Wood Handled Skillet (10)		221	3 pt. Sidney Coffee Pot
S-1081	Skillet Cover (deep skillet) (8)		222	2 qt. Sidney Coffee Pot
S-1082	Skillet Cover (deep skillet) (9)		223	3 qt. Sidney Coffee Pot
S-1088	Deep Skillet (8)		224	4 qt. Sidney Coffee Pot
S-1089	Deep Skillet (9)		228	5 pt. French Style Coffee Pot
S-1090	Deep Skillet (10)		229	3 pt. French Style Coffee Pot
S-1103	Flat Bacon Fryer with press		230	1 pt. "Sidney" Pattern Tea Pot
S-1107	Handled Griddle (7)		232	2 pt. Sidney Tea Pot
S-1108	Handled Griddle (8)		233	3 pt. Sidney Tea Pot
S-1109	Handled Griddle (9)		234	4 pt. Sidney Tea Pot
S-1110	Handled Griddle (10)		236	6 pt. Sidney Tea Pot
S-1120	Bailed Griddle (10)		246	5 1/2 pt. Drip Drop Round Roaster
S-1122	Bailed Griddle (12)		247	8 1/2 pt. Drip Drop Round Roaster
S-1124	Bailed Griddle (14)		248	9 2/3 pt. Drip Drop Round Roaster
S-1126	Bailed Griddle (16)		248	Dutch Oven Trivet
S-1147	Long Griddle (7)		248-C	9 2/3 pt. Combination Cooker
S-1148	Long griddle (8)		249	12 1/2 pt. Drip Drop Round Roaster
S-1149	Long Griddle (9)		250	17 pt. Drip Drop Round Roaster
S-1150	Long Griddle (10)		250	Dutch Oven Trivet
S-1151	Long Griddle (11)		251	22 1/2 pt. Drip Drop Round Roaster
S-1317	Krusty Korn Kob (tea size)		246-251	Trivets for Roasters with the same No's.
S-1318	Krusty Korn Kob (senior size)		261	6 5/8" x 11" Drip Drop Oval Roaster
S-1319	Krusty Korn Kob (junior size)		263	8" x 12 1/8" Drip Drop Oval Roaster
S-1323	Pop - Over Pan (style B)		265	9 1/4" x 14 1/8" Drip Drop Oval Roaster
S-1326	Bread Stick Pan (style E)		265-T	9 1/4" x 14 1/8" Oval Roaster and Baker with tray
S-1327	Small Stick Pan (style EE)		267	10 7/8" x 15 5/8" Drip Drop Oval Roaster
S-1335	5-Cup Pop-Over Pan (style Q)		269	12 1/4" x 18 3/8" Drip Drop Oval Roaster
S-1336	8-Cup Pop-Over Pan (style R)		261,	
S-1337	11-Cup Pop-Over Pan (style S)		3,5,7,9	Trivets for Oval Roasters with the same No's.
S-1390	Lamb Cake Mold		272	4 1/2 in. Round Casserole
S-1401	Top Skillet for Combination Fryer/Roaster		273	5 inch Round Casserole
S-1402	Deep Skillet for Combination Fryer/Roaster		274	6 inch Round Casserole

ALUMINUM

			275	7 1/16" Round Casserole
01	Sugar Scoop		281	6" x 8 1/4" Oval Casserole
2M	Dutch Oven Trivet		282	7" x 9 5/8" Oval Casserole
105	6 pt. Colonial Tea Kettle (automatic cover)		283	8 3/16" x 11 1/4" Oval Casserole
106	8 pt. Colonial Tea Kettle (automatic cover)		291	7 3/4" Shallow Round Casserole
107	10 pt. Colonial Tea Kettle (automatic cover)		292	8 3/4" Shallow Round Casserole
108	12 pt. Colonial Tea Kettle (automatic cover)		295	8 1/2" Double Casserole
108	Ice Scoop		298	Butter Slicer
109	16 1/2 pt. Colonial Tea Kettle (automatic cover)		300	Cheese Slicer
115	6 pt. Colonial Tea Kettle (swing cover)		301	6 1/8" 8 1/4" Shallow Oval Casserole
116	8 pt. Colonial Tea Kettle (swing cover)		302	6 7/8" x 9 3/8" Shallow Oval Casserole
117	10 pt. Colonial Tea Kettle (swing cover)		303	6 7/8" x 10 7/8" Shallow Oval Casserole
118	12 pt. Colonial Tea Kettle (swing cover)		311	4 1/2" Shirred Egg Pan
119	16 1/2 pt. Colonial Tea Kettle (swing cover)		312	5 1/2" Shirred Egg Pan
127	10 pt. Puritan Tea Kettle (automatic cover)		321	2 7/8" Custard Cup
128	12 pt. Puritan Tea Kettle (automatic cover)		322	3 1/4" Custard Cup
132	2 qt. Sidney Tea Kettle (loose lid)		331	6 1/2" Casserole Pan
133	3 qt. Sidney Tea Kettle (loose lid)		332	7 1/2" Casserole Pan
134	4 qt. Sidney Tea Kettle (loose lid)		332 1/2	Round Sizzling Platter
135	5 qt. Sidney Tea Kettle (loose lid)		333	Al Carders Sizzling Steak Platter
136	6 qt. Sidney Tea Kettle (loose lid)		334	Al Carders Sizzling Steak Platter
138	8 qt. Sidney Tea Kettle (loose lid)		335	Al Carders Sizzling Steak Platter
134-B	4 qt. Sidney Tea Kettle (with double boiler)		335	9 3/4" Pie Casserole
135-B	5 qt. Sidney Tea Kettle (with double boiler)		336	Child's Warm Plate
136-B	6 qt. Sidney Tea Kettle (with double boiler)		340	Al Carders Steak Platter
138-B	8 qt Sidney Tea Kettle (with double boiler)		343	3 pt. Pudding Pan
144	4 qt. Sidney Tea Kettle (swing lid)		344	4 pt. Pudding Pan
145	5 qt. Sidney Tea Kettle (swing lid)		345 1/2	5 1/2 pt. Pudding Pan
146	6 qt. Sidney Tea Kettle (swing lid)		347	7 pt. Pudding Pan
148	8 qt. Sidney Tea Kettle (swing lid)		349	9 pt. Pudding Pan
156	7 pt. Grand Prize Tea Kettle (swing lid)		351	7 in. Shallow Pan
157	9 1/2 pt. Grand Prize Tea Kettle (swing lid)		352	8 in. Shallow Pan
158	12 pt. Grand Prize Tea Kettle (swing lid)		353	9 in. Shallow Pan
165	3 pt. or 4 cup Two-Way Coffee Maker		353 1/2	9 3/4" Shallow Pan
166	2 qt. or 6 cup Two-Way Coffee Maker		354	10 1/2 " Shallow Pan
167	3 qt. or 10 cup Two-Way Coffee Maker		361	6 5/8 Pie Pan
168	4 qt. or 12 cup Two-Way Coffee Maker		362	8 1/4" Pie Pan
169	6 qt. or 17 cup Two-Way Coffee Maker w/bail handle		363	9 7/8" Pie Pan
171	2 pt. or 5 cup Tall Colonial Coffee Percolator		364	10 5/8" Pie Pan
172	3 pt. or 7 cup Tall Colonial Coffee Percolator		371	8 1/2" Cake Pan
173	4 1/2 pt. or 9 cup Tall Colonial Coffee Percolator		372	9 1/4" Cake Pan
185	3 pt. or 4 cup Low Colonial Coffee Percolator		381	5" x 81/4" Bread or Cake Pan
186	2 qt. or 6 cup Low Colonial Coffee Percolator		382	5" x10" Bread or Cake Pan
187	3 qt. or 10 cup Low Colonial Coffee Percolator		383	5 3/4" x 11 1/4" Bread or Cake Pan
188	4 qt. or 12 cup Low Colonial Coffee Percolator		385	3 3/16" Handled Ramequin
191	3 pt. Colonial Coffee Pot		401	2" x 2 3/4", Small Cup
192	2 qt. Colonial Coffee Pot		402	2 1/8" x 3 1/4", Small Cup
193	3 qt. Colonial Coffee Pot		403	2 3/8" x 3 3/8", Large Cup
194	4 qt. Colonial Coffee Pot		404	2 1/2" x 3 7/8", Large Cup
195	6 qt. Colonial Coffee Pot		406	3" x 3 3/4", Tall Cup
196	7 qt. Colonial Coffee Pot		408	5 1/4 pt. Water Bottle with Cast Cover
202	2 pt. Colonial Tea Pot		409	2 1/2 qt. Water Pitcher
			410	4 qt. Water Pitcher
			411	5 pt. Water Carrier

No.	Description	No.	Description
421	4 3/4" x 3" Round Jelly Mould	674	4 qt. Deep Sauce Pan
422	6" x 5" Round Jelly Mould	680	Three Section Sauce Pan
423	7" x 3" Round Jelly Mould	682	2 qt. Lipped Sauce Pan
424	5 3/4" x 8" x 2 1/2" Round Jelly Mould	683	3 qt. Lipped Sauce Pan
425	9 1/4" x 21/4" Round Jelly Mould	684	4 qt. Lipped Sauce Pan
426	3 3/4" x 7" x 2 3/4" Square Jelly Mould	685	5 qt. Lipped Sauce Pan
432	3 qt. Mixing Bowl	686	6 qt. Lipped Sauce Pan
433	4 qt. Mixing Bowl	687M	Wooden Handle Sauce Pan
434	5 qt. Mixing Bowl	691	5 pt. Convex Sauce Pan
435	6 qt. Mixing Bowl	692	7 pt. Convex Sauce Pan
442	3 qt. Oyster Stew Bowl	693	8 1/2 pt. Convex Sauce Pan
443	4 qt. Oyster Stew Bowl	695	1 qt. Paul Revere Sauce Pan
444	5 qt. Oyster Stew Bowl	697	15 1/8" Egg Whip or Beating Spoon
448	10" Bundt Cake Mould	699	14 1/2" Cake or Egg Beater
450	3 5/8" Fruit Juice Extractor (without holes)	701	1 qt. Double Boiler
452	3 5/8" Fruit Juice Extractor (with holes)	702	2 qt. Double Boiler
453	6 1/4" Fruit Juice Extractor	703	3 qt. Double Boiler
454	7 1/4" x 7 1/4" x 91/4" Sink Strainer	704	4 qt. Double Boiler
456	Krusty Korn Cob Senior	706	14 1/2" Chafing Dish Spoon
458	Krusty Korn Kob Junior	708	9 1/2" Soup Ladle
459	Krust Korn Kob Tea Size	709	11" Flat Spoon
460	Bread Stick Mould (EE)	710	13" Flat Spoon
462	Bread Stick Mould (E)	711	15" Flat Spoon
464	Little Gem Pan (9-cups)	713	11" Spoon with Hook
466	Little Gem Pan (12-cups)	714	13" Spoon with Hook
468	Pop-Over Pan, Style B	716	11 1/2" Tom & Jerry Ladle without Hook
470	French Roll Pan, Style D	717	11 1/2" Tom & Jerry Ladle with Hook
472	Golfball Pan, Style F	718	10" Spoon (double knobbed handle)
474	Vienna Roll Pan, Style I	719	Cake or Egg Beater
476	Pop-Over Pan, Style Q	720	Jar Filler
478	Pop-Over Pan, Style R	722	3 1/2" x 12" Long Handled Ladle
480	Pop-Over Pan, Style S	723	3 3/4" x 15" Long Handled Ladle
481	1/2P Sauce Pan	724	4 1/8" x 15" Long Handled Ladle
500	Bacon and Egg Breakfast Skillet (Wood Handle)	726	3 1/2" x/12" Strainer Ladle
503	Wooden Handled Skillet (3)	727	3 3/4" x/15" Strainer Ladle
504	Wooden Handled Skillet (4)	728	4 1/8" x 15" Strainer Ladle
505	Wooden Handled Skillet (5)	730	7" Fruit or Gravy Ladle
506	Wooden Handled Skillet (6)	731	7" Fruit Ladle with Hook
507	Wooden Handled Skillet (7)	732	2 qt. Lipped Kettle
507c	Skillet Cover (7)	733	3 qt. Lipped Kettle
508-OS	Oven-Skillet	734	4 qt. Lipped Kettle
508	Wooden Handled Skillet (8)	736	6 qt Lipped Kettle
508c	Skillet Cover (8)	736-C	6 qt. Cooking and Baking Kettle
509	Wooden Handled Skillet (9)	738	8 qt. Lipped Kettle
509c	Skillet Cover (9)	740	10 qt. Lipped Kettle
509M	Chicken Fryer (9)	740-C	10 qt. Cooking and Baking Kettle
510	Wooden Handled Skillet (10)	R-740	Baking Rack
515	Buffet Skillet (5)	742	12 qt. Lipped Kettle
516	Buffet Skillet (6)	742-C	12 qt. Cooking and Baking Kettle
520	French Fry Skillet	744	14 qt. Lipped Kettle
521	French Fry Skillet	746	16 qt. Lipped Kettle
522	French Fry Skillet	750	20 qt. Lipped Kettle
523	French Fry Skillet	754	24 qt. Lipped Kettle
524	French Fry Skillet	767	6 qt. Flat Bottom Kettle
537	Flaring Skillet (7)	768	7 qt. Flat Bottom Kettle
538	Flaring Skillet (8)	769	9 qt. Flat Bottom Kettle
539	Flaring Skillet (9)	772	2 qt Scotch Bowl
557	Handled Griddle (7)	773	3 qt. Scotch Bowl
558	Handled Griddle (8)	774	4 qt. Scotch Bowl
559	Handled Griddle (9)	775	5 qt. Scotch Bowl
560	Handled Griddle (10)	781	5 pt. Convex Kettle
568	Chicken Fryer	782	7 pt. Convex Kettle
578	National Skillet (8)	783	8 1/2 pt. Convex Kettle
579	Kitchen Cook All	784	10 pt. Convex Kettle
600	13" Griddle-Broiler	791	5 pt. Convex Pot
610	Bailed Griddle (10)	792	7 pt. Convex Pot
612	Bailed Griddle (12)	793	81/2 pt. Convex Pot
614	Bailed Griddle (14)	794	10 pt. Convex Pot
616	Bailed Griddle (16)	796	12 1/4 in. Wood Handled Dipper
617	Wood Handled Griddle (7)	798	151/2 in. Wood Handled Ladle
618	Wood Handled Griddle (8)	800	91/2" Cover
619	Wood Handled Griddle (9)	801	101/2" Cover
620	Wood Handled Griddle (10)	802	11 1/2" Cover
630	Rapid Heating Griddle	803	6 qt. Steam Cooker
631	11 in. Rapid Heating Griddle	804	3 qt. (ea.) Triplicate Sauce Pan Set
637	7 5/8" x 16 3/4" Long Griddle	805	2 qt. (ea.) Triplicate Sauce Pan Set
638	8 7/8" x 19 1/4" Long Griddle	820	9 1/4" Omelet Pan
639	10" x 21 3/8" Long Griddle	821	12" Omelet Pan
640	12 3/8" x 24 1/4" Long Griddle	827	6 5/8" Round Waffle Iron (low base) (7)
642	Wood Handled Round Broiler	828	7 9/16" Round Waffle Iron (low base) (8)
644	3 section Egg Poacher	829	8 5/8" Round Waffle Iron (low base) (9)
646	6 section Egg Poacher	837	6 5/8" Round Waffle Iron (high base) (7)
648	3/4 pt. Sauce Pan; also Wax Ladle when Wood Handled	838	7 9/16" Round Waffle Iron (high base) (8)
651	2 pt. Sauce Flaring Pan	839	8 5/8" Round Waffle Iron (high base) (9)
652	2 1/2 pt. Sauce Flaring Pan	840	Square Waffle Iron (high base)
653	3 pt. Sauce Flaring Pan	841	Cake or Omelet Baker
661	2 1/2 pt. Buffet Sauce Pan	842	Omelet Pan
662	1/2 pt. Buffet Sauce Pan	843	(heart, hexagon, round) Boxed Swedish Cake and Patty Moulds
672	2 qt. Deep Sauce Pan	844	Boxed Swedish Cake and Patty Moulds (heart, hexagon)
673	3 qt. Deep Sauce Pan	845	Boxed Swedish Cake and Patty Moulds (hexagon, round)

No.	Description
846	Crisp Card Moulds (4 card shapes)
848	Crisp Patty Moulds (deep heart and round)
850	Toy Skillet
851	Toy Bailed Griddle
852	Toy Waffle Iron
853	Toy Kettle
854	Toy Handled Griddle
855	Toy Handle Griddle
861	10 qt. Steam Pressure Cooker
862	15 qt. Steam Pressure Cooker
863	20 qt. Steam Pressure Cooker
864	25 qt. Steam Pressure Cooker
	Complete cooker includes two insert pans, a meat rack, lifting hook, canning trivet, and cook book.
900	3" x 8 1/2" Sugar Scoop
901	4 x 10" Sugar Scoop
901 1/2	4 x 11" Sugar Scoop
902	5 x 12" Sugar Scoop
903	5 1/2" x 14" Sugar Scoop
904	6 1/4" x 15 1/4" Sugar Scoop
906	4 1/2" x 12" Salt Scoop
907	8 3/4" x 15 7/8" Flaring Coffee Scoop
908	2 3/4" x 9" Narrow Scoop
911	3 x 8" 1/2" Solid Coffee Scoop
911A	Coffee Scoop
911 1/2	3 1/2" x 9 1/2" Solid Coffee Scoop
912	4 x" Solid Coffee Scoop
913	4 1/2" x 11" Solid Coffee Scoop
914	5" x 13 3/4" Solid Coffee Scoop
915	6" x 14" Solid Coffee Scoop
921	3" x 8 1/2" Wood Handled Coffee Scoop
921 1/2	3 1/2" x 9 1/2" Wood Handled Coffee Scoop
922	4" x 10" Wood Handled Coffee Scoop
923	4 1/2" x 11 1/8" Wood Handled Coffee Scoop
924	5 1/8" x 13 3/4" Wood Handled Coffee Scoop
925	6" x 14 1/2" Wood Handled Coffee Scoop
926	2 3/4" x 8 3/8" Solid Confectionery Scoop
928	2 1/2" x 8" Wood Handled Confectionery Scoop
930	3" x 7 1/4" Thumb Scoop
932	3" x 10 1/4" Solid Ice Scoop
934	3" x 9 3/4" Wood Handled Ice Scoop
936	2 1/2" x 4 1/2" Drug Scoop
937	3" x 4 7/8" Drug Scoop
938	3 1/4" x 5 3/8" Drug Scoop
939	3 5/8" x 5 3/4" Drug Scoop
940	11 3/4" Solid Ice Cream Spade
942	10 1/2" Wood Handled Ice Cream Spade
944	1 pt. Ice Cream Pail (Sefton Wire Bail)
945	1 qt. Ice Cream Pail (Sefton Wire Bail)
946	1 pt. Ice Cream Pail (Yale and Northland)
946	1 1/2 pt. Ice Cream Pail (Yale and Northland)
947	1 qt. Ice Cream Pail (Yale and Northland)
948	1 pt. Ice Cream Pail (Tall or Regular)
948	1 1/2 pt. Ice Cream Pail (Tall or Regular)
949	1 qt. Ice Cream Pail (Tall or Regular)
950	1 pt. Ice Cream Pail (Crunden)
951	1 qt. Ice Cream Pail (Crunden)
960	1 1/2 pt. Mixing Cup
962	7 3/4" x 9" x 1" Candy Tray
963	7 3/4" x 11" x 1" Candy Tray
964	7 3/4" x 13" x 1" Candy Tray
965	7 3/4" x 19" x 1" Candy Tray
966	7 3/4" x 9" x 1 1/2" Candy Tray
967	7 3/4" x 9" x 2 3/8" Candy Tray
968	8" x 21" x 2 1/2" Candy Tray
968-1	8" x 24" x 2 1/2" Candy Tray
968-2	8" x 20" x 2 1/2" Candy Tray
972	3 1/2" x 10 1/2" Solid Lard Spade
973	3 1/8" x 12 3/8" Wood Handled Lard Spade also Cake or Meat Turner
974	6 3/8" x 9 1/2" Transfer Ladle
975	3 1/4" x 9" Lard Ladle
976	4" x 10" Lard Ladle
978	1 pt. Small Dipper
979	1 qt. Small Dipper
980	2 qt. Large Dipper
981	4 qt. Large Dipper
982	5 1/2 qt. Large Dipper
984	1 pt. Measure
985	1 qt. Measure
986	2 qt. Measure
987	4 qt. Measure
988	1 pt. Funnel
989	1 qt. Funnel
990	2 qt. Funnel
991	4 qt. Funnel
992	1 pt. Pickle Dipper
998	1 qt. Measure (Canadian)
999	2 qt. Measure (Canadian)
1000	Picnic Grill
1001	6" x 12" Baker's Peel
1002	9" x 18" Baker's Peel
1003	7" x 30" Baker's Peel
1004	8" x 36" Baker's Peel
1005	2 1/4" x 9 3/4" x 13 3/4" Counter Pan
1006	2 1/4" x 10 3/4" x 14 1/2" Counter Pan
1007	2 1/4" x 11 1/2" x 16 1/2" Counter Pan
1008	2 1/4" x 12 3/4" x 18 1/4" Counter Pan
1009	Lamb Cake Mould (aluminum)
1819	Pot, 34 qt. (cast aluminum)
1820	Deep Sauce Pan
1832	Shallow Sauce Pan
1954	Heavy Duty Prison Pan
2188	Hotel Skillet, 18 1/4: dia
3192	Coffee Percolator
3254	Kook All, Kettle & Skillet
4052	Bun Warmer

HAMMERED ALUMINUM

No.	Description
HS1268	Dutch Oven
2127	5 qt. Tea Kettle
3127	Tea Kettle
3248	Round Roaster (8)
3249	Round Roaster (9)
3254	Kook All
3254M	Kook All Insert
3266	Oval Roaster (6)
3266	Oval Roaster Cover
3266M	Oval Roaster Cover
3341	Sizzling Steak Platter
3342	Sizzling Steak Platter
3503	No.3 Wood Handle Skillet
3581	5 Star Skillet Bottom
3682	2 qt. Lipped Kettle w/ lid
3683	3 qt. Lipped Kettle w/ lid
3684	4 qt. Lipped Kettle w/ lid
3685	5 qt. Lipped Kettle w/ lid
3686	6 qt. Lipped Kettle w/ lid

MAGNALITE

No.	Description
4000	Child's Warm Plate
4004	Bake & Serve Pan
4005	9 5/8" x 15 3/8" Deep Roaster Pan
4007	12 7/8" x 13 3/8" Bake and Roast Pan
4052	Salad Bowl
4054	2 qt. Round Casserole
4056K	Round Casserole w/ glass lid
4133	Tea Kettle
4192	Coffee Pot
4248	Round Roaster (8)
4249	Round Roaster (9)
4263	Oval Roaster (3)
4265	Oval Roaster (5)
4267	Oval Roaster (7)
4269	Oval Roaster (9)
4341	Sizzling Steak Platter
4342	Sizzling Steak Platter
4343	Sizzling Host Platter
4344	Sizzling Vegetable Platter
4506	8" Covered Skillet (6)
4507	8" Chef Skillet
4508	10" Covered Skillet (8)
4509	10" Chef Skillet
4509-C	10" Chef Skillet Cover
4510	Square Skillet w/ lid
4510	Baking Pan
4512	12" Covered Skillet
4569	10 1/2" Covered Chicken Fryer
4570	12" Covered Chicken Fryer
4602	12" x 12 1/2" Broiler-Griddle
4672	2 qt. Covered Gourmet Pan
4680	1 qt. Covered Petite Gourmet Pan
4681	1 1/2 qt. Covered Sauce Pan
4682	2 qt. Covered Sauce Pan
4683	3 qt. Covered Sauce Pan
4684	4 qt. Covered Sauce Pan
4702	Sauce Pan
4738	7 1/2 qt. Deep Kettle Dutch Oven

THE GRISWOLD MANUFACTURING COMPANY
Erie, Pennsylvania

The Boston Department Store, Erie, PA window display, circa 1930s.

Matthew Griswold (b. June 6, 1833) moved to Erie, Pennsylvania in 1865, after thirty years on the family farm in Old Lyme, Connecticut. His move was prompted not only by business considerations, but also by family relationships. His second cousin, Samuel Selden (b. July 9, 1821, in Erie) had returned there to join the paper manufacturing business after several years of managing a plantation in Cuba. Samuel's brother, John Card Selden (b. November 28, 1825, in Erie), had worked during his early adulthood as a store clerk in Troy, New York, before joining his brother George in California in 1850. He had returned to Erie in 1853, and joined his father in the mercantile business. In addition, John C. Selden was married to Matthew Griswold's sister, Lydia. After Matthew relocated to Pennsylvania, he entered into a partnership with his two cousins.

By 1868, the company formed by the partnership of Matthew Griswold and the Selden brothers was manufacturing separable butt hinges and other articles of light hardware, working in a building known as the "Butt Factory." Situated on West 10th Street, on the bank of the Erie Extension Canal west of Chestnut Street, the original factory was a picturesque old frame building partly enclosed in the rear by a long rail fence.

The closing of the Erie Extension Canal in 1871 opened up the west side streets of Erie, thus allowing for expansion of the Butt Factory. Building succeeded building until the plant extended to Walnut Street.

The name "Butt Factory" was dropped in 1873, when the company became know as the Selden & Griswold Manufacturing Company. At that time, its force of employees numbered twenty.

Samuel Selden died in 1882, and in 1884 Matthew Griswold bought out the interests held by John Card Selden and by Samuel Selden's heirs to become the sole owner. At that time, the business employed about a hundred men, who worked in facilities including a foundry (100' x 150'), a two-story finishing room (30' x 90'; the upper floor was for machinery and a mounting room), a two-story storeroom (30' x 40'), a second two-story storeroom (60' x 95'), and an engine and boiler room with a fifty-horsepower engine.

Fire swept through this old plant on August 8, 1885, but it was repaired and remodeled the same year. The firm was reorganized two years after the fire, and the Griswold Manufacturing Company was chartered. Matthew Griswold's son, Marvin Griswold, left his position as treasurer of the Shaw Piano Company to join the Griswold Manufacturing Co. as treasurer.

In 1903 the old plant was abandoned, and the firm moved into the Shaw Piano Company buildings on the corners of 12th and Raspberry Streets. Numerous other buildings were added, and by 1909 the plant occupied the entire square between Cascade, 12th, Raspberry, and the railroad tracks.

One Griswold employee, Charles A. Massing, was to become one of the driving forces of the company. Initially hired in 1899 as a clerk, Massing was given the opportunity to become a salesman. Subsequently he became a sales manager, and then vice president in charge of sales. Over the course of his career, he was responsible for several patents. Massing retired in 1955, after 56 years of service.

Matthew Griswold, Sr. stepped down from his position as president in 1905, but remained as chairman until his death on May 19, 1919. Matthew Griswold, Jr. took his father's place as president in 1905, and kept the position until he left the company in 1914. He was replaced by his brother Marvin. Marvin Griswold is credited with making the firm an acknowledged leader in the manufacture of cast iron cookware. He, together with such field representatives as Charles Massing, John Holland, and S.E. Lent, contributed the driving energy and foresight that produced Griswold's growth.

Marvin Griswold died in 1926, after which Matthew, Jr.'s son Roger Griswold served as president until 1945. Roger foresaw that electricity would be the ideal heat source for cooking operations, prompting Griswold to manufacture a commercial electric waffle baker. The line was expanded to include a complete commercial electric cooking line.

In the summer of 1937, a prolonged labor strike arose because company officials refused to recognize the CIO, a large labor union. After weeks of negotiations in which city officials and police took an active part, the strike was settled. For the first time in Erie's industrial history, laborers demands for better working conditions and higher wages had made a serious impact.

Roger Griswold, who had been the Griswold Manufacturing Company's president since 1927, died suddenly of a heart attack in December of 1944. His brother Ely Griswold, who was the controlling stock holder, assumed the presidency. Shortly thereafter, Ely announced that the company was to be sold because he wanted to retire. This prompted bitter lawsuits between the two branches of the Griswold family. Nonetheless, Ely Griswold succeeded in his goal, and the Griswold Manufacturing Company was sold in 1946 to a syndicate of New York City investors. By 1947 all members of the Griswold family had left the company, which was then headed by Isador Tachna, president, and Abe S. Weissman, general manager and treasurer.

In March of 1957, the historic Griswold Manufacturing Co. was purchased by the McGraw Edison Company of Chicago, Illinois. Within six months, McGraw Edison had sold the Housewares Division and the Griswold name and trademarks to Griswold's strongest competitor, the Wagner Manufacturing Company of Sidney, Ohio. McGraw Edison subsequently closed out the electrical cooking division, deciding to combine its entire Erie facilities with other units in Illinois.

The Wagner Manufacturing Company continued the Griswold name and trademark, but dropped the phrase "Erie, Pa." from their manufactured pieces. It was now the Griswold Manufacturing Company, Division of Wagner Manufacturing Company, Sidney, Ohio.

In January of 1959, the Wagner Manufacturing Company transferred all Griswold trademark rights to Textron Inc. of Providence, Rhode Island. For the next ten years, cast iron cookware marketed with the Griswold trademark continued to be manufactured in the Sidney, Ohio plant under the auspices of the Randall Company, a subsidiary of the Textron Corporation.

The General Housewares Corporation acquired all rights to both the Griswold and Wagner trademarks in August of 1969.

Griswold Foundryman, Frank Buterbaugh, operates a Bull Ladle which fills the foundrymans ladles used in pouring castings, circa 1940s.

Griswold Manufacturing Company Hollow Ware Department Employees.

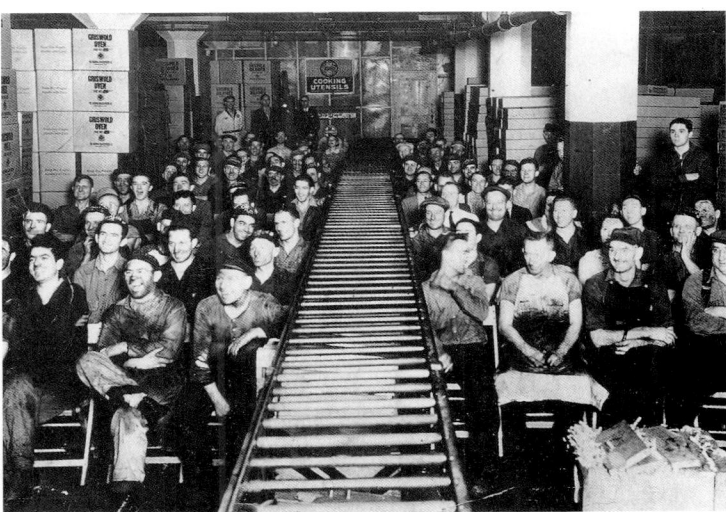

Griswold workers assemble for a meeting, circa 1955.

SKILLETS & SAUCE PANS

"ERIE" or ERIE
c. 1870s to 1900

No. 6	$150-$200
No. 7	$50-$75
No. 8	$30-$40
No. 9	$30-$40
No. 10	$75-$100
No. 11	$150-$200
No. 12	$100-$150

ERIE
(with inset heat ring)

No. 5	$175-$200
No. 6	$50-$75
No. 7	$30-$50
No. 8	$30-$50
No. 9	$40-$60
No. 10	$75-$100
No. 11	$150-$200
No. 12	$150-$200

All skillet values based on pieces in excellent condition.

GRISWOLD'S ERIE
c. 1890 to 1910

No. 5	$175-$200
No. 6	$50-$75
No. 7	$30-$50
No. 8	$30-$50
No. 9	$40-$60
No. 10	$75-$100
No. 11	$150-$200
No. 12	$150-$200

Slant/ERIE PA USA
(with heat ring)
c. 1909 to 1929

No. 2	$500-$600
No. 3	$30-$40
No. 4	$80-$100
No. 5	$30-$50
No. 6	$30-$50
No. 7	$30-$50
No. 8	$30-$50
No. 9	$30-$50
No. 10	$60-$75
No. 11	$150-$200
No. 12	$75-$100
No. 13	$1000-$1200
No. 14	$700-$800
No. 20	$700-$800

Slant/ERIE
c. 1907 to 1912

No. 1	Rare
No. 2	$400-$500
No. 3	$25-$35
No. 4	$100-$150
No. 5	$30-$40
No. 6	$30-$40
No. 7	$40-$50
No. 8	$30-$40
No. 9	$30-$50
No. 10	$50-$75
No. 11	$150-200
No. 12	$100-$150
No. 13	$600-$700
No. 14	$600-$700

Slant/ERIE PA USA (with smooth bottom)
c. 1939 to 1944

No. 2 $400-$500
No. 3 $50-$60
No. 5 $40-$50
No. 8 $40-$50
No. 9 $60-75

Block/ERIE PA USA (with heat ring)
c. 1920—1930

No. 0 $75-$100
No. 2 $1000-1500
No. 3 $20-$30
No. 4 $450-$500
No. 5 $400-$500
No. 6 $75-$100
No. 7 $25-45
No. 8 $30-$40
No. 9 $30-$40
No. 10 $60-$75
No. 11 $150-$200
No. 12 $75-$100
No. 13 $1200-$1500
No. 14 $100-$150
No. 20 $500-$600

Block/ERIE PA USA (with smooth bottom)
c. 1930 to 1939

No. 2 $350-$400
No. 3 $10-$20
No. 4 $60-$80
No. 5 $10-$20
No. 6 $20-$30
No. 7 $20-$30
No. 8 $20-$30
No. 9 $20-$30
No. 10 $60-80

Small logo (early handle)
c. 1939 to 1944

No. 3 $5-$15
No. 5 $10-$20
No. 6 $10-$20
No. 7 $10-$20
No. 8 $10-$20
No. 9 $20-$30
No. 10 $20-$30
No. 12 $50-$75
(with heat ring)

Small logo
(late handle)
c. 1944 to 1957

No. 3	$5-$15
No. 4	$30-$50
No. 5	$15-$20
No. 6	$15-$20
No. 7	$15-$20
No. 8	$15-$20
No. 9	$20-$30
No. 10	$30-$40

Wood Handle
(various logos)
c. 1885 to 1940

No. 2	Rare
No. 3	$175-$200
No. 4	$200-$250
No. 5	$100-$125
No. 6	$100-$125
No. 7	$75-100
No. 8	$75-$100
No. 9	$50-$75
No. 10	$100-$125
No. 11	$200-$250
No. 12	$200-$250

Small logo (with hinge tab)
c. 1940s to 1957

No. 3	$30-$50
No. 5	$50-$60
No. 6	$60-$70
No. 7	$60-$70
No. 8	$40-$50
No. 9	$60-$70

Small logo
(grooved handle)
c. 1944 to 1957

No. 3	$5-$15
No. 4	$30-$40
No. 5	$15-$20
No. 6	$15-$20
No. 7	$15-$20
No. 8	$15-20
No. 9	$20-$30

VICTOR
(fully marked)
c. 1920 to 1935

No. 5	$400-$500
No. 6	$150-$200
No. 7	$35-$60
No. 8	$35-$60
No. 9	$35-$60

Deduct 30% for other Victors

REGULAR SKILLET-Size: No.8, 10 1/2" dia. x 2" deep; **p/n**: none; **Markings**: "ERIE", B 8; **Finish**: iron; **Circa**: 1890; **VALUE: $35-$34**. Note unusual handle reinforcement.

REGULAR SKILLET-Size: No.8; **p/n**: none; **Markings**: "ERIE", C, 8, B; **Finish**: iron; **Circa**: 1880; **VALUE: $40-$50**. Lay-out lines can be seen around the skillet bottom.

WOOD HANDLE SKILLET-Size: No.6; **p/n**: 3349; **Markings**: ERIE ALUMINUM, 3349; **Finish**: aluminum; **Circa**: 1920s; **VALUE: $40-$50; No.7, $50-$60; No.8, $50-$60**.

WOOD HANDLE SKILLET-Size: No.9; **p/n**: 727; **Markings**: ERIE, 727, 9E; **Finish**: iron; **Circa**: 1895-1910; **VALUE: $75-$100; No.8; $60-$75; No.10, $100-$125**. Handle probably not original. Most early handles were round.

STEEL SKILLET-Size: 6" dia., 5 1/2 handle; **p/n:** 32; **Markings:** Early spider logo; **Finish:** steel with fused markings; **Circa:** 1900; **VALUE:** $500-$600.

ODORLESS SKILLET-p/n: 869; **Markings:** ODORLESS, PATD OCT 17, 1893; **Finish:** iron; **Circa:** 1890s; **VALUE:** $75-$100. A cover was an option.

A cover was an option for the Odorless Skillet. **VALUE: $50-$75**.

This Odorless Skillet was found with the letters JR raised on the bottom. These are very similar to those on the Regular Griddle on page 55 of *The Book of Griswold & Wagner*. **Value: $100-$125**.

WOOD HANDLE SKILLET-**Size**: No.8, 10 1/2"; **p/n**: 208C; **Markings**: 8, slant logo, CAST, 208C; **Finish**: aluminum; **Circa**: 1920s; **VALUE: $35-$40**.

SHALLOW SKILLET-**Size**: No.107; **p/n**: 200; **Markings**: 107, slant logo, 200; **Finish**: iron; **Circa**: 1940s; **VALUE: $75-$100**.

ODORLESS SKILLET-**Size**: 11 3/8" x 1 7/8" deep; **p/n**: none; **Markings**: Faint E__E, 9, PAT APPLIED FOR on handle; **Finish**: iron; **Circa**: 1900; **VALUE: $75-$100**. This skillet is either Griswold or made from a Griswold Skillet.

WOOD HANDLE SKILLET-Size: No.9; **p/n**: 209; **Markings**: stamped logo, 9, 209; **Finish**: aluminum; **Circa**: 1920s; **VALUE: $25-$40**.

WOOD HANDLE SKILLET-Size: No.7, 9 7/8" dia.; **p/n**: 207; **Markings**: small logo, ERIE PA., U.S.A., NO.7, PAT NO. 207; **Finish**: aluminum; **Circa**: 1930s; **VALUE: $30-$40**.

REGULAR SKILLET-Size: No.9; **p/n**: 710; **Markings**: 9, slant logo, 710B; **Finish**: iron; **Circa**: 1909; **VALUE: $60-$70**. Note no ERIE or ERIE PA, USA.

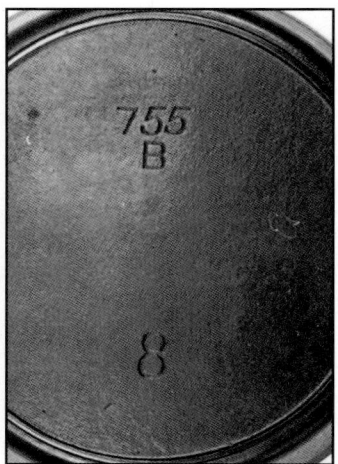

REGULAR SKILLET-Size: No.8, 10" dia. x 1 3/4" deep; **p/n**: 755B; **Markings**: 755B, 8; **Finish**: iron; **Circa**: 1920s; **VALUE: $45-$60**. This is from the unmarked series referred to on page 25 of *The Book of Griswold & Wagner*.

IRON MOUNTAIN SKILLET-Size: No.3; **p/n**: 1031; **Markings**: 3, 1031; **Finish**: aluminum; **Circa**: 1940; **VALUE: $15-$25**.

COLONIAL BREAKFAST SKILLET-Size: 9" x 9"; **p/n**: 666; **Finish**: aluminum; **Circa**: post 1957; **VALUE: $15-$20**. Note no Erie, PA, USA.

REGULAR SKILLET-Size: No.3; **p/n**: 709; **Markings**: block logo, CAST IRON SKILLET, ERIE PA, U.S.A., 709; **Finish**: aluminum; **Circa**: 1940s; **VALUE: $20-$25**.

MERIT REGULAR SKILLET-Size: No.10; **p/n**: 1506; **Markings**: MERIT, 10, 1506; **Finish**: iron; **Circa**: 1940s; **VALUE: $30-$40**.

COLONIAL BREAKFAST SKILLET-Size: 9" x 9"; **p/n**: A566; **Markings**: block logo, COLONIAL BREAKFAST SKILLET, ERIE, PA., U.S.A., PATENT APPLIED FOR, A566; **Finish**: aluminum with wood handle; **Circa**: 1930s; **VALUE: $30-$40**.

DEEP SKILLET WITH COVER-Size: No.8; **p/n**: 2028, Cover-2098; **Markings**: No.8, block logo, ERIE PA., U.S.A. 2028; Cover-Griswold, 2098; **Finish**: Hammered Chrome; **Circa**: 1940s; **VALUE: $100-$125**.

REGULAR SKILLET-Size: No.8; **p/n**: 667; **Markings**: 100TH ANNIVERSARY, NO.8, G.W. CO., 667; **Finish**: iron; **Circa**: unknown; **VALUE: $75-$100**.

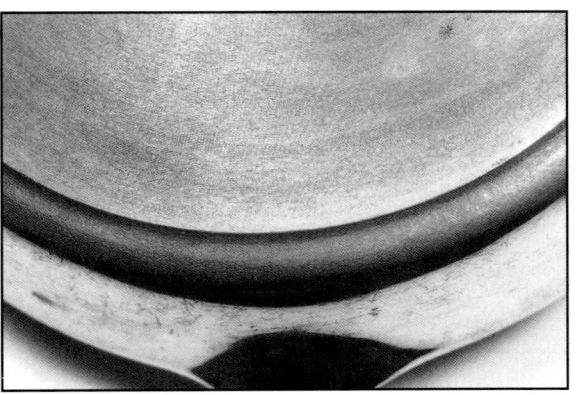

MILLED BOTTOM SKILLET-Size: No.8; **p/n**: 715; **Markings**: 715, GRISWOLD under the handle; **Finish**: iron; **Circa**: 1930s-1940 **VALUE: $150; No.4, $200; No.6, $200; No.10, $250; No.13, $300-$350**. These were designed for use on electric ranges.

REGULAR SKILLET-Size: No.14; **p/n**: 718; **Markings**: CAST IRON SKILLET, 14, block logo, ERIE PA., U.S.A., 718; **Finish**: **Circa**: 1959s; **VALUE: $150**. Note late style handle.

REGULAR SKILLET-Size: NO.14; **p/n**: none; **Markings**: block logo, CAST IRON SKILLET, A, 15 1/2 INCH; **Finish**: iron; **Circa**: 1960s **VALUE: $100-$125**. This particular skillet was made in the Sidney, OH foundry but was purchased with a marked Griswold Erie, PA plain cover. This verifies that when Wagner purchased the Griswold Mfg. Co., it also purchased their inventory.

REGULAR SKILLET WITH COVER-Size: No.8; **p/n**: 704; **Markings**: small logo, 704, No.8.; Cover-8, Self Basting, block logo, 1098B; **Finish**: chrome; **Circa**: 1950s; **VALUE: $50-$75**. Note recessed area around the cover handle.

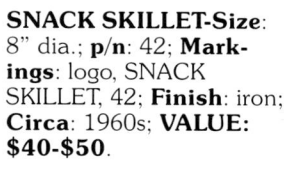

SNACK SKILLET-Size: 8" dia.; **p/n**: 42; **Markings**: logo, SNACK SKILLET, 42; **Finish**: iron; **Circa**: 1960s; **VALUE: $40-$50**.

SQUARE SKILLET-Size: 9 9/16" square; **p/n**: 28; **Markings**: medium logo, SQUARE FRY SKILLET, 28, A.; **Finish**: iron; **Circa**: 1950s; **VALUE: $30-$40**.

LOTH'S SKILLET-Size: No.10; **p/n**: none; **Markings**: CAST IRON SKILLET, 10, LOTH'S, THE W.J. LOTH STOVE CO., WAYNESBORO VIRGINIA, raised "5" bottom right of circle; **Finish**: iron; **Circa**: 1950s; **VALUE: $75**. Griswold did not make this skillet. Apparently, a Griswold skillet was used as a pattern.

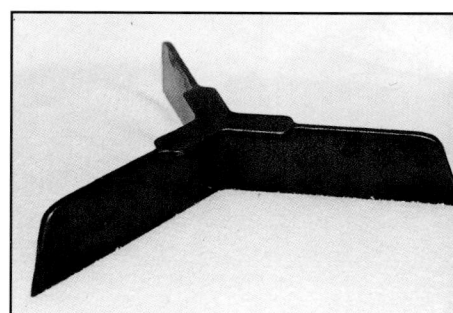

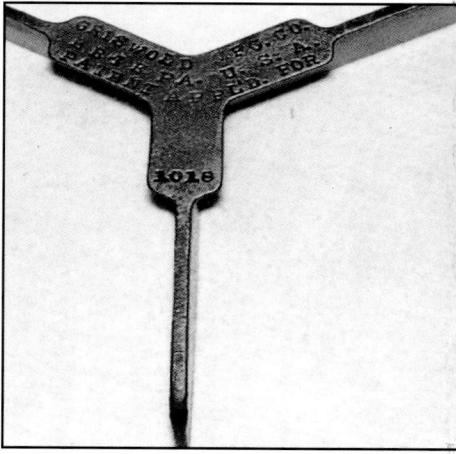

SKILLET DIVIDER-Size: fits No.8 or No.208 aluminum skillet; **p/n**: 1018; **Markings**: GRISWOLD MFG. CO., ERIE PA., U.S.A., PATENT APPL'D FOR, 1018; **Finish**: iron; **Circa**: 1931; **VALUE: $300-$350**.

SOMETHING NEW IN COOKING UTENSILS
...for Perfectly Cooked Foods with Economy and Convenience

"NEVERSTICK" LOAF PAN
Made in Plain or Chrome Finish

The GRISWOLD "NEVERSTICK" LOAF PAN is for oven or top stove cooking. Cakes, bread, meat and fish loaves, baked macaroni, scalloped potatoes and all casserole dishes, French fried potatoes, etc., cooked perfectly and WITHOUT STICKING.

Made of high grade cast iron smooth casting, not polished, in either plain or chrome finish. Size pan: Length 9⅝"; Width 5⅜"; Depth 2½"; Capacity 2 qts.; Net weight 4¾ lbs.

Women everywhere are interested in cooking utensils that produce healthful, flavorsome, perfectly cooked foods with convenience and economy. These utensils have been designed for these exacting requirements.

SKILLET FOOD DIVIDER
Fits No. 8 Griswold Skillet
Patent Applied for

Do you have a No. 8 Cast Iron or No. 208 Cast Aluminum GRISWOLD SKILLET in your home? You can make dinner skillets of either of them with the SKILLET FOOD DIVIDER. You can then cook three foods at one time over one fire.

There is a new flavor, new health value, new cooking ease and economy in cooking foods in the NEW GRISWOLD DINNER SKILLET with it's SELF-BASTING COVER. Vegetables are cooked in their own juices, meats gently browned and full flavored. A new joy in cooking is yours using the "ALL-IN-ONE" DINNER SKILLET—it will cook THREE FOODS at ONE TIME over ONE FIRE. SAVES TIME AND FUEL.

DINNER SKILLET
Cooks three foods at one time over one fire
Patent Applied for

Griswold Advertising Brochure includes Skillet Food Divider.

PURITAN SKILLET-Size: No.10; **p/n**: 1516; **Markings**: 10, PURITAN, 1516; the top is plain with no markings; **Finish**: iron; **Circa**: 1940s; **VALUE**: $50-$60.

NO.3 SKILLET COVER & BOX-Circa: 1940-1960; **VALUE**: Cover-$125-$150; Box-$50-$75.

HINGED DEEP SKILLET-Size: 10 9/16" dia. x 3" d.; **p/n**: 1102; **Markings**: No. 8, small logo, ERIE PA, 1102B; **Finish**: iron; **Circa**: 1940s-1950s; **VALUE**: $25-$35.

DEEP SKILLET OR CHICKEN PAN-Size: 10 3/4" dia. x 3" deep; **p/n**: A28; **Markings**: DEEP SKILLET OR CHICKEN PAN, 28, block logo, ERIE PA., U.S.A., A28; **Finish**: aluminum; **Circa**: 1940s; **VALUE**: $75-$85.

ARISTOCRAFT SKILLET WITH COVER-Size: 10 1/4" diameter x 2" deep; **p/n**: A1208; Cover-1208C; **Markings**: small logo, A1208; Cover -1208C; **Finish**: aluminum; **Circa**: 1940-1950s; **VALUE: $50-$60**.

ARISTOCRAFT CHICKEN FRYER-Size: 10 1/4" dia. x 3" deep; **p/n**: 128; cover-A5528; **Markings**: small logo, Aristocraft Ware; Cover-A5528CE; **Finish**: aluminum with wood handle; **Circa**: 1940s-1950s; **VALUE: $75-$100**. Note paper sticker-Purina Custom Mix, 100 Pointer.

SAUCE PAN-Size: 2 qt., 7 5/8" dia. x 4 1/2" deep; **p/n**: none; **Markings**: (in raised letters), ERIE, 2 QTS; **Finish**: aluminum with wood handle; **Circa**: 1898; **VALUE: $75-$100**.

SAUCE PAN-Size: 2 1/2 Qt., 6 5/8" dia. x 4 3/4" deep; **p/n**: 432 1/2; cover-A411C; **Markings**: 2 1/2 QT., CAST ALUMINUM, block logo, ERIE PA., U.S.A., 432 1/2; **Finish**: aluminum; **Circa**: 1930s; **VALUE: $35-$45**.

SAUCE PAN-Size: 2 Qt.; **p/n**: A2142; (cover) A2142C; **Markings**: block logo, 2 QT., ERIE PA., A2142; Cover GRIS-WOLD, A2142C; **Finish**: Hammercast Aluminum with wood handle; **Circa**: 1940s **VALUE: $45-$60**.

SAUCE PAN-Size: 4 Qt., 8 7/8" dia. x 3 3/4" deep; **p/n**: 414, (cover) A414C; **Markings**: slant logo, SAUCE PAN, 4 QT, CAST ALUMINUM, ERIE PA., U.S.A.; **Finish**: aluminum; **Circa**: 1930s; **VALUE: $75 with cover**.

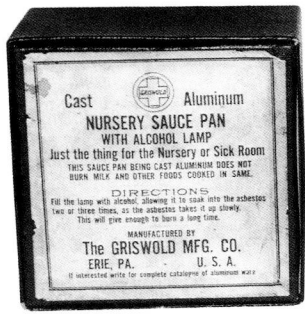

NURSERY SAUCE PAN SET-Size: 1 pint, 4 1/4" dia. x 2 3/8" deep; Handle, 3 1/4"; **p/n**: 41; Burner Stand, 3379, **Markings**: 'ERIE', 41, 1PT; Stand-3379; **Finish**: aluminum; **Circa**: 1910; **VALUE: $1,000-$1,200; Pan only, $75-$100.** Sauce Pan also came with p/n 3362.

SAUCE PAN-Size: 8" dia. x 2 3/4" deep; **p/n**: none; **Markings**: GHC logo, General Housewares Corp., MADE IN USA, Griswold logo; **Finish**: iron; **Circa**: 1980s; **VALUE: $20-$25**. This piece was not made in the Griswold foundry.

SAUCE PAN-Size: 7 1/2" dia. x 3 3/8" deep; **p/n**: 84; **Markings**: block logo, 84; **Finish**: iron; **Circa**: 1950s; **VALUE: $75-$100**. This piece is usually porcelainized.

OMELET PAN-Size: 9 5/16" open x 15 3/4" long including handles; **p/n**: A53L, A53R; **Markings**: Stamped logo, A53R, A53L; **Finish**: aluminum with wood handles; **Circa**: 1950s; **VALUE: $60-$75**.

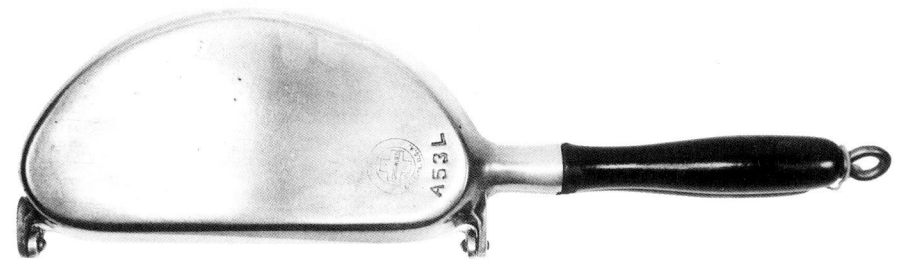

GRIDDLES

BAIL HANDLE GRIDDLE-Size: No.10; **p/n**: 776; **Markings**: Diamond Logo, N0.10, 776; **Finish**: iron; **Circa**: 1884-1910; **VALUE: $100-$150**; No.12, $75-$100; No.14, $75-$100; No.16, $100-$150.

BAIL HANDLE GRIDDLE-Size: No.10, 10 3/4" dia.; **p/n**: 776; **Markings**: 10, "ERIE", 776, GRISWOLD; **Finish**: iron; **Circa**: 1915; **VALUE: $100-$125**. Notice ghost marks of both center and bottom position logos, plus "X" bottom reinforcement.

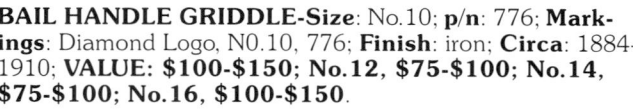

HANDLE GRIDDLE-Size: No.8; **p/n**: 738; **Markings**: slant logo, 8, ERIE, 738A; **Finish**: iron; **Circa**: 1909; **VALUE: $45-$60**; No.7, $55-$65; No.9, $55-$65; No.10, $65-$75.

HANDLE GRIDDLE-Size: No.8; **p/n**: 738; **Markings**: slant logo, 8, "ERIE", 738; **Finish**: iron; **Circa**: 1909; **VALUE: $40-$50**; No.9, $50-$60; No.10, $60-$75. Note single hole handle.

WOOD HANDLE GRIDDLE-**Size**: No.9; **p/n**: 309; **Markings**: slant logo, 9, 'ERIE', 309; **Finish**: aluminum; **Circa**: 1930s; **VALUE: $45-$60**.

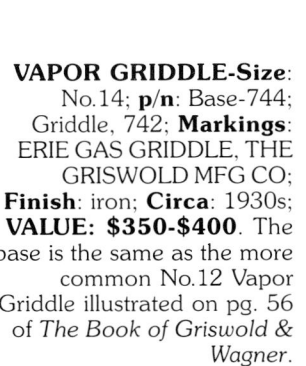

VAPOR GRIDDLE-**Size**: No.14; **p/n**: Base-744; Griddle, 742; **Markings**: ERIE GAS GRIDDLE, THE GRISWOLD MFG CO; **Finish**: iron; **Circa**: 1930s; **VALUE: $350-$400**. The base is the same as the more common No.12 Vapor Griddle illustrated on pg. 56 of *The Book of Griswold & Wagner*.

HANDLE GRIDDLE-**Size**: No.8; **p/n**: none; **Markings**: ERIE ALUMINUM, 8; **Finish**: aluminum; **Circa**: 1898-1910; **VALUE: $30-$40; No.9, $50-$60; No.10, $60-$75**. Handle is also of aluminum but is riveted on.

MERIT REGULAR GRIDDLE-**Size**: No.9; **p/n**: 1508; **Markings**: MERIT, 9 1508; **Finish**: iron; **Circa**: 1930-1940; **VALUE: $45-$60; No.7, $45-$60; No.8, $35-$40**. Made for Sears Roebuck & Co.

BEST MADE REGULAR GRIDDLE-Size: No.9; **p/n**: 1245; **Markings**: BEST MADE, No.9, 1245; **Finish**: iron; **Circa**: 1940s; **VALUE: $50-$60**.

GOOD HEALTH REGULAR GRIDDLE-Size: No.8; **p/n**: 620; **Markings**: GOOD HEALTH, GRIDDLE, 8, 620; **Finish**: iron; **Circa**: 1931-1936; **VALUE: $50-$70; No.9, $55-$65**.

BEST MADE REGULAR GRIDDLE-Size: No.9; **p/n**: 1245; **Markings**: BEST MADE, S.R. AND CO. No.9, 1245; **Finish**: iron; **Circa**: 1930s-1940; **VALUE: $50-$60**. Made for Sears Roebuck & Co.

REGULAR GRIDDLES-Size: right-No.8; left, No.9; **p/n**: 2039; **Markings**: No.8; No.9, block logo, ERIE PA, 2039; **Finish**: hammered iron; **Circa**: 1940s; **VALUE: $100-$125**. Same identical size and pattern number, but one is marked No.8, the other No.9.

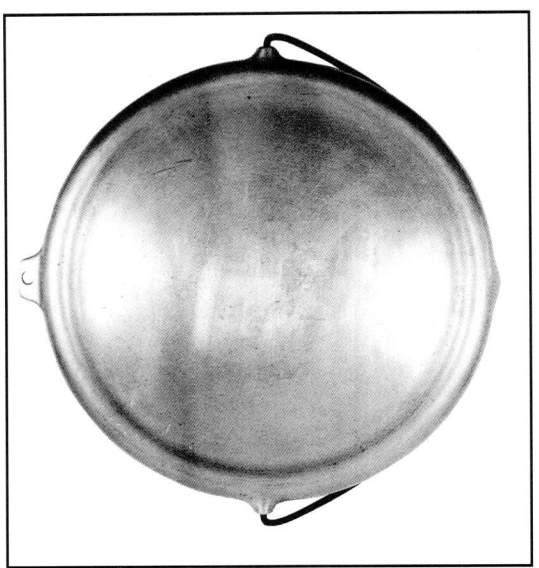

ALUMINUM GRIDDLE/ BROILER-Size: 13 5/8" dia.; **p/n**: A3514; **Markings**: small logo, ERIE PA., U.S.A., A3514; **Finish**: aluminum; **Circa**: 1932; **VALUE: $60-$75**.

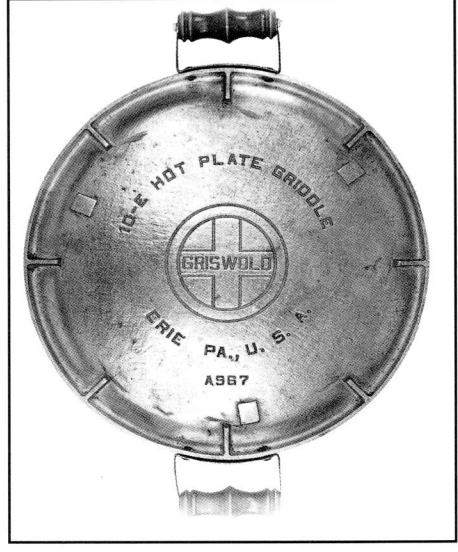

HOT PLATE GRIDDLE-Size: 9 3/8" dia.; **p/n**: A967; **Markings**: block logo, HOT PLATE GRIDDLE, ERIE PA., U.S.A., A967; **Finish**: aluminum; **Circa**: 1930; **VALUE: $75-$100**.

PLETT PAN-Size: 9 7/16" dia. x 5/16" deep; **p/n**: 2980; **Markings**: SCANDINAVIAN IMPORTING CO. BOSTON MASS, PLETT PAN, 2980; **Finish**: iron; **Circa**: 1920s; **VALUE: $50-$65**. Note early style handle.

PLETT PAN- p/n: 2980; **Markings**: No.34, slant logo, 2980X; **Finish**: aluminum; **Circa**: 1930s; **VALUE: $30-$40**.

Top left: **LONG GRIDDLE-Size**: No.8, 19 5/8" x 9 1/2" plus handles; **p/n**: 745; **Markings**: 8, 745, ERIE; **Finish**: iron; **Circa**: 1900-1909; **VALUE: $30-$40; No.7, $30-$40; No.9, $30-$40; No.10, $65-$75**.

Top center: **LONG GRIDDLE-Size**: No.8, 19 5/8" x 9 1/2" plus handles; **p/n**: 745; **Markings**: 8, slant logo, ERIE, 745A; **Finish**: iron; **Circa**: 1909; **VALUE: $30-$40; No.7, $30-$40; No.9, $35-$45**.

Top right: **LONG GRIDDLE-Size**: No.8, **p/n**: 745; **Markings**: slant logo, 8, CASE IRON GRIDDLE, ERIE PA., U.S.A., 745; **Finish**: iron; **Circa**: 1930; **VALUE: $35-$45; No.9, $60-$75; No.11, $100-$150**.

Bottom left: **PURITAN LONG GRIDDLE-Size**: No.9, 21 1/2" x 10 1/8"; **p/n**: 1511; **Markings**: PURITAN, 9,1511; **Finish**: iron; **Circa**: 1930s; **VALUE: $30-$40; No.8, $30-$40**. Puritan was made for Sears Roebuck & Co.

Bottom center: **LONG GRIDDLE-Size**: No.8, 10 1/8" x 7 3/4"; **p/n**: 771; **Markings**: 8, CAST IRON GRIDDLE, block logo, ERIE PA., U.S.A., 771; **Finish**: iron; **Circa**: 1940s; **VALUE: $25-$35; No.7, $30-$35; No.9, $35-$45; No.10, $60-$70**.

NO. 18 CAST IRON GRILL-Size: 16 3/4" x 10"; **p/n**: 1108; **Markings**: No.18, CAST IRON GRILL, block logo, ERIE PA., U.S.A., 1108; **Finish**: iron; **Circa**: 1955; **VALUE: $150-$200** with the Anniversary sticker.

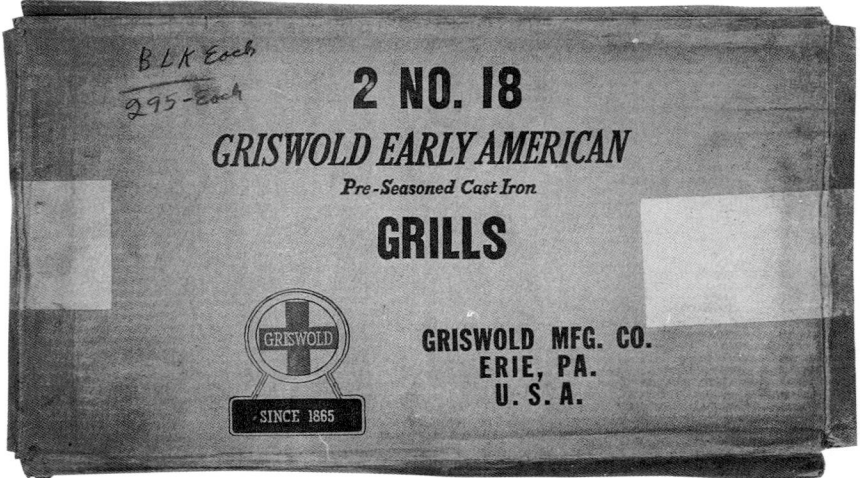

Grills were shipped two in a carton.

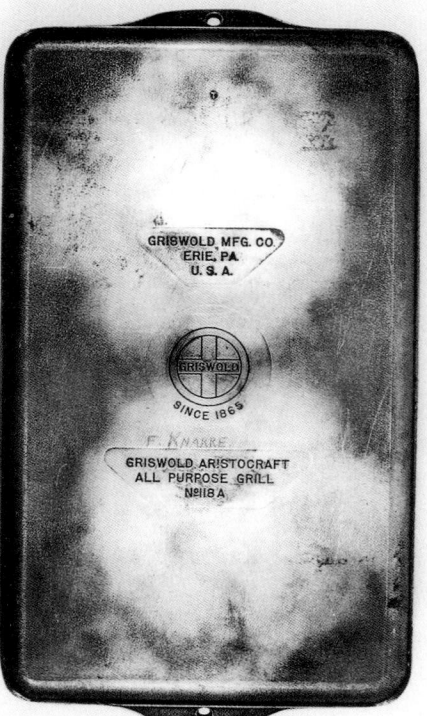

ARISTOCRAFT GRILL-Size: 17" x 10 1/8"; **p/n**: 118A; **Markings**: GRISWOLD MFG CO., ERIE PA, U.S.A., Griswold logo, SINCE 1865, GRISWOLD ARISTOCRAFT ALL PURPOSE GRILL, NO.118A; **Finish**: aluminum; **Circa**: 1940s-1950s; **VALUE: $125-$175**.

DUTCH OVENS & OVAL ROASTERS

DUTCH OVEN-Size: No.9; **p/n**: none; **Markings**: "ERIE", 9; Cover: 9; **Finish**: iron; **Circa**: 1890-1910; **VALUE: $100-$125; No.8, $75-$100; No.10, $125-$150**. Note shape of handles.

CHUCKWAGON DUTCH OVEN COVER-Size: 11; **p/n**: 844; **Markings**: THE GRISWOLD MFG. CO., 11, CAST IRON FLANGE COVER, ERIE PA., U.S.A., 844, block logo; **Finish**: iron; **Circa**: 1920s; **VALUE: $150**. Block logo, and "Flange Cover" unusual. Also came in size 10.

DUTCH OVEN-Size: No.8; **p/n**: 833; **Markings**: "ERIE", 8; (cover) 837; **Finish**: aluminum; **Circa**: 1910; **VALUE: $45-$60**.

TITE TOP DUTCH OVEN-Size: No.8; **p/n**: 833C; **Markings**: This piece is unusual in that Dutch is misspelled and reads DUTOH; **Finish**: iron; **Circa**: 1930-1940; **VALUE: $100-$150**.

DUTCH OVEN-Size: No.8; **p/n**: 833; (cover) A-2551; **Markings**: block logo, ERIE PA., U.S.A., PAT'D MARCH 16, 20, 833; (cover) slant logo, ERIE PA., U.S.A., A2551 in raised letters; **Finish**: chrome; **Circa**: 1930s; **VALUE: $75-$100**. Slant logo cover with applied handle is very unusual with chrome finish. This piece is a true factory marriage.

DUTCH OVEN-Size: No.7; **p/n**: 2603; (cover) 2604; **Markings**: Fully marked, block logo; **Finish**: plated outside, black iron interior; **Circa**: 1930s; **VALUE: $45-$50**.

MERIT DUTCH OVEN-Size: No.9, 11 1/8" dia. x 4 1/4" deep; **p/n**: 479; (cover) 1521; **Markings**: MERIT, 9, 479; (cover) MERIT, 1521; **Finish**: iron; **Circa**: 1930s; **VALUE: $90-$125**. Note broken Hear rings under cover.

DUTCH OVEN WITH HINGED COVER-Size: No.8; **p/n**: 2058; (cover) 2098; **Markings**: block logo, No.8, ERIE PA., U.S.A., 2058; (cover) GRISWOLD, 2098; **Finish**: hammered chrome; **Circa**: 1940s; **VALUE: $60-$75**.

OVAL ROASTER-Size: 9 3/8" x 12 7/8" x 4 7/8" deep; **p/n**: A2; Cover: A2c; **Markings**: block logo, EXTRA HEAVY, A2; (cover) PAT'D FEB 10, 1920, A2C; **Finish**: aluminum; **Circa**: 1940s; **VALUE: $100-$150**.

DUTCH OVEN-Size: No.8; **p/n**: 465; (cover) A465C-D; **Markings**: small logo, ERIE PA., U.S.A., NO.8, PAT NO. 465; (cover) PAT'D FEB 10, 1920, A465-C-D; (trivet) unmarked; **Finish**: aluminum; **Circa**: 1950s; **VALUE: $60-$70**.

OVAL ROASTER-Size: No.5, 14 3/8" x 9 1/2" x 4 1/4" deep; **p/n**: A485; (cover) A485C; **Markings**: THE GRISWOLD MFG. CO., CAST 5 ALUMINUM, OVAL ROASTER, ERIE PA., U.S.A., A485; (cover) PAT 1,330,209., A485C; **Finish**: aluminum; **Circa**: 1940s; **VALUE: $75-$100**.

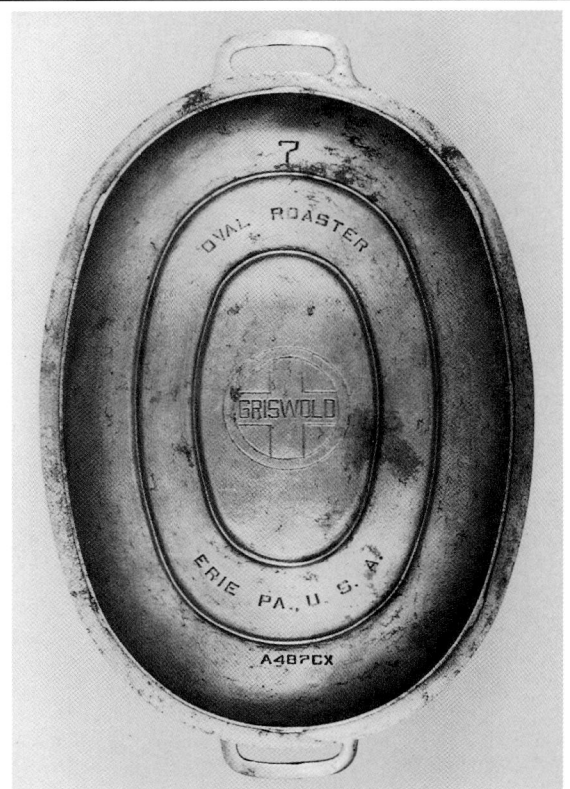

OVAL ROASTER-Size: No.5; **p/n**: A2185; (cover) A2185C; **Markings**: No.5, block logo, ERIE PA., A2185; (cover) GRISWOLD, A2185C; **Finish**: Hammer Cast Aluminum; **Circa**: 1940s; **VALUE: $65-$85**.

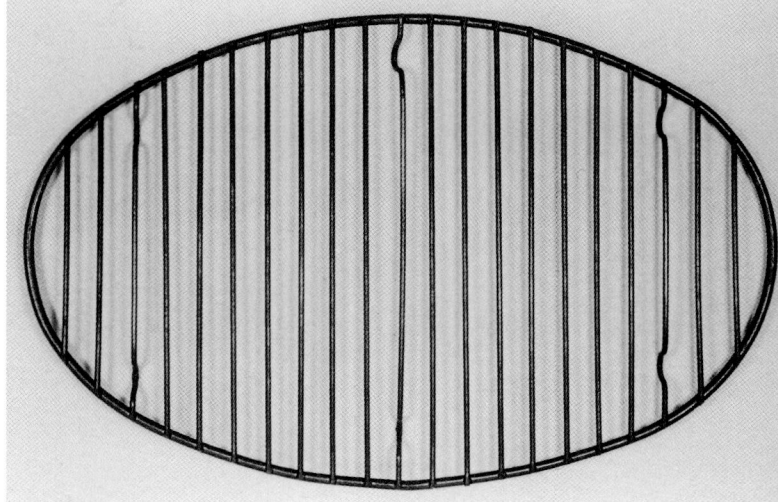

OVAL ROASTER-Size: No.7; **p/n**: 487; (cover) A487C; **Markings**: small logo, THE GRISWOLD MFG CO, ERIE PA., U.S.A., NO.7 PAT 487; **Finish**: aluminum; **Circa**: 1950s; **VALUE: $125-$150**. Note wire trivet of this time period, and original sticker.

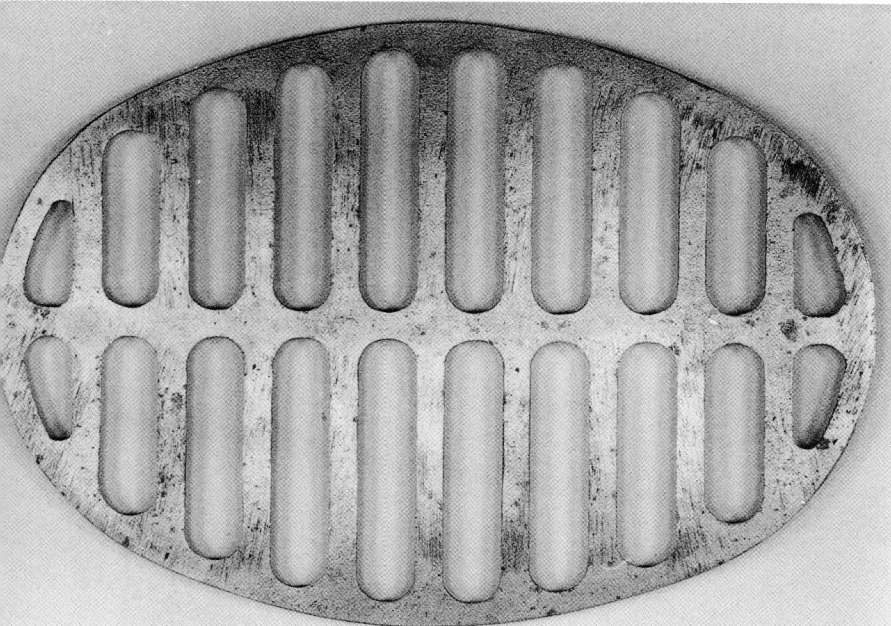

SYMBOL WARE OVAL ROASTER-Size: 16 3/8" x 10 1/4" x 5 3/8" deep; **p/n**: 99; **Markings**: GRISWOLD, 99; cover and trivet not marked; **Finish**: aluminum with enameled steel cover; **Circa**: 1950s; **VALUE: $60-$75**.

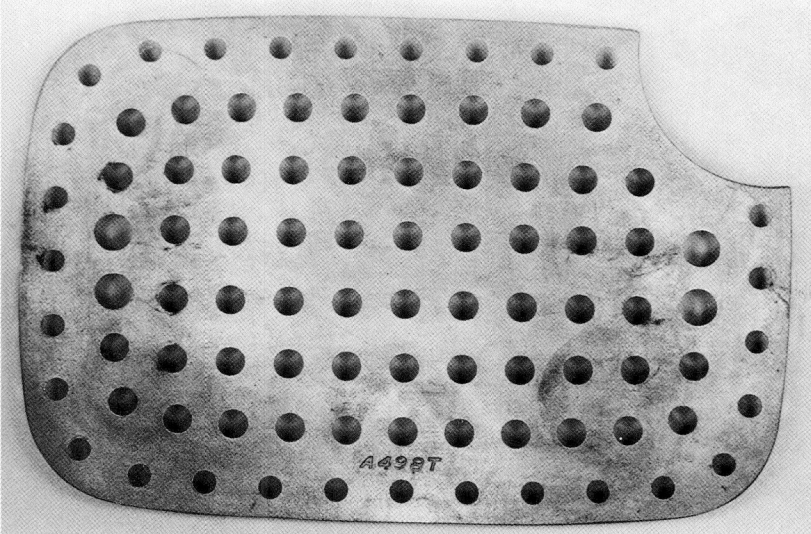

ARISTOCRAFT ROASTER-Size: 16 1/8" x 12 1/16" x 4 1/2" deep; **p/n**: A498; (cover) A498C; Trivet A498T **Markings**: THE GRISWOLD MFG. CO., ERIE PA., U.S.A.; (cover) A498C, PAT 1,330,209; Trivet: A498T **Finish**: aluminum; **Circa**: 1950s; **VALUE: $100-$150**. Cover came with either smooth or hammered top panel.

KETTLES

SAFETY KETTLE TRI-FOLD BROCHURE; VALUE: $35-$50.

SAFETY KETTLE-Flat Bottom-Size: 11 5/16" dia. x 7 3/4" deep; **p/n**: 861; **Markings**: SAFETY, 861, 9; Trivet stamped, 9; **Finish**: iron with tin trivet; **Circa**: 1920s; **VALUE: $150-$200 complete with trivet**.

SAFETY KETTLE- Size: No.9, 9" high x 11 1/2" dia.; **p/n**: 830; **Markings**: ERIE SAFETY, 830, PAT'D MAR 10, 91, 9; **Finish**: iron; **Circa**: 1890s; **VALUE: $125; with cover $200**. This appears to be the earliest style. Note cast iron pour spout. Also, cover retainers are on the top of the kettle ears so the cover fits on top rather than being inset as with later models.

SAFETY KETTLE TRIVETS-Finish: tin; **Circa**: 1920s; **VALUE: $35-$50**. The trivet with the small holes is rarely seen.

152

SKINNER SAFETY KETTLE-Size: No.10, 12 1/8" dia. x 8 3/4" deep; **p/n**: 862; **Markings**: SKINNER SAFETY CO, 862, ERIE PA, 10; **Finish**: iron; **Circa**: 1920s; **VALUE: $75-$100**. Note the Griswold instruction sticker on the bottom.

SCOTCH BOWL-Size: No.5, 12" dia. x 4 3/4" deep; **p/n**: 783; **Markings**: ERIE No 5, 783; **Finish**: iron; **Circa**: late 1800s; **VALUE: $75-$100**. Note the unusual position of the pattern number.

SCOTCH BOWL MASTER PATTERN-Size: No.5, 12 1/16" dia. x 4 11/16" deep; **p/n**: 783A; **Markings**: SCOTCH 5 BOWL. block logo ERIE PA., U.S.A., 783A; **Finish**: iron with brass kettle ears, bottom ring. There is a trace of brass on the ingate connection. Layout lines are visible. The pour ring attachment and the ingates have been broken off; **CIRCA:** 1920 (?); **VALUE: $500-$700**. **See picture in color section.**

Brass kettle ears were inlaid and soldered.

SCOTCH BOWL-Size: ; **p/n**: No.5, 12" dia. x 4 3/4" deep; **Markings**: GRISWOLDS ERIE, 783, No.5; **Finish**: iron; **Circa**: 1888-1904; **VALUE: $100-$125**.

MASLIN KETTLE-Size: 12 qt.; **p/n**: 6797; **Markings**: ERIE (raised letters), 6797, 12 QTS; **Finish**: aluminum; **Circa**: 1900-1910; **VALUE: $200-$250**. Note heat ring and pour ring.

SCOTCH BOWL-Size: No.2; **p/n**: 6790; **Markings**: 6790, No 2; **Finish**: aluminum; **Circa**: 1920s; **VALUE: $40-$60**.

TRIVET-Size: 9 7/16" dia.; **p/n**: A765B; **Markings**: block logo, ERIE PA., U.S.A., PATENTED FEB 10, 1920, A765B; **Finish**: aluminum; **Circa**: 1930s; **VALUE: $75-$100**. This is the upper trivet from the Combination Cooker.

MASLIN KETTLE-Size: 24 qt., 15 3/8" x 9 3/4" deep; **p/n**: A4524; (cover) A4524C; **Markings**: slant logo, THE GRISWOLD MFG. CO., CAST 24 ALUMINUM, MASLIN KETTLE, ERIE PA., U.S.A.; (cover) block logo, PAT'D SEPT 22, 1925, ERIE PA., U.S.A., PAT'D FEB 10, 1920, A4524C; **Finish**: aluminum; **Circa**: 1920s; **VALUE: $300-$400**.

Page from 1928 catalog illustrating the Combination Cooker.

BAKING KETTLE-Size: No.8, 11 1/2" dia. x 6" deep; **p/n**: A1458; **Markings**: block logo, THE GRISWOLD MFG. CO., CAST 8 ALUMINUM BAKING KETTLE, ERIE PA., U.S.A., A1458; (cover) BAKING KETTLE COVER, SELF BASTING, block logo, A1458CX; **Finish**: aluminum; **Circa**: 1930s; **VALUE: $200-$250**. Note temperature gauge in the cover.

Waterless Cooking Kettle bi-fold Brochure with recipes- Value: $25-$35.

WATERLESS COOKING KETTLE-Size: No.11, 11 7/8"dia, x 7 5/8" deep; **p/n**: A1411; (cover) A1411C; (trivet) A466T; **Markings**: block logo, THE GRISWOLD MFG. CO., CAST ALUMINUM, 11, WATERLESS COOKING KETTLE, ERIE PA., U.S.A., PAT'D MAR 16,10, A1411; (cover) WATERLESS COOKING KETTLE COVER, block logo, A1411C; **Finish**: aluminum; **Circa**: 1930s; **VALUE: $300-$325**.

TEA KETTLES, COFFEE POTS, & PITCHERS

TEA KETTLE-**p/n**: A56; **Markings**: large block logo, A56; **Finish**: aluminum; **Circa**: 1930s; **VALUE: $40-$50**.

COLONIAL TEA KETTLE-**Size**: 5 qt., 9" dia.; **p/n**: 525; **Markings**: block logo, 5QT, COLONIAL DESIGN, CAST ALUMINUM, ERIE PA., U.S.A., 525; (cover) 525C; **Finish**: aluminum; **Circa**: 1920s; **VALUE: $100-$125**. Handle is riveted. Cover removable.

COFFEE POT-**Size**: 6 1/2" dia. x 8" high; **p/n**: unmarked (A113); **Markings**: slant logo; **Finish**: aluminum; **Circa**: 1910; **VALUE: $75-$95**.

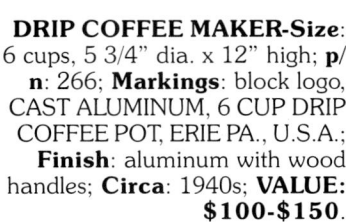

DRIP COFFEE MAKER-**Size**: 6 cups, 5 3/4" dia. x 12" high; **p/n**: 266; **Markings**: block logo, CAST ALUMINUM, 6 CUP DRIP COFFEE POT, ERIE PA., U.S.A.; **Finish**: aluminum with wood handles; **Circa**: 1940s; **VALUE: $100-$150**.

COFFEE POT-**Size**: 6 3/8" dia x 9" high; **p/n**: 103; **Markings**: stamped logo, No.103; **Finish**: aluminum; **Circa**: 1910; **VALUE: $75-$95**.

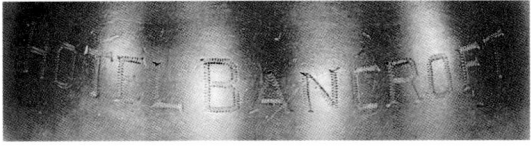

BAILED WATER PITCHER-Size: 2 1/2 qts., 8" high; **p/n**: A172; **Markings**: A172, SAMUEL LEWIS HOTEL SUPPLIES, 73 BARCL___T, NY; HOTEL BANCROFT across the front; **Finish**: aluminum; **Circa**: unknown; **VALUE: $150-$200**.

WAFFLE IRONS

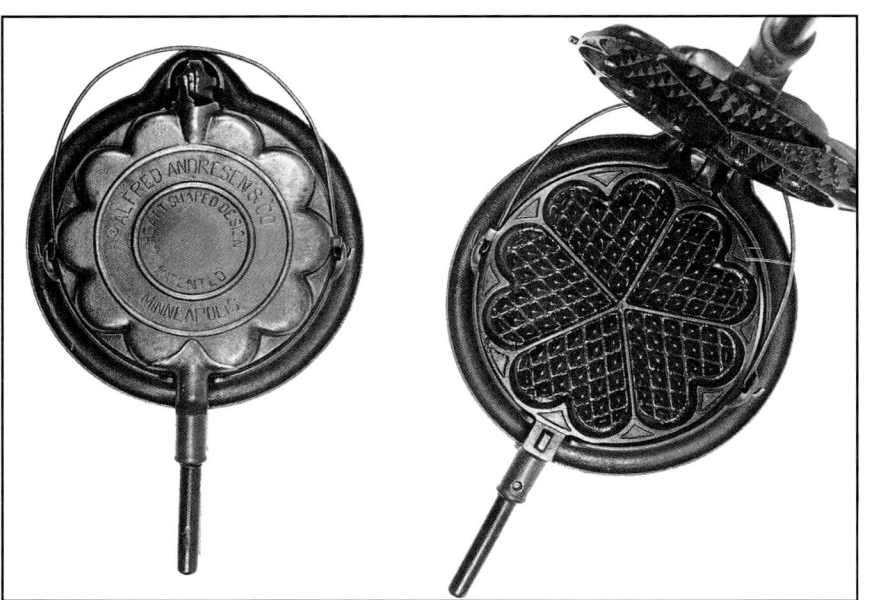

ANDRESEN WAFFLE IRON-Size: No.8; **p/n**: none, (base) 235; **Markings**: ALFRED ANDRESEN & CO, HEART SHAPED DESIGN PATENTED MINNEAPOLIS; Base: THE GRISWOLD MFG. CO. ERIE PA., U.S.A., NO 8, 235; **Finish**: iron with wood handles; **Circa**: 1910; **VALUE: $95-$125**. This waffle has the acorn hinge.

Design Patent-Andresen Heart Pattern-Date: Dec. 27, 1904.

WAFFLE IRON-Size: No.8, (paddles) 7 1/2" dia.; **p/n**: (high base) 914; (paddles) 885, 886; **Markings**: (base) GRISWOLD, 914; (paddles) standard markings; **Finish**: iron; **Circa**: 1920s; **VALUE: $150-$200**. This base is unusual. Note the design and how pins fit into bail attachment.

KRUM KAKE IRON-Size: No.8, 7 3/4" dia.; **p/n**: 2424 & 2423; (base) 975c; **Markings**: ALFRED ANDRESEN & CO., MINNEAPOLIS, KORNU KOPIA KRUMB KAKE, PATEND; (base) GRISWOLD 8, 975C; **Finish**: iron with wood handles; **Circa**: 1914; **VALUE: $90-$100**.

AMERICAN WAFFLE IRON-Size: No.9; **p/n**: 316 & 317; high base: 319; **Markings**: PAT DEC 1, 1908, AMERICAN No 9; **Finish**: (paddles) nickel; (base) iron; **Circa**: 1920s; **VALUE: $75-$100**.

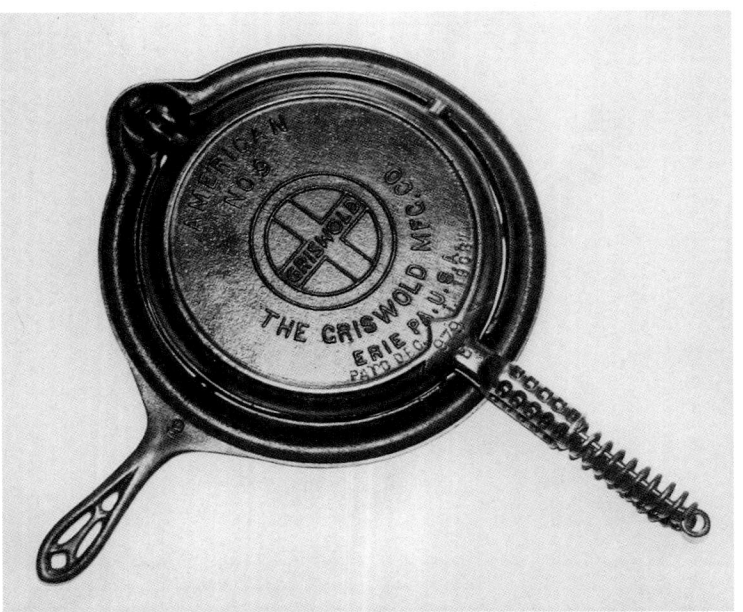

AMERICAN WAFFLE IRON-Size: No. 8; **p/n**: 628N; (base) 152A; **Markings**: AMERICAN, NO. 628N, block logo, THE GRISWOLD MFG CO. ERIE PA., U.S.A.; **Finish**: aluminum paddles, iron base; **Circa**: 1930s; **VALUE** $45-$60.

AMERICAN WAFFLE IRON-Size: No.9; **p/n**: 980, 979, (base) 978; **Markings**: AMERICAN N0 9, slant logo, THE GRISWOLD MFG. CO., ERIE PA, U.S.A., PAT'D DEC. 1, 1908, 979B, 980A, (base) 978; **Finish**: iron; **Circa**: 1908-1920; **VALUE: $75-$100**.

BROCHURE-Size: 3 1/4" x 6 1/4", 12 pages; **Circa:** 1920s; **VALUE:** $100-$125. This brochure has very nice color and graphics.

HEARTS STAR WAFFLE IRON-Size: No. 708; **p/n**: A708F, A708M; **Markings**: HEART STAR, ERIE PA., U.S.A., 708, PAT'D MAY 18-20; **Finish**: aluminum on iron base; **Circa**: 1920; **VALUE**: $75-$100.

ELECTRIC WAFFLE IRON-Size: 7 1/2" dia; (base) 9 1/2" dia.; **p/n**: A-2 -E; **Markings**: THE GRISWOLD MFG. CO., ERIE PA., U.S.A., Griswold logo, VOLT 110, WATT 660, A-2-E; **Finish**: chrome; **Circa**: 1928-1930s; **VALUE: $75-$100**. Aluminum plates, steel body and base.

BEST MADE WAFFLE IRON-Size: ; **p/n**: 1250; (base) 1251; **Markings**: BEST MADE, S.R. AND CO., No.8, 1250; base: PAT 1251, BEST MADE S.R & CO; **Finish**: iron; **Circa**: 1940s; **VALUE: $50-$60**.

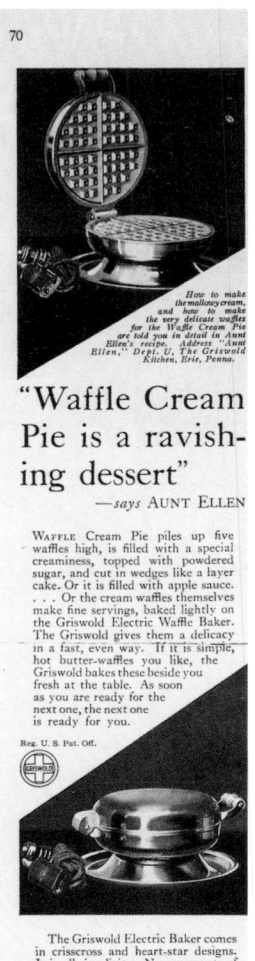

Magazine Advertisement, c.1928

MAJESTIC WAFFLE IRON-Size: No.8; **p/n**: 885M, 886M; (base) 975D; **Markings**: MAJESTIC MFG. CO., MAJESTIC, ST LOUIS, MO, PATENTED DEC 1, 1908, 885M, 886M; (base) GRISWOLD, 8, 975-D; **Finish**: iron; **Circa**: 1920s; **VALUE: $100-$150**.

ELECTRIC WAFFLE IRON, Model 1-8-E-Size: (plates) 7 3/16" dia.; **p/n**: A923; (electric shield) A932; **Markings**: THE GRISWOLD MFG. CO, ERIE PA., U.S.A.; (brass plate) Volts 110, Watts 660, No.1-8-E; **Finish**: aluminum; **Circa**: 1931; **VALUE: $100-$150**.

MUFFIN PANS

GOLF BALL GEM PAN-Size: 10 1/2" x 7 1/8"; **p/n**: 947; **Markings**: 947 under handle and on one cup, 1891 inscribed on bottom of one cup; **Finish**: iron; **Circa**: 1880s; **VALUE: $350-$400**. The 1891 date is rare.

POPOVER PAN-Size: 11 1/8" x 7 5/8"; **p/n**: none; **Markings**: ERIE No 10 (on top of handles; **Finish**: iron; **Circa**: 1890s; **VALUE: $75-$100**. Note two dots under the "o" in No. 10. This creates a very interesting variation.

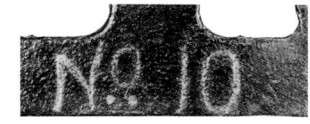

NO.16 GEM PAN-Size: 6 1/2" x 9"; **p/n**: 6139; **Markings**: GRISWOLD NO.16, GRISWOLD MFG CO., ERIE PA., U.S.A., 6139; **Finish**: aluminum; **Circa**: 1910-1920; **VALUE: $300-$350**.

POPOVER PAN-Size: 11 1/18 x 7 1/2; **p/n**: none; **Markings**: ERIE, No 10 (on top of handles); **Finish**: aluminum; **Circa**: 1900-1910; **VALUE: $50-$75**. Two dots under "o" in No.10. One dot is not visible in this photograph.

CORN STICK PAN-p/n: 2073; **Markings**: NO 273, GRIS-WOLD, CRISPY CORN STICK PAN, ERIE PA., U.S.A., 2073; **Finish**: chrome or black iron; **Circa**: 1940a; **VALUE: chrome $350; black iron $400**.

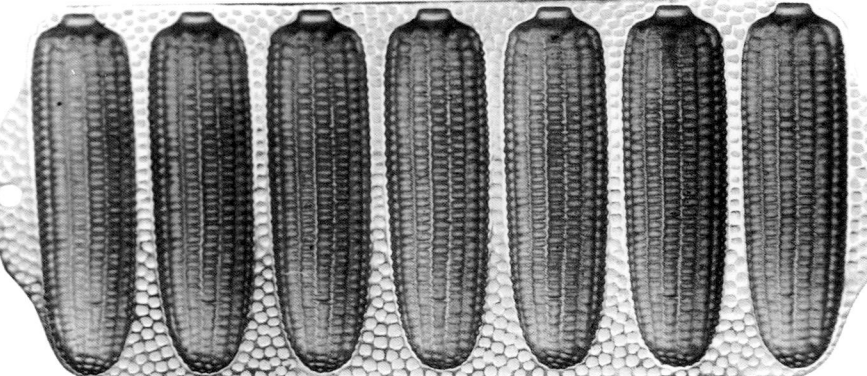

POPOVER PAN-Size: 11 2/8" x 7 3/4"; **p/n**: 8010; **Markings**: ERIE, 8010; **Finish**: aluminum; **Circa**: 1920; **VALUE: $45-$60**.

NO.10 POPOVER PAN-Size: 11 5/8" x 8" x 15/8" deep; **p/n**: none (948); **Markings**: ERIE, NO 10.; **Finish**: iron; **Circa**: 1920s; **VALUE: $100-$125**. Outside frame is uncommon.

TOYS & MINIATURES

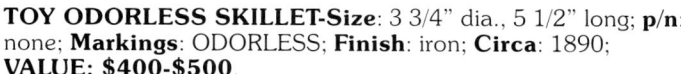

TOY ODORLESS SKILLET-**Size**: 3 3/4" dia., 5 1/2" long; **p/n**: none; **Markings**: ODORLESS; **Finish**: iron; **Circa**: 1890; **VALUE: $400-$500**.

SAFETY KETTLE-Salesman Sample-**Size**: 4 3/4" dia. x 2 3/4" deep; **p/n**: none; **Markings**: SAFETY; **Finish**: iron with tin cover; **Circa**: 1900; **VALUE: $2,500-$3,000**.

Miniature Safety Kettles with full size No.9 Safety Kettle. Notice tin trivet in both.

TOY DUTCH OVEN-Size: 4 3/8" dia. x 1 3/4" deep; **p/n**: 568, (cover) 569; **Markings**: THE GRISWOLD MFG. CO., ERIE PA., U.S.A., CAST IRON TITE TOP DUTCH OVEN, 0, PAT'D MAR 16,20, 268, block logo; (cover) PAT'D FEB 10, 1920, ERIE PA., U.S.A., 569, block logo **Finish**: iron; **Circa**: 1930; **VALUE: $500-$600**. Plain cover for '0' Dutch oven is very unusual. Acorn shaped knob is unusual.

REPRODUCTION TOY SKILLET-Size: No.0; **p/n**: 562; **Markings**: standard markings; **Finish**: poor, rough quality. Also notice the interior is rough, uneven and not polished.

NO.2 SIZE TOY SKILLET-Size: 2 3/4" dia.; **p/n**: none; **Markings**: stamped logo; **Finish**: aluminum; **Circa**: 1920s; **VALUE: $100-150**.

NO.2 SIZE TOY SKILLETS-Size: 2 3/4" dia.; **p/n**: none; **Markings**: (left & center) USE ERIE WARE THE BEST; (right) ERIE; **Finish**: iron or nickel; (center) aluminum; **Circa**: 1920s; **VALUE: (left & center) $200; (right) $250**.

SERVING PIECES, CASSEROLES, & PATTY BOWLS

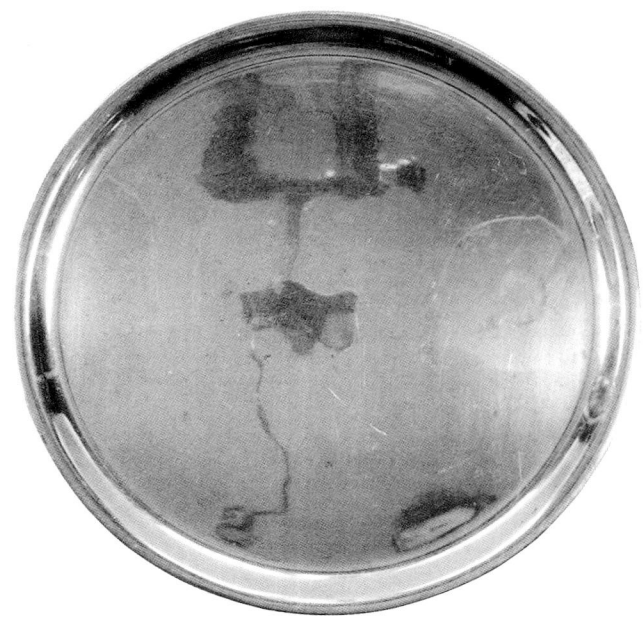

ROUND TRAY-Size: 13" dia. x 1/2" deep; **p/n**: 35; **Markings**: 35 (appears to be hand inscribed); **Finish**: aluminum; **Circa**: 1898; **VALUE: $250-$300**. This piece is listed in a 1898 catalog as a Chafing Dish or Serving Waiter, "Especially designed to be used under a chafing dish. For a serving tray it cannot be surpassed: highly polished."

SHIRRED EGG DISH-Size: 6 1/8" dia.; **p/n**: 56; **Markings**: slant logo, 56; **Finish**: aluminum; **Circa**: 1920s; **VALUE: $60-$70**.

STEAK PLATTER-p/n: 849; **Markings**: STEAK PLATTER, logo, ERIE PA., U.S.A., 849; **Finish**: DuChro; **Circa**: 1950; **VALUE: $50-$60**. Wood holders were available as an option, and after market.

RAREBIT DISHES-Size:(top) 5 1/8" x 10 1/16", (bottom) 4 5/16" x 8 7/8"; **p/n**: (top) 1529, (bottom) 1528; **Markings**: (both) RAREBIT DISH, block logo, ERIE PA., U.S.A., pattern number; **Finish**: (top) polished chrome, (bottom) Du-Chro; **Circa**: 1940s; **VALUE: $125-$150**.

RAREBIT DISH-**p/n**: 1529; **Finish**: chrome; **Circa**: 1940s; **VALUE: $150-$200 with original sticker**.

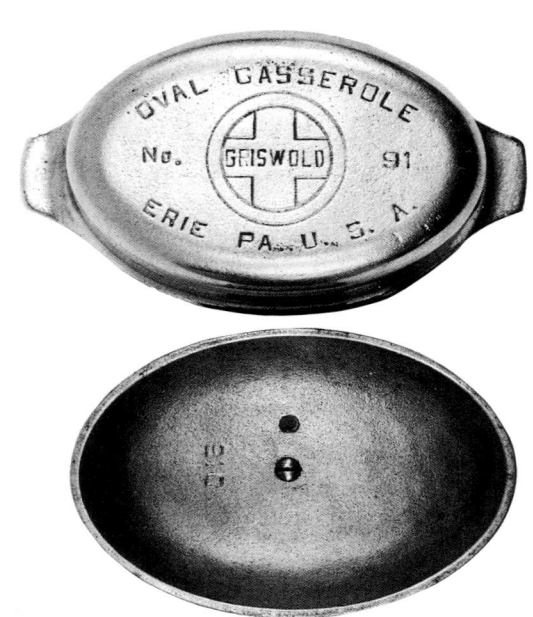

OVAL CASSEROLE-Size: 3 13/16" x 6 1/2" x 2 3/8: deep; **p/n**: 91; **Markings**: block logo, OVAL CASSEROLE, No.91, ERIE PA., U.S.A.; (cover) 91C; **Finish**: chrome; **Circa**: 1940s-1950s; **VALUE: $250-$300**.

OVAL CASSEROLE-Size: 3 15/16" x 6 1/2" x 2 3/8" deep; **p/n**: 91; **Markings**: OVAL CASSEROLE, No.91, block logo, ERIE PA., U.S.A.: (cover) 91C; **Finish**: iron; **Circa**: 1940s; **VALUE: $350-$400**. Loop handle cover is scarce. Also, note holes and handles.

AL CARDERS SERVING KETTLE-Size: 4 1/4" dia. x 1 7/8" deep; **p/n**: 580; (cover) 581; **Markings**: AL CARDERS SERVING KETTLE, 580, (cover) 581; **Finish**: iron with nickel plated knob; **Circa**: 1940s; **VALUE: $125-$150**. Raised letter cover is unusual.

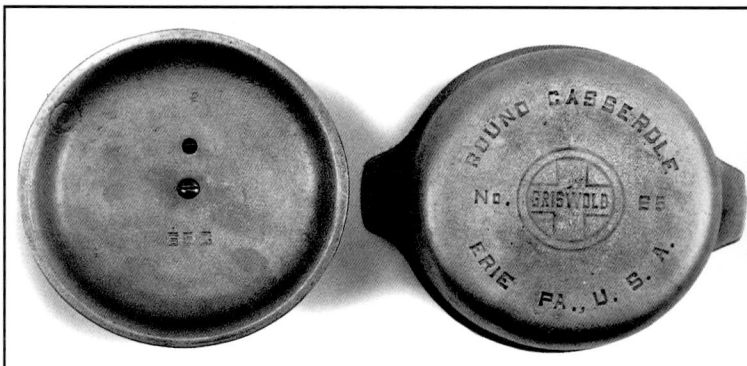

ROUND CASSEROLE-Size: 5 1/8" dia. x 2 1/8" deep; **p/n**: 65, (cover) 65C; **Markings**: block logo, ROUND CASSEROLE, No.65, ERIE PA, U.S.A., (cover) 65C; **Finish**: chrome; **Circa**: 1950s; **VALUE: $75-$100**.

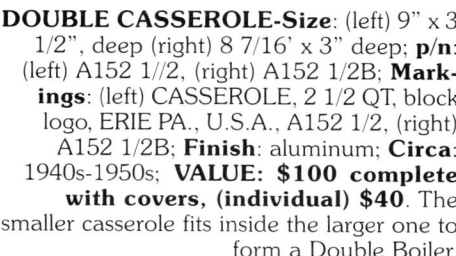

DOUBLE CASSEROLE-Size: (left) 9" x 3 1/2", deep (right) 8 7/16' x 3" deep; **p/n**: (left) A152 1//2, (right) A152 1/2B; **Markings**: (left) CASSEROLE, 2 1/2 QT, block logo, ERIE PA., U.S.A., A152 1/2, (right) A152 1/2B; **Finish**: aluminum; **Circa**: 1940s-1950s; **VALUE: $100 complete with covers, (individual) $40**. The smaller casserole fits inside the larger one to form a Double Boiler.

DOUBLE CASSEROLE COVERS-p/n: (left) A152 1/2C, (right) A425C; **Markings**: (left) GRISWOLD CASSEROLE COVER, PATD FEB 10, 1920, ERIE PA., U.S.A., A152 1/2C, (right) block logo, SELF BASTING, PAT'D FEB 10, 1920, ERIE PA., U.S.A., A425C; **Finish**: aluminum; **VALUE: $20-$30**.

No.0 SERVICE KETTLE-Size: 4 1/2" dia. x 1 9/16" deep; **p/n**: 580, (cover) 581; **Markings**: block logo, No.0 SERVICE KETTLE, ERIE PA., U.S.A., 560, (cover) 581; **Finish**: chrome; **Circa**: 1940s; **VALUE: $100-$150**.

No.00 SERVICE KETTLE-Size: 4 1/4" dia. x 1 1/2" deep; **p/n**: 579, (cover) 581; **Markings**: block logo, No.00 SERVICE KETTLE, ERIE PA., U.S.A., 579, (cover) 581; **Finish**: chrome; **Circa**: 1940s; **VALUE: $100-$150**. Notice three short legs.

BOWL-Size: 11 5/8" dia. x 2 3/4" deep; **p/n**: none; **Markings**: Hearthstone, U.S.A. 4 QUART, GHC logo, GRISWOLD, A; **Finish**: iron; **Circa**: 1980s; **VALUE: $25-$30**. This piece was made by the General Housewares Corporation in the Wagner foundry.

No.000 SERVICE KETTLE-Size: 4 1/4" dia. x 1 1/16" deep; **p/n**: 575, (cover) 581; **Markings**: block logo, o.000 SERVING KETTLE, ERIE PA., U.S.A., 575, (cover) 581; **Finish**: chrome; **Circa**: 1940s; **VALUE: $150-$200**. Legs longer than No.00. All three Service Kettles are the same height.

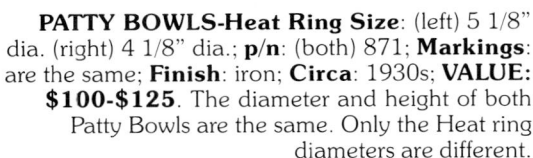

PATTY BOWLS-Heat Ring Size: (left) 5 1/8" dia. (right) 4 1/8" dia.; **p/n**: (both) 871; **Markings**: are the same; **Finish**: iron; **Circa**: 1930s; **VALUE: $100-$125**. The diameter and height of both Patty Bowls are the same. Only the Heat ring diameters are different.

FOOD CHOPPERS

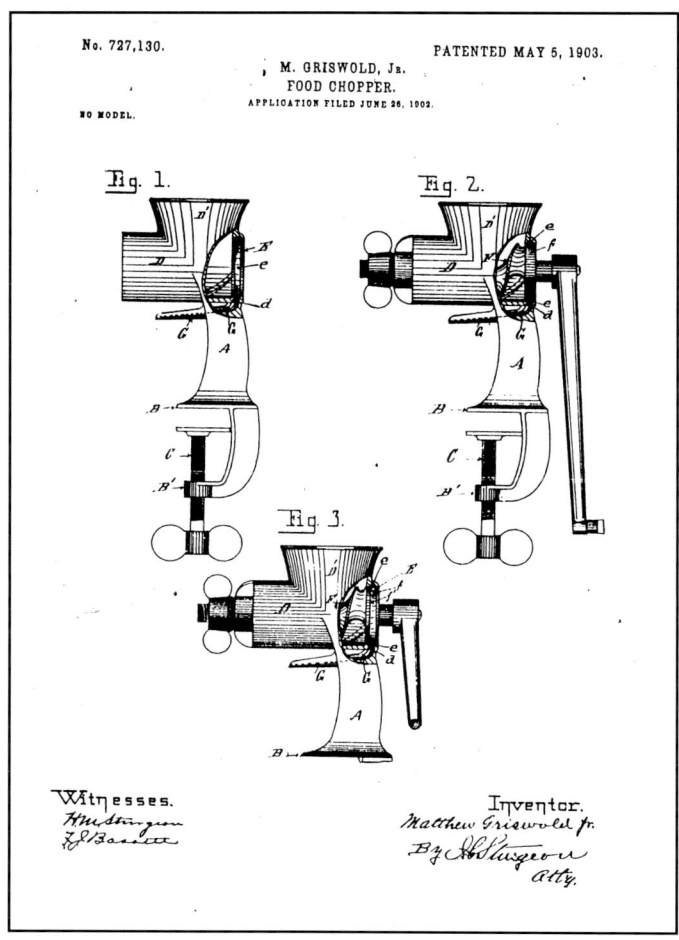

U.S. Patent for Food Chopper, dated May 6, 1903

No.10 FOOD CHOPPER-Size: 7 5/8"; **p/n**: 2460, (crank) 2458; **Markings**: No.10, GRISWOLD, (crank) 2458; **Finish**: galvanized; **Circa**: 1910; **VALUE: $25-$35**. This was the smallest in this series.

No.0 FOOD CHOPPER-Size: 7"; **p/n**: 401, (crank) 403; **Markings**: logo, GRISWOLD, 401, (crank) THE GRISWOLD MFG CO, ERIE PA, 403; **Finish**: galvanized; **Circa**: 1920s; **VALUE: $45**.

"ERIE" FOOD CHOPPER-Size: 8 1/2" high, (hopper) 3" x 2 1/4"; **p/n**: none; **Markings**: CLASSIC NO.1, GRISWOLD MFG. CO, ERIE PA; **Finish**: galvanized; **Circa**: 1905; **VALUE: $25-$30**. Note spout under the grinder chamber to channel drippings.

PURITAN FOOD CHOPPER-p/n: 2468; **Markings**: No.11, PURITAN, (crank) GRISWOLD MFG. CO., ERIE PA. U.S.A.; **Finish**: galvanized; **Circa**: 1920s; **VALUE: $10-$15**.

No.1113 FOOD CHOPPER-Size: 10"; **p/n:** 458; **Markings:** logo, GRISWOLD, 458, N0 1113, (crank) THE GRISWOLD MFG. CO. ERIE PA., U.S.A.; **Finish:** galvanized; **Circa:** 1919-1923; **VALUE: $10-$15**. This is the late style with the blade retaining ring.

FOOD CHIPPER BROCHURE- bi-fold; **Value: $30-$35**.

STOVES & HEATERS

ERIE 100 GAS HEATER-Size: 19" high x 7" dia.; **Markings:** ERIE 100; **Finish:** tin with iron base and top; **Circa:** 1910; **VALUE: $150-$200**.

Classic No.616 PARLOR STOVE-Size: 23" high x 17 1/2" wide; **p/n:** 616; **Markings:** CLASSIC NO. 616; **Finish:** tin body with iron treatments; **Circa:** 1910; **VALUE: $300-$350**.

CLASSIC No.44 HEATER- Size: 33" high x 20" wide; **p/n:** unknown; **Markings:** CLASSIC NO. 44; **Finish:** iron; **Circa:** 1920s; **VALUE: $400-$500** as is; complete $800-$1000. The top is missing on this piece.

CLASSIC GAS HEATER- Size: 33 1/2" high x 21" wide; **p/n:** unknown; **Markings:** CLASSIC, GRISWOLD MFG. CO., ERIE PA., USA; **Finish:** tin back and sides, the rest is cast iron; **Circa:** 1900-1920; **VALUE: $300-$350**.

WIZZARD HOT PLATE- Size: 13" wide x 12" deep; **p/n:** 1000D, (burner) 1036; **Markings:** WIZZARD on plate, (bottom) GRISWOLD MFG. CO, ERIE PA; **Finish:** iron; **Circa:** 1920s; **VALUE: $125-$150**.

Classic No. 60 RADIATOR- Size: 29" high; **p/n:** (base) 163, (top) 165; **Markings:** CLASSIC NO. 60, 163, 165; **Finish:** tin tubes with iron top and base, black with nickel trim; **Circa:** 1920s; **VALUE: $1250-$1500**.

GRATE FROM WIZZARD HOT PLATE- p/n: 1008; **Markings:** 1008, GRISWOLD, ERIE PA in raised letters on the underside.

LAUNDRY STOVE-Size: 18" high x 26" wide; **p/n:** unknown; **Markings:** (plate) ERIE, No202; **Finish:** iron; **Circa:** 1901-1920; **VALUE: $200-$250**. Legs are unusual.

4 BURNER HOT PLATE-Size: 24 1/2" wide x 22" deep; **p/n:** unknown; **Markings:** (plate) GRISWOLD; **Finish:** iron; **Circa:** 1920s-1940; **VALUE: $400-$500**.

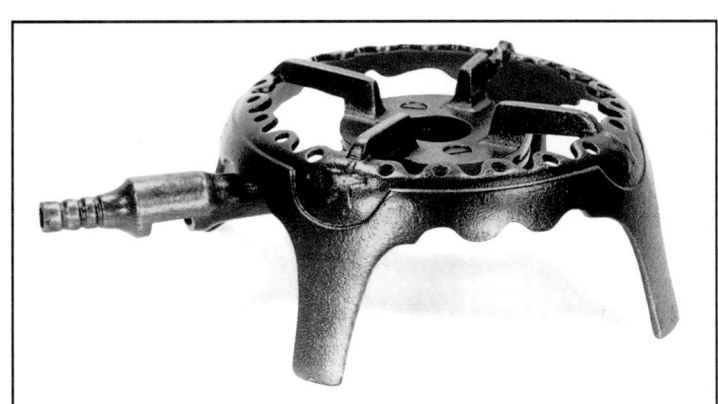

ELEVATED HOT PLATE- p/n: 7082; **Markings:** 7082, EMPIRE; **Finish:** japanned; **Circa:** 1920s; **VALUE: $150-$200**.

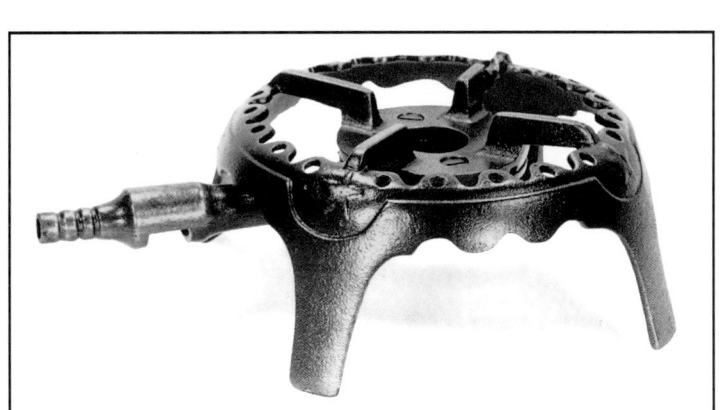

NURSERY HOT PLATE- Size: 5" dia. x 3" high; **p/n:** (burner) 243; **Markings:** 243; **Finish:** iron; **Circa:** 1920s-1930s; **VALUE: $250-$300**.

SINGLE BURNER HOT PLATE-Size: No.31; **p/n:** 1131, (burner) 1130; **Markings:** GRIS-NO 31-WOLD; **Finish:** japanned; **Circa:** 1930s-1940s; **VALUE:** $100-$150. Legs are wired for shipping.

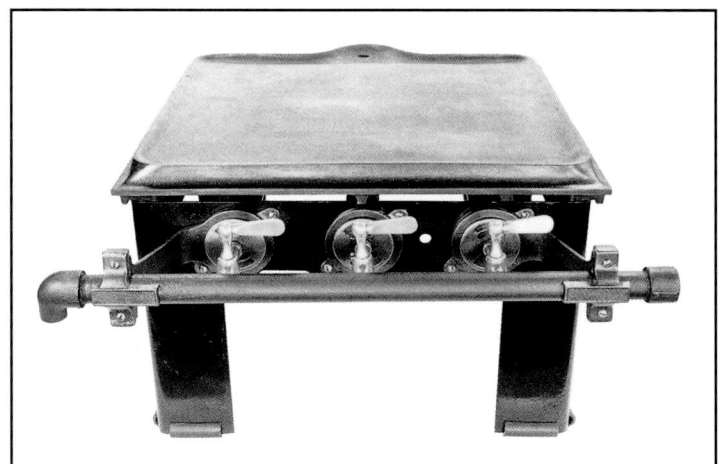

No.230 GAS GRIDDLE-Size: 12" high x 18" wide; **p/n:** (griddle) 230; **Markings:** (brass plate) GRISWOLD MFG. CO, ERIE PA., USA, NO 230, (griddle) block logo, ERIE PA., U.S.A., 230; **Finish:** japanned; **Circa:** 1930s; **VALUE:** $250-$300.

ELECTRIC HOT PLATE-Size: 11 5/8" wide x 13" deep x 9" high; **p/n:** N261; **Markings:** (metal plate) logo, CATALOG NO N 261, VOLTS 208, WATS 2KW; **Finish:** chrome; **Circa:** 1940s; **VALUE:** $100-$150.

ELECTRIC OVEN-Size: 14 1/2" x 12" x 11' deep; **p/n:** none; **Markings:** THE GRISWOLD MFG. CO. ERIE, PA., USA., (brass plate) logo, 110 volt, 900 watt; **Finish:** japanned; **Circa:** 1920s; **VALUE:** $200-$250.

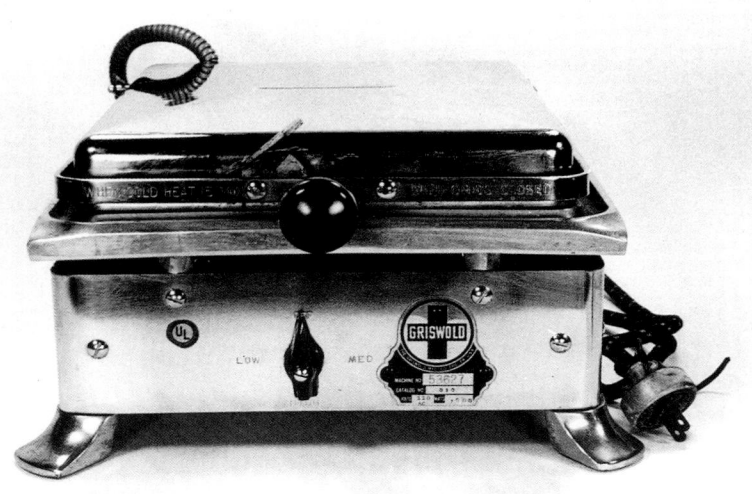

ELECTRIC SANDWICH GRILL-Size: 11 5/8" wide x 6 3/4" deep x 6 1/5" high; **p/n:** catalog No.70; **Markings:** (metal tag) logo, 110 VOLTS, 660 WATTS; **Finish:** chromed steel; **Circa:** 1930-1940; **VALUE:** $200-$250.

ELECTRIC SANDWICH GRILL-Size: 11 1/2" wide x 13 1/4" deep x 7" high closed; **p/n:** 810; **Markings:** (plate on front) logo, CATALOG NO. 810, VOLTS 110AC, WATTS 1000; **Finish:** chrome; **Circa:** 1935-1955; **VALUE:** $200-$250.

ROLL WARMER-Size: 26" wide x 15" deep x 20" high; **p/n:** none; **Markings:** (metal tag) logo, CAT NO. 1105, 115 VOLT, 1000 WTS; **Finish:** stainless steel; **Circa:** 1940-1950s; **VALUE:** $200-$250.

HOT FOOD SERVER-Size: 13' wide x 17" deep x 21" high; **p/n:** none; **Markings:** (metal tag) logo, CAT. NO 1304; **Finish:** stainless steel; **Circa:** 1930s-1940s; **VALUE:** $225-$250.

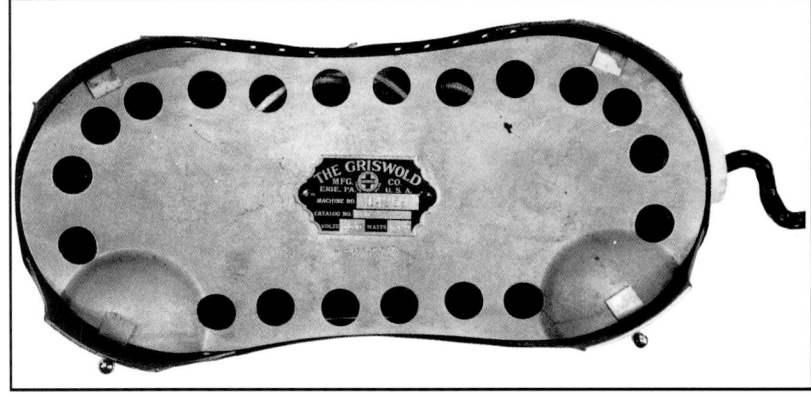

ELECTRIC EGG COOKER-Size: 11" wide x 14" high; **p/n:** Catalog No.9; **Markings:** (metal tag) logo, CATALOG NO 9; **Finish:** nickel plated steel; **Circa:** 1930 -1940s; **VALUE: $350-$450**.

STOVE PIPE DAMPERS AND LID LIFTERS

STOVE PIPE THIMBLE, OR SAFE HEAD-Size: 9 5/8" outside dia.; **p/n:** none; **Markings:** GRISWOLD MFG. CO. ERIE PA. 6 INCH BUTTLES PATENT; **Finish:** iron ring - front & back, tin spacers; **Circa:** 1890; **VALUE: $250-$350**.

STOVE PIPE DAMPER-Size: 5 inch; **p/n:** none; **Markings:** AMERICAN, ERIE PA, PAT MAR 23, 1875, MAR 13, 1877, APR 10 1880; **Finish:** iron with steel spindle, and wood handle; **Circa:** 1880s; **VALUE: $75-$100**.

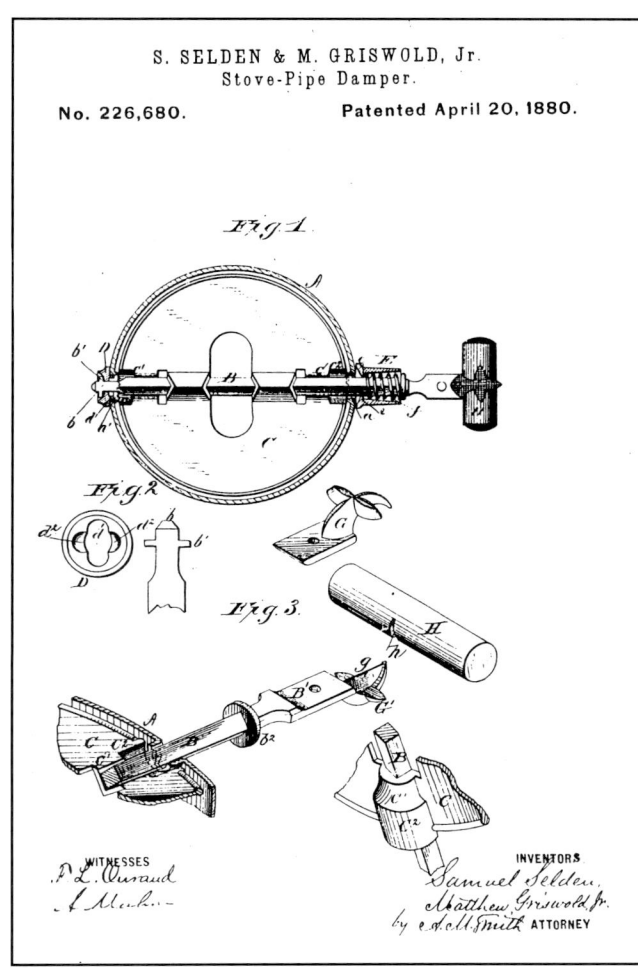

U.S. Patent for Stove Pipe Damper dated April 20, 1880.

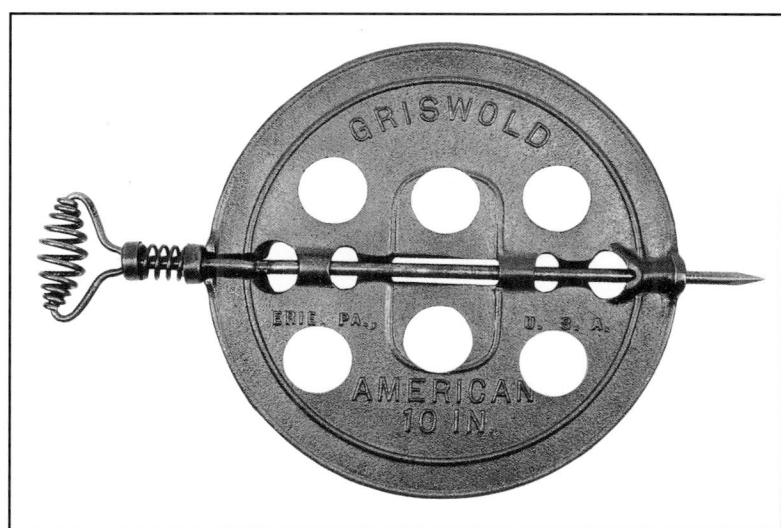

10 INCH STOVE PIPE DAMPER-Size: 9 5/8" dia.; **p/n:** 59_; **Markings:** GRISWOLD AMERICAN, 10 INCH, ERIE PA., U.S.A., PT'D JULY 20, 1915; **Finish:** iron; **Circa:** 1910; **VALUE: $35-$45**. Six holes is unusual.

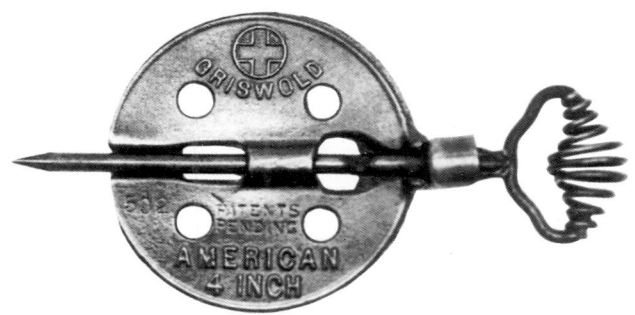

STOVE PIPE DAMPER-Size: 4 inch; **p/n:** 502; **Markings:** Logo, GRISWOLD, AMERICAN 4 INCH, PATENT PENDING; **Finish:** iron; **Circa:** 1910-1920s; **VALUE: $30-$35**. Four holes is unusual.

STOVE PIPE DAMPER-Size: 5 inch; **p/n:** 6408; **Markings:** GRISWOLD, ERIE PA., USA, 5 IN, NEW AMERICAN, (reverse) REVERSIBLE STEEL SPINDLE; **Finish:** iron; **Circa:** 1910-1920; **VALUE: $35-$40**. Six holes is unusual.

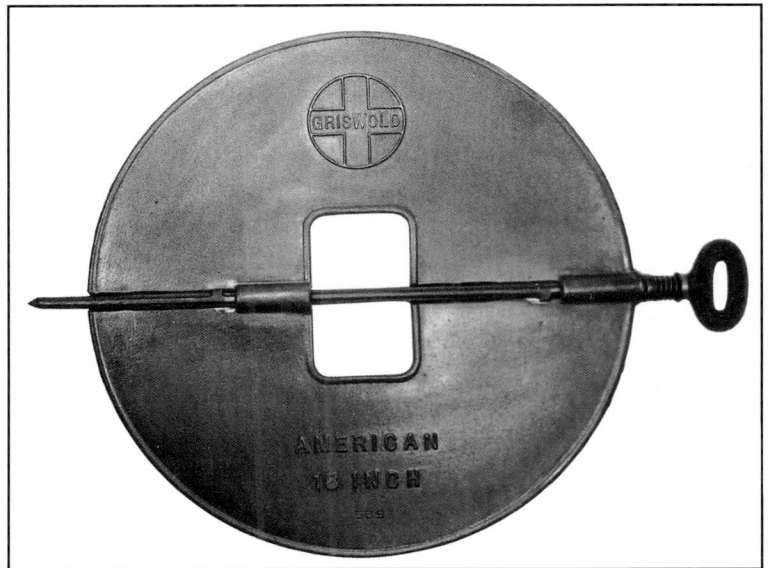

18 INCH STOVE PIPE DAMPER-Size: 18 inch; **p/n:** 589, (handle) 590; **Markings:** logo, AMERICAN 18 INCH, 589; **Finish:** iron; **Circa:** 1920-1940s; **VALUE: $150-$200**.

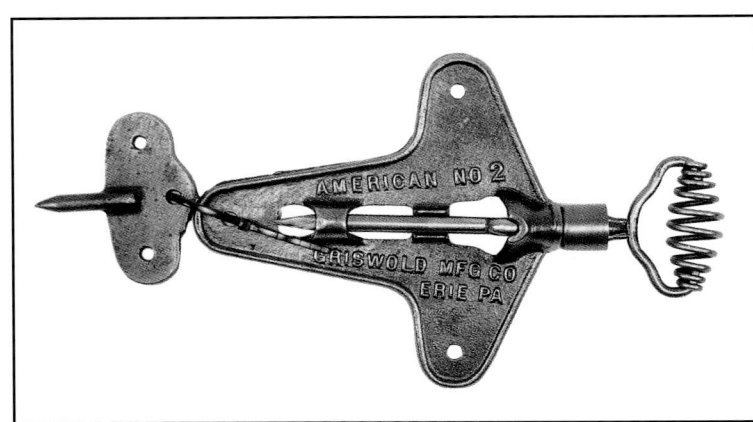 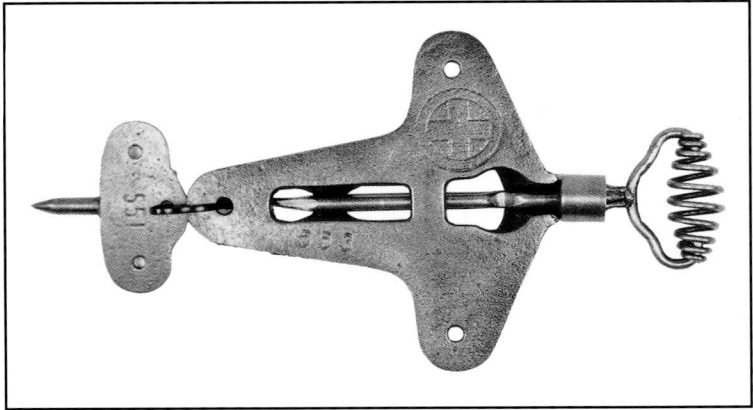

TWO PART DAMPER CLIP- p/n: 553, (tip) 551; **Markings:** AMERICAN NO 2, GRISWOLD MFG. CO., ERIE PA, logo, 553; **Finish:** iron; **Circa:** 1905; **VALUE: $75-$100**.

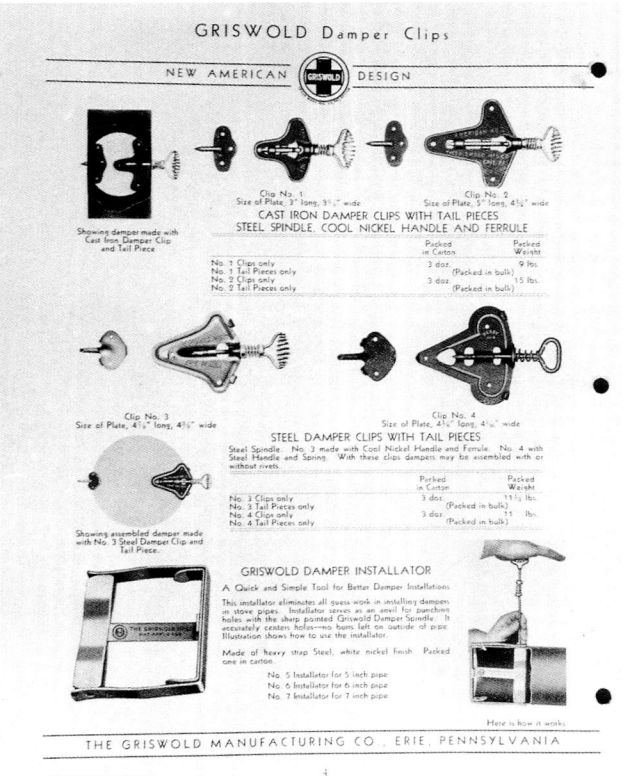

Page from 1840 Griswold Catalog.

STOVE PIPE DAMPER INSTALLER-Size: 5 3/4" high x 6 5/8" wide; **p/n:** none; **Markings:** logo, THE GRISWOLD MFG. CO., ERIE PA., U.S.A., DAMPER INSTALLER, NO 6, PAT APPLIED FOR; **Finish:** stainless steel; **Circa:** 1940s; **VALUE: $450-$550**. Used to align steel spindle in the stove pipe.

STOVE LID LIFTER-Size: 9 1/16"; **p/n:** none; **Markings:** ERIE, NO 80; **Finish:** nickel; **Circa:** 1900-1930s; **VALUE: $200-$300.**

STOVE LID LIFTER-Size: 8 1/2"; **p/n:** none; **Markings:** star between bars at the end; **Finish:** iron; **Circa:** 1890-1910; **VALUE: $50-$75.** Many early pieces were not marked.

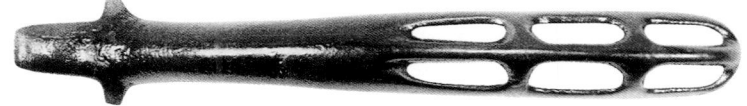

MISCELLANEOUS

SKILLET GRILL-Size: 8 1/2" dia.; **p/n:** 299; **Markings:** (top) GRISWOLD, (bottom) SKILLET GRILL, ERIE PA., U.S.A., PATENT APPLIED FOR, 299; **Finish:** iron; **Circa:** 1930; **VALUE: $100-$150.** There are two variations of the Skillet Grill. The other is shown on pg. 178 of *The Book of Griswold & Wagner*.

GREASE RECEPTACLE-Size: 3 7/8" square x 3 3/4" h.; **p/n:** 1482; **Markings:** THE GRISWOLD MFG. CO., ERIE PA., 1482; **Finish:** iron; **Circa:** 1950s; **VALUE: $75-$100.** For use on a commercial griddle.

PERCOLATOR PLATE-Size: 7" dia.; **p/n:** none; **Markings:** PERCOLATOR PLATE, THE GRISWOLD MFG. CO., ERIE PA., U.S.A.; **Finish:** steel; **Circa:** 1950s; **VALUE: $65-$85**.

GASOLINE STOVE-WARE ADJUSTER-Size: Available in No.8 for No.s 7,8, or 9 ware; **p/n:** none; **Markings:** none; **Finish:** iron; **Circa:** 1890s; **VALUE: $300-$350**. According to an 1890-91 catalog, "specially adopted to fit all round bottom ware and round waffle irons on gasoline or oil stoves."

SAD IRON HEATER-Size: 10 1/2" dia.; **p/n:** 1313; **Finish:** iron; **Circa:** 1920s; **VALUE: $125-$150**.

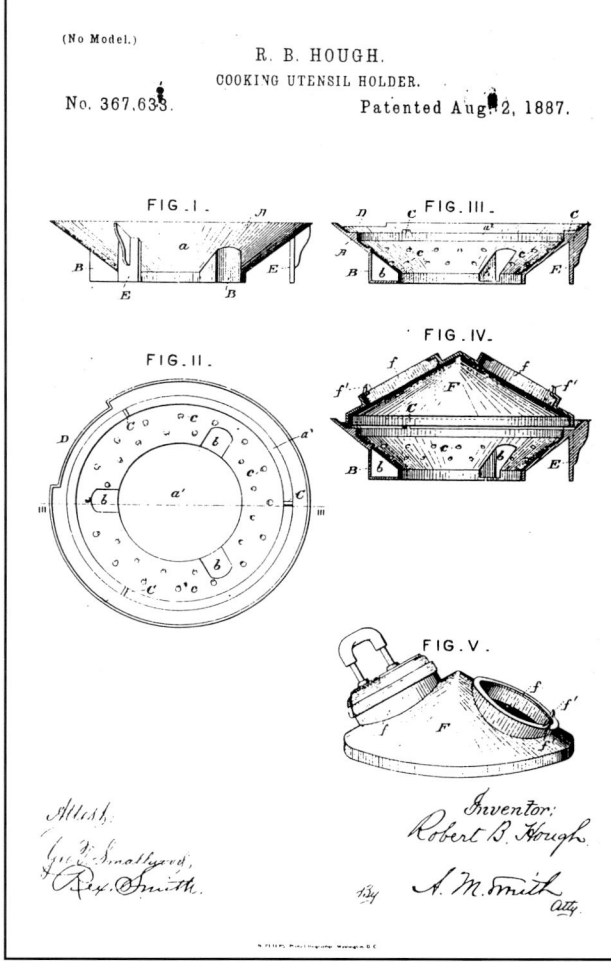

U.S. Patent Drawing for Cooking Utensil Holder-The patent reads in part, "This invention relates to attachments for supporting utensils upon gasoline or other stoves while said utensils and their contents are being heated; and the object to the invention is to produce an attachment which will accommodate utensils of different sizes and properly deflect the heat or flame around the base of the utensil." This piece will accommodate skillets, waffle irons and kettles (both flat bottom and round bottom).

SAD IRON STAND-Size: 5 7/8" x 4 1/4"; **p/n:** 1604; **Markings:** 1604; **Finish:** iron; **Circa:** 1910; **VALUE: $75-$85**.

SAD IRON HANDLE-**p/n:** 1310; **Markings:** ERIE, 1310; **Finish:** iron with wood; **Circa:** 1910; **VALUE: $200-$225**. It is unusual for a Sad Iron Handle to be marked ERIE.

REPRODUCTION ASHTRAY-**Size:** 00; **p/n:** 570; **Markings:** block logo, 00, 570, PAT NO. 100,021; **Finish:** aluminum; **Circa:** unknown; **VALUE: $5**. This piece has the same pattern number as the ashtray with a match holder. The third cigarette rest has been added.

DECORATIVE TRIVET-**p/n:** 1727; **Markings:** GRISWOLD TRIVET, NO 1727; **Finish:** aluminum; **Circa:** 1940s; **VALUE: $30**.

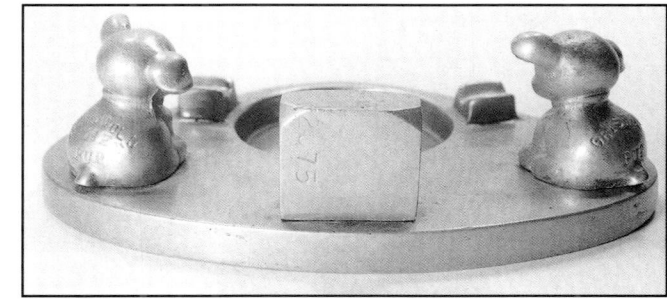

PUP ASHTRAY WITH MATCH BOX HOLDER-**Size:** 6 7/8" long by 4 3/4" wide; **p/n:** 2075 (match holder); **Markings:** 2075, (pups) GRISWOLD, PUP, (faint HINES); **Finish:** aluminum; **Circa:** unknown; **VALUE: $150-$200**. There is some concern if this was made by Griswold. The pups and holder are attached with screws.

WIND PROOF ASHTRAYS-**Size:** (left) No.33 5 3/16" dia., (right) No.32 4 5/16" dia.; **p/n:** (left) 33, (right) 32; **Markings:** Wind Proof Ashtray, small logo, pattern number; **Finish:** japanned iron with brass grill; **Circa:** 1950s; **VALUE: No.33, $50-$60; No. 32, $40-$50**.

FIXED HANDLE FLUTER WITH BASE-Size: (base) 5 13/16" x 3 1/16"; **p/n:** none; **Markings:** THE ERIE FLUTER, base not marked; **Finish:** nickel; **Circa:** 1900; **VALUE: $400-$500.**

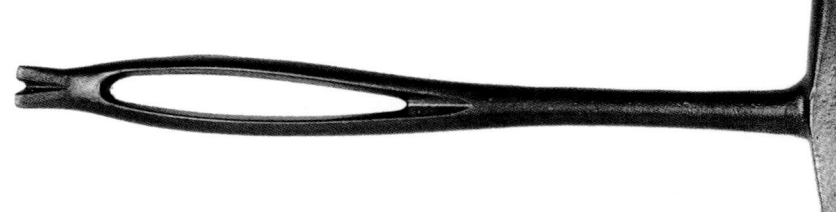

TACK HAMMER-Size: 8 1/2"; **p/n:** none; **Markings:** none; **Finish:** iron; **Circa:** 1890-1905; **VALUE: $75-$100.** There were two sizes of this item listed in a 1890-91 Griswold catalog.

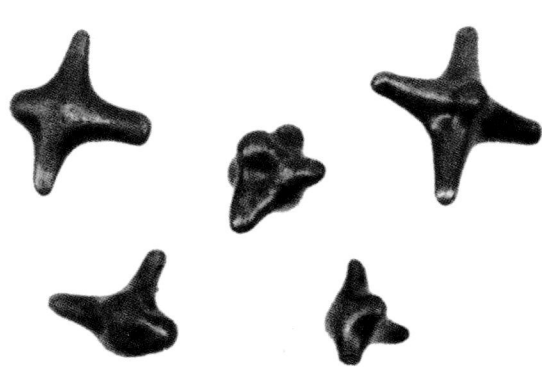

POLISHING STARS-Size: 3/4"; **Finish:** iron; **Circa:** 1920-1950s; **VALUE: $5 each.** These stars were put in a tumbling and with water and castings, and tumbled. The tumbling polished the rough edges off the castings. The stars were worn also, as these pieces show. These stars were dug from the dirt floor of the Griswold Foundry.

No.2 COFFEE ROASTER-Size: cylinder 8" x 5 1/2"; **p/n:** none; **Markings:** GRISWOLD MFG. CO. ERIE PA., COFFEE ROASTER NO. 2; **Finish:** iron base, tin cylinder; **Circa:** 1898-1918; **VALUE: $1000, $1500 with handle.** The handle is rare.

HAND TAMPER-Size: 14" long x 3 3/4" dia.; **p/n:** none; **Markings:** G.M.C., hand inscribed; **Finish:** hardwood; **Circa:** unknown; **VALUE: $150-$200**. Tampers were used to pack sand around the pattern. This tamper came from the Erie PA area. GMC could represent Griswold Mfg. Co.

RURAL MAILBOX-Size: 24" long x 8 1/2" wide x 8" tall; **p/n:** none; **Markings:** MFG BY THE RANDALL CO, SIDNEY OHIO, 04-68; **Finish:** green enamel; **Circa:** 1960s; **VALUE: $60-$75**.

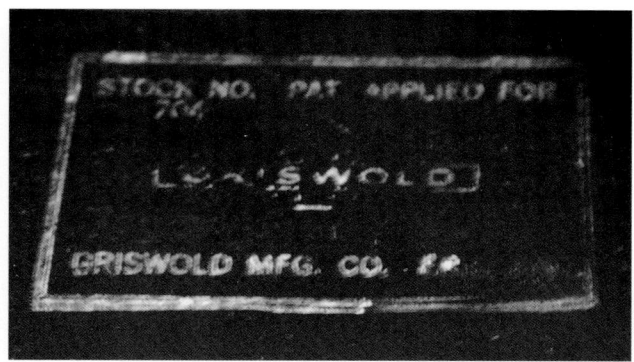

CONTEMPORARY MAILBOX-Size: 16 7/16" x 6 3/4"; **p/n:** none; **Markings:** STOCK NO 704, PAT APPLIED FOR, GRIS-WOLD MFG. CO; **Finish:** painted steel; **Circa:** 1960s; **VALUE: $40-$60**.

GRISWOLD COLOR

STORE DISPLAY POSTER-Size: 18 1/2" x 13 1/2"; **Finish:** Cardboard Lithograph: **Value:** $700-$800.

Values of porcelain pieces are based on pieces in pristine condition. Any damage or chips greatly reduce the value.

REGULAR SKILLET-Size: No.10; **p/n:** 716; **Markings:** CAST IRON SKILLET, 10, block logo, ERIE PA. USA; **Finish:** dark blue porcelain, inside & outside; **Circa:** 1940s; **VALUE: $100-$150**.

REGULAR SKILLET-Size: No.8; **p/n:** 704; **Markings:** block logo, ERIE PA. U.S.A., CAST IRON SKILLET, 8; **Finish:** dark blue exterior, light blue interior; **Circa:** 1940s; **VALUE: $50-$75**.

REGULAR SKILLET-Size: No.5; **Markings:** slant logo, ERIE, 5; **Finish:** red porcelain, outside and interior; **Circa:** unknown; **VALUE: $50-$75**.

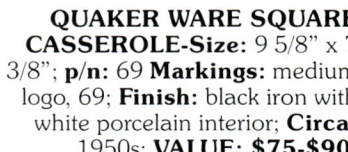

QUAKER WARE SQUARE CASSEROLE-Size: 9 5/8" x 7 3/8"; **p/n:** 69 **Markings:** medium logo, 69; **Finish:** black iron with white porcelain interior; **Circa:** 1950s; **VALUE: $75-$90**.

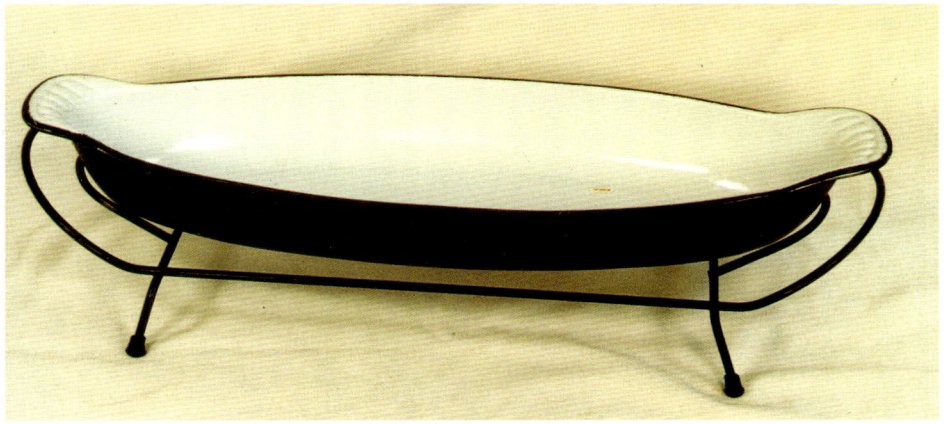

QUAKER WARE FISH BAKING DISH-Size: 17" x 6 1/4"; **p/n:** 82; **Markings:** medium logo, 82; **Finish:** iron with white porcelain interior; **Circa:** 1950s; **VALUE:** **$100-$125 with stand**.

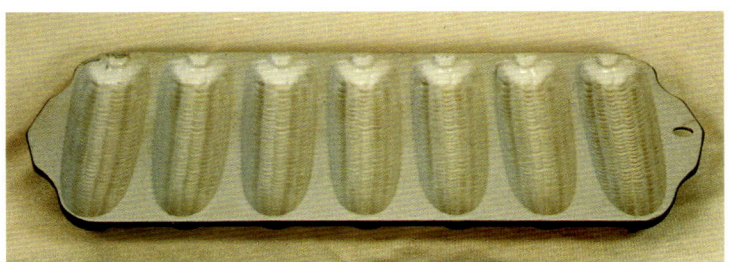

QUAKER WARE CORN STICK PAN Pan-p/n: 273; **Markings:** No. 273, GRISWOLD CRISPY CORN STICK PAN, ERIE PA., U.S.A., 930; **Finish:** iron with white porcelain interior; **Circa:** 1950s; **VALUE: $75-$90**.

QUAKER WARE COLONIAL BREAKFAST SKILLET, SQUARE EGG SKILLET & No.0 SKILLET- p/n: 666, 129, 562; **Finish:** iron with white porcelain interior; **Circa:** 1950s; **VALUE: No. 666, $75-$100; No. 129, $100-$125; No. 562, $75-$100**.

QUAKER WARE SQUARE SKILLETS-Size: No.s 3, 6, 8; **p/n:** 2103, 2106, 2108; **Markings:** medium logo, SQUARE FRY SKILLET, ERIE PA; **Finish:** iron with white porcelain interior; **Circa:** 1950s; **VALUE: No. 2103, $100; No. 2106, $150; No. 2108, $60-$75**.

QUAKER WARE SKILLET GRIDDLE-Size: No.107; **p/n:** 200; **Markings:** slant logo, 200, 107; **Finish:** iron with white porcelain interior; **Circa:** 1950s; **VALUE: $75-$100**.

QUAKER WARE OVAL CASSEROLE-p/n: 95, (cover); **Markings:** medium logo, 95; **Finish:** iron with white porcelain interior; **Circa:** 1950s; **VALUE: $100-$150**. Note Griswold sticker inside.

DEEP DUTCH OVEN-Size: 7" high x 10 1/4" dia.; **p/n:** 918; **Markings:** block logo, 918, logo knob glass cover; **Finish:** Flamingo Red porcelain with cream interior; **Circa:** 1950; **VALUE: $150-$200**.

SKILLET GRIDDLE-Size: No.109; **p/n:** 202; **Markings:** small logo, CAST IRON SKILLET GRIDDLE, 109, ERIE PA., 202, A; **Finish:** iron with blue porcelain interior; **Circa:** 1960s; **VALUE: $75-$100**.

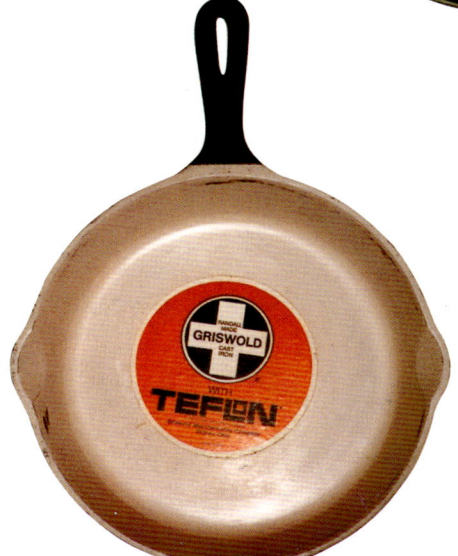

SAUCE PAN- p/n: 84; **Markings:** block logo, 84; **Finish:** Buttercup Yellow porcelain with Dove Gray interior; **Circa:** 1977-1960; **VALUE: $60-$75**. Hollow handle is unusual.

REGULAR SKILLET- Size: 10 1/2" dia.; **p/n:** none; **Markings:** 10 1/2 INCH SKILLET, (sticker) Randall Made, GRISWOLD CAST IRON, GRISWOLD MANUFACTURING COMPANY, SIDNEY OHIO; **Finish:** iron with cream Teflon interior; **Circa:** 1960s; **VALUE: $30**. Not an Erie PA. piece.

AHSTRAY WITH MATCH HOLDER- Size: No.00; **p/n:** unknown; **Markings:** Griswold logo; **Finish:** Robins Egg Blue porcelain with cream interior; **Circa:** 1950s; **VALUE: $35-$45.**

SKILLET-Size: 8" dia.; **p/n:** 2705; **Markings:** block logo, 2795, (cover) not marked; **Finish:** chrome, (cover) copper anodized aluminum; **Circa:** 1850s; **VALUE: $50-$65.**

AHSTRAY-Size: 3 5/8" dia.; **p/n:** unknown; **Markings:** Griswold logo; **Finish:** black with white speckled porcelain; **Circa:** 1960s; **VALUE: $15-$20.**

SYMBOL WARE SAUCE PAN-Size: 2 qt., 7 1/2" dia. x 4 1/2" high; **p/n:** 92; **Markings:** GRISWOLD in sunburst, 2 QT, 92; **Finish:** aluminum with enameled cover, plastic knob and handle; **Circa:** 1950s; **VALUE: $50-$75; 1 Qt, $40-$50.**

CIGAR TRIMMER (top view)- Notice the blade protruding in the holes as the lever is pressed down. The blade would trim the tip of the cigar.

SCOTCH BOWL - MASTER PATTERN-
Size: No.5; **Finish:** Iron with brass ears, and bottom ring; **Circa;** VALUE: $500-$700.

PUP ASHTRAY WITH MATCH BOX HOLDER-When the box of wooden matches is pressed down on the column, the box opens. There is some question if this was made by Griswold. The pups and holder are attached with screws.

DEEP LONG PAN- MASTER PATTERN-Size: No.9, 23 3/8" x 13 7/16"; **p/n:** 386X; **Markings:** 9, 386X; **Finish:** brass; **Circa:** 1900; **VALUE:** Rare. This master pattern is missing the bottom plate.

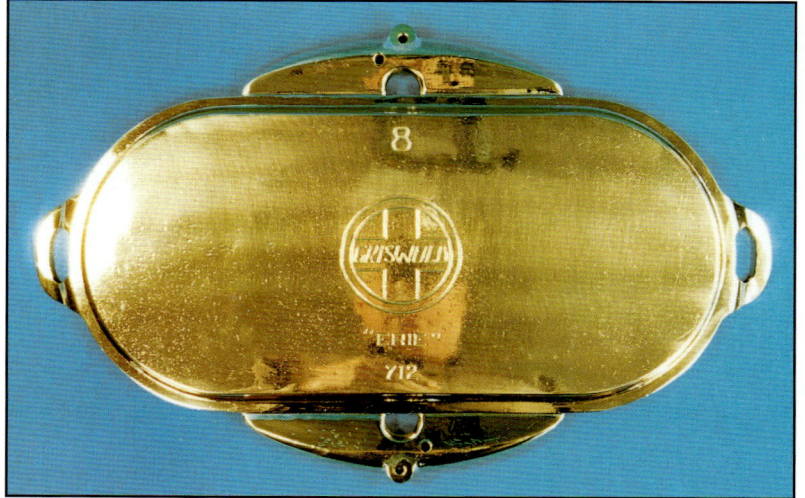

SHALLOW LONG PAN - MASTER PATTERN-Size: 21 1/16" x13 1/4"; **p/n:** 712; **Markings:** slant logo, "ERIE", 8, 712; **Finish:** brass; **Circa:** 1900-1910; **VALUE:** Rare.

SCOTCH BOWL-Size: NO.5; **Markings:** original sticker; **Finish:** iron; **Circa:** 1930s; **VALUE:** $75-$100.

FAKE ALARM CLOCK-This item is a Fake! This is an old clock with a fake face which appears aged. This clock has been faked with other faces such a Winchester, etc.

FOOD CUTTER DISPLAY STAND-Size: 45" high x 36" wide; **p/n:** (diamond plate) 47; **Markings:** diamond logo, GRISWOLD FOOD CUTTERS; **Finish:** (diamond plate) aluminum; **Circa:** 1910; **VALUE:** $1,000-$1,200.

ELECTRIC HOT PLATE-Size: 21" l. x 11" w. x 6" d.; **p/n:** none; **Markings:** (metal tab) THE GRISWOLD MFG. CO., ERIE PA., U.S.A., 110 VOLT; **Finish:** japanned with green knobs; **Circa:** 1930s; **VALUE:** $250-$300.

BROCHURE-Size: 3 1/4" x 6 1/4", 19 pages; **Circa:** 1927; **VALUE:** $65-$85. Wonderful color graphics.

BROCHURE-Size: 3 3/8" x 6 1/4"; **Circa:** unknown; **VALUE:** $45-$65.

AUNT ELLEN COOK BOOK-Size: 5 1/2" x 7 1/4", 47 pages; **Circa:** 1928; **VALUE:** $100-$150.

BROCHURE-Size: 3 1/2" x 6 3/8, tri fold; **Circa:** 1920; **VALUE:** $45-$65.

BROCHURE-Size: 6 1/4" x 6", unfolds to 12 3/4" x 12"; **Circa:** 1940s; **VALUE:** $45-$65.

RECIPE BOOK-Size: 5 1/8" 6 7/8", 16 pages; **Circa:** 1919; **VALUE: $45-$65.**

BROCHURE-Size: 3 1/2" x 6 1/4", unfolds to 6 7/8" x 11 1/4"; **Circa:** 1930s-1940s; **VALUE: $35-$45.**

BROCHURE-Size: 3 3/8" x 6 1/4"; **Circa:** 1920s; **VALUE: $45-$60.**

BROCHURE-Size: 3 1/8" x 6 1/4", unfolds to 9 1/2" x 12"; **Circa:** 1940s; **VALUE: $45-$65.**

BROCHURE-Size: 3 1/4" x 6 1/8", 32 pages; **Circa:** 1910; **VALUE: $45-$65.**

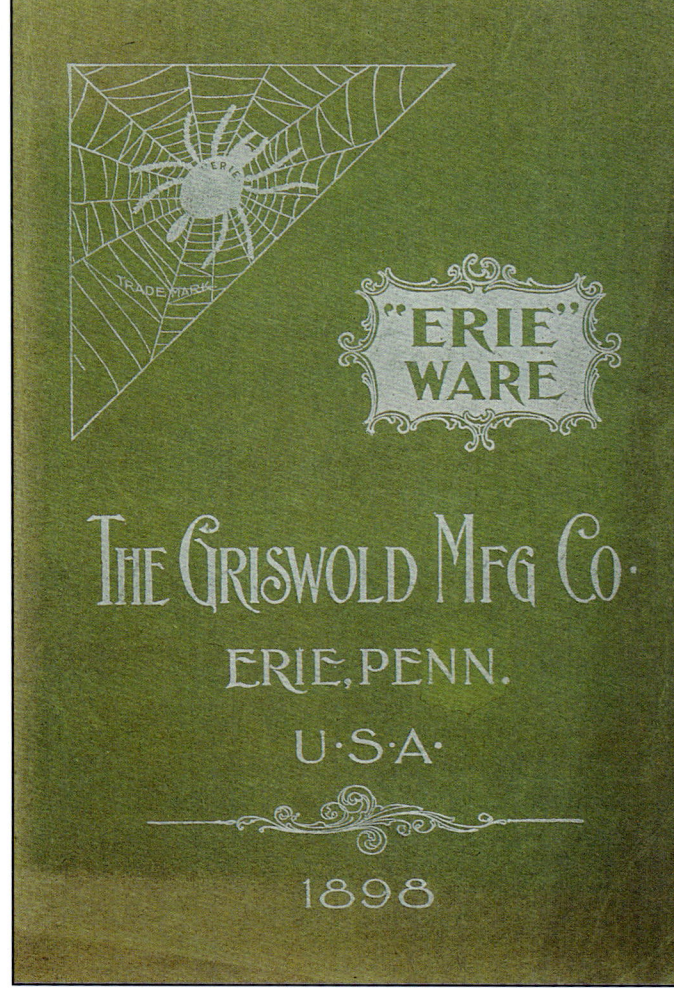

CATALOG-Size: 6" 9", 80 pages; **Circa:** 1898; **VALUE:** $500.

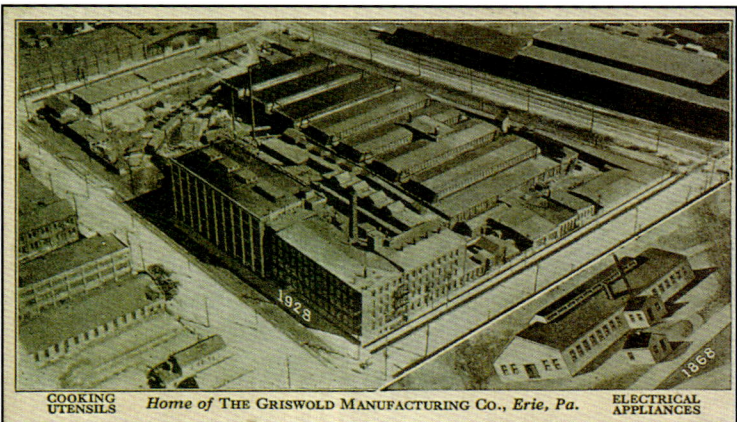

POST CARD-Size: 3 14" x 5 1/2"; **Circa:** 1928; **VALUE:** $35-$40.

Top left: **BROCHURE-Size:** 3 1/4" x 6 1/4", bifold; **Circa:** 1920s; **VALUE:** $25-$35.

Top center: **BROCHURE-Size:** 3 1/2" x 6", 6 pages; **Circa:** 1934; **VALUE:** $25-$35.

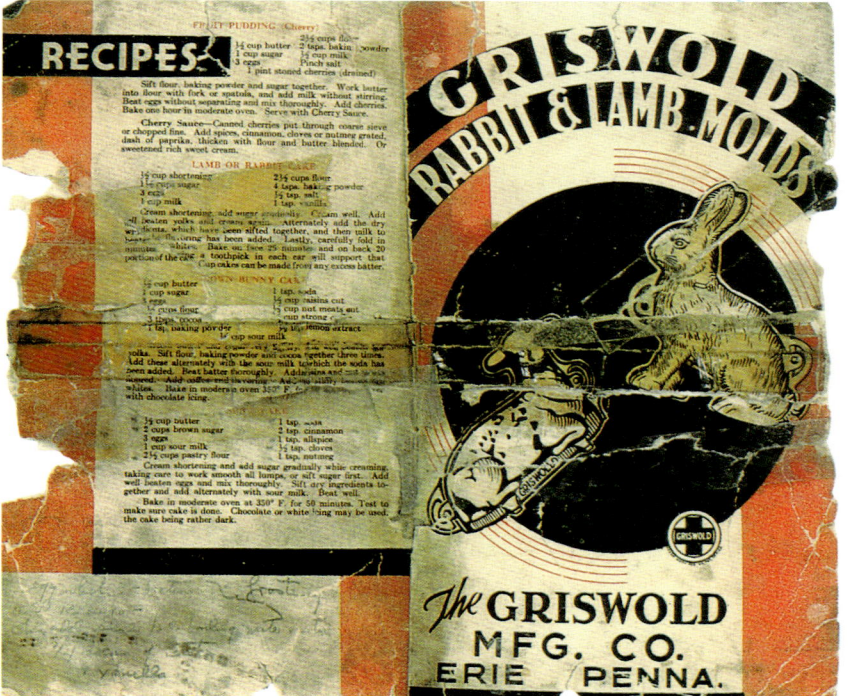

BROCHURE-Size: 3 1/2" x 5 3/4", bifold; **Circa:** 1945; **VALUE:** $50-$75.

GRISWOLD PATTERN NUMBERS

Cast Iron

Pattern Number		Piece
9		Electric Egg Cooker
28		Square Fry Skillet
30		Griswold Pup
31		Cowboy Hat Ashtray
32		Wind Proof Ashtray
32		No.32 Gas Hot Plate
33		Wind Proof Ashtray
35		Coffee Grinder Drawer Front
40		Base for No.2 Fruit & Lard Press
41	2	Strainer Plate for No.2 Fruit and Lard Press
42	2	Plunger Plate for No.2 Fruit and Lard Press
42		Snack Skillet
43	2	Cross Bar for No.2 Fruit and Lard Press
43		Chef Skillet
45	2	Lever Handle for No.2 Fruit and Lard Press
47		Base for 4 Qt. Fruit and Lard Press
48		Strainer Plate for 4 Qt. Fruit and Lard Press
49		Plunger plate for 4 Qt. Fruit and Lard Press
50		Cross Bar for 4 Qt. Fruit and Lard Press
52		Lever Handle for 4 & 6 Qt. Fruit and Lard Press
52		16 inch American Damper
53		Square Egg Skillet
54		Base for No.10 Fruit and Lard Press
55		Strainer Plate for No10 Fruit and Lard Press
56		Plunger Plate for No.10 Fruit and Lard Press
57		Cross Bar for No.10 Fruit and Lard Press
59		Lever Handle for No.10 Fruit and Lard Press
63		Table Service Pot
65		Round Casserole
67		Casserole dish
68		Cover for Casserole Dish
69		Casserole Dish
70		Electric Sandwich Grill
71		Deep Patty Bowl
72		Deep Patty Bowl
77		Base for No.6 Fruit and Lard Press
78		Strainer Plate for No.6 Fruit and Lard Press
79		Plunger Plate for No.6 Fruit and Lard Press
80		Cross Bar for No.6 Fruit and Lard Press
82		Oval Service Dish
83		Service Casserole Dish
84		Sauce Pan
86		Base for Erie Fluter
87		Fish Service Dish
89		Casserole Dish
90		Oval Casserole, Cover 90C
91		Oval Casserole Dish
93		Tea Ball Tea Pot
93		Oval Bean Pot
100		Base for No.110 Fruit and Lard Press
100		Gas Heater Base
100		Table Service Kettle, 00
101		Coffee Pot, 1 qt.
101		Strainer Plate for No.110 Fruit and Lard Press
102		Plunger Plate for No.110 Fruit and Lard Press
102		Coffee Pot, 2 qt
103		Coffee Pot, 3 qt.
103		Cross Bar for No.110 Fruit and Lard Press
104		Lever Handle for No.110 Fruit and Lard Press
104		Coffee Pot, 4 qt.
105		No.3 Mailbox Lid
106		No.3 Mailbox Door
107		No.3 Mailbox Body
109		"0" Table Service Dutch Oven
111	603	3 Pt. Casserole
112		Casserole Lid for p/n 111
114		Fire Pot for Gas Heaters, No.s 100 and 200
115		Coffee Mill, wall mounted
125		Coal and/or Wood Oven
129		Square Egg Skillet
130		Stove for No.13 Waffle Iron
133		2 pt. Tea Kettle
135		Ring surrounding valve at end of burner on has hot plate
141		No.6 Waffle Iron
142		No.6 Waffle Iron Frame, low with bail handle
143		No.6 Waffle Iron Frame, low with side handle
145		Coffee Mill, wall mounted
146		No.7 Waffle Iron
147		No.7 Waffle Iron Frame, low with bail handle
148		No.77 Waffle Iron Frame, high with bail handle
149		No.7 Waffle Iron Frame, low with side handles
150		No.77 Waffle Iron Frame, high with side handles
151		No.8 Waffle Iron
152		No.8 Waffle Iron Frame, low with bail handle
153		No.88 Waffle Iron Frame, high with bail handle
154		No.8 Waffle Iron Frame, low with side handles
155		No.88 Waffle Iron Frame, high with side handles
156		No.9 Waffle Iron
157		Waffle Iron Frame, low with bail handle
158		No.99 Waffle Iron Frame, high with bail handle
159		No.9 Waffle Iron Frame, low with side handles
160		No.99 Waffle Iron Frame, high with side handles
161		No.11 Square Waffle Iron
162		No.11 Sq. Waffle Iron Frame, low base
163		No.11 Sq Waffle Iron Base, high base
163		Base for Classic Radiator Stove
164		Waffle Iron, rectangular, three section
165		Top for Classic Radiator Stove
166		Base for No.13 Waffle Iron
171		Size 8 Waffle Iron, hammered surface
172		Size 8 Waffle Iron, hammered surface
173		Size 8 Waffle Iron Base, hammered, low with side handles
178		No.8 Waffle Iron Base, Delux
180		No.10 Dutch Oven, with legs
185		No.201 Gas Hot Plate, single burner
187		No.203 Gas Hot Plate, three burner
188		Size 8 Trivet for Dutch Oven
189		No. 9 "Puritan" Dutch Oven Trivet
191		Burner for Gas Hot Plate
200		Base for No.40 Kerosene Heater
200		No.107 Skillet Griddle
201		No.108 Skillet Griddle
202		No.109 Skillet Griddle
203		No.110 Skillet Griddle
204		No.6 Dutch Oven Trivet
205		Top for No.40 Kerosene Heater
205		No.7 Dutch Oven Trivet
206		No.8 Dutch Oven Trivet
207		No.9 Dutch Oven Trivet
208		No.10 Dutch Oven Trivet
209		No.11 Dutch Oven Trivet
210		No.12 Dutch Oven Trivet
211		No.13 Dutch Oven Trivet
212		Sausage Griddle for use on commercial stove
214		Griddle for No.130 Stove
218		No.3 Oval Roaster
230		Gas Griddle
233		Grate for use on commercial stove
234		No.8 Waffle Iron, CLOWS; both sides are same p/n
235		No.8 Waffle Iron Base, low with bail handle, no notches for leveling pins
236		No.9 Waffle Iron, CLOWS; both sides are same p/n
237		No.9 Waffle Iron Base, low with bail handle, no notches for leveling pins
238		Clamp tabs for wire supports on 5-Tier Dutch Oven Display Stand

No.	Description	No.	Description
239	Feet for Dutch Oven Display Stand	374	Nut Cracker Handle
243	Nursery Hot Plate	376	No.6 Handle Griddle
245	5 Qt. Colonial Tea Kettle, Iron	380	No.1 Mailbox body
250	Lemon Squeezer	381	No.1 Mailbox door
251	Lemon Squeezer	382	No.1 Mailbox lid
257	No.1 Classic Ice Shave body	385	No.2 Tobacco Cutter base
258	No.1 Classic Ice Shave top	386	Deep Long Pan, No.9
259	Classic Ice Shave, blade clamp	386	No.2 Tobacco Cutter upper body, back half
260	7 Burner Hotel/Restaurant Gas Stove	387	No.2 Tobacco Cutter upper body, front half
261	Classic Ice Shave No.2 Body	388	No.2 Tobacco Cutter Handle
262	Classic Ice Shave No.2 Cover	389	No.2 Tobacco Cutter blade clamp
274	No.3 Oval Roaster Trivet	390	No.2 Tobacco Cutter blade pivot
275	No.5 Oval Roaster Trivet	391	No.3 Tobacco Cutter base
276	No.7 Oval Roaster Trivet	392	No.3 Tobacco Cutter side plate
277	No.9 Oval Roaster Trivet	393	No.3 Tobacco Cutter side plate
287	Grease Catcher for grill	394	No.3 Tobacco Cutter blade clamp
297	The Erie Fluter fluting iron bottom	395	No.8 Waffle Iron, marked VICTOR or GOOD HEALTH
298	The Erie Fluter, top	396	Size 8 Waffle Iron Base, low with side handle, no drop ring
299	Skillet Grill	397	No.3 Tobacco Cutter Handle
300	Heat Regulator	398	No.8 Waffle Iron Base, low with bail handle
301	Stove Lid Lifter	401	No.0 Food Chopper Body
302	Double Gas Hot Plate	402	No.0 Food Chopper Scroll
305	No.6 Waffle Iron	403	No.0 Food Chopper Crank
306	No.6 Waffle Iron	404	No.0 Food Chopper nut butter knife
307	No.6 Waffle Iron Base, low with bail handle	406	'0' size Toy Waffle Iron (male ball joint)
308	No.7 Waffle Iron	407	'0' size Toy Waffle Iron (female ball joint)
309	No.7 Waffle Iron	408	'0' size Toy Waffle Iron Base, low with side handle
310	No.7 Waffle Iron Base, low with bail handle	410	Food Chopper Scroll
310	No.10 Dutch Oven with three legs, bail handle	411	No.1 Toy Skillet
311	No.7 Waffle Iron Base, high with bail handle	432	Wing Nut for No.s 0,1,2,3, and 4 Food Choppers
312	No.8 Waffle Iron	450	No.1 Food Chopper body
313	No.8 Waffle Iron	451	No.1 Food Chopper ring
314	No.8 Waffle Iron	453	No.2 Food chopper body
314	No.8 Cake or Omelet Baker Iron	453S	8 inch American Damper
315	No.8 Cake or Omelet Baker Iron	454	No.s 2 & 3 Food Chopper ring
315	No.8 Waffle Iron	456	No.3 Food Chopper body
316	No.9 Waffle Iron	458	No.4 Food Chopper body
317	No.9 Waffle Iron	459	No.4 Food Chopper ring
318	No.9 Waffle Iron Base, low with bail handle	463	No.3 Self Basting Skillet Cover
319	No.9 Waffle Iron Base, high with bail handle	465	No.5 Self Basting Skillet Cover
320	No.8 Waffle Ring for use on stoves No.s 150-160	466	No.6 Self Basting Skillet Cover
321	No.9 Waffle Ring for use on stoves No.s 150-160	467	No.7 Self Basting Skillet Cover
322	No.111 Sq. Waffle Iron Base, low	468	No.8 Self Basting Skillet Cover
324	No.6 Waffle Iron Base, low with side handle	469	No.9 Self Basting Skillet Cover
325	No.7 Waffle Iron Base, low with side handle	470	No.10 Self Basting Skillet Cover
326	No.7 Waffle Iron Base, high with side handles	471	No.11 Self Basting Skillet Cover
327	No.8 Waffle Iron Base, low with side handle	472	No.12 Self Basting Skillet Cover
328	No.8 Waffle Iron Base, high with side handles	474	No.14 Self Basting Skillet Cover
329	No.9 Waffle Iron Base, low with side handle	478	No.8 Puritan Dutch Oven
330	No.9 Waffle Iron Base, high with side handles	479	No.9 Dutch Oven, unmarked
331	No.8 Waffle Iron (not marked Griswold)	479	No.9 "Puritan" Dutch Oven
332	No.8 Waffle Iron, W.M.C. CO.	482	No.9 Dutch Oven Cover, unmarked
333	No.8 "Puritan" Waffle Iron	491	No.9 Dutch Oven, unmarked
334	No.8 Waffle Iron, marked Rav-O-Noc, H.S.B & Co.	494	No.9 Dutch Oven Cover, unmarked
335	No.8 Waffle Iron, marked Rav-O-Noc, H.S.B & Co.	500	3 inch Damper
336	No.8 Waffle Iron (not marked)	502	Stove Pipe Damper, 4 inch
339	No.8 Waffle Iron Base, low with no handle	506	No.6 Handle Griddle
341	No.6 Wood Handled Griddle	508	5 inch Damper
342	No.7 Wood Handled Griddle	510	3 inch Oval Damper
343	No.8 Wood Handle Griddle	511	5 1/2 inch Damper
345	No.8 Good Health Waffle Iron (both sides)	514	Reversible Solid Damper for Oil Burner
347	No.2 Mailbox body	517	6 inch Damper
348	No.2 Mailbox Lid	517C	6 inch American Damper
350	No.2 Mailbox Hinge Block	520	6 inch Damper
352	No.3 Main Box (Figural)	521	7 inch Oval Damper
353	Mailbox top	522	3 inch Damper
354	No.4 Mailbox Body	523	4 inch Damper
355	No.4 Mailbox Top	538	6 inch Damper
356	No.4 Mailbox Door	541	4 inch Oval Damper
357	Sundial	545	9 inch Damper
357	Mailbox	551	Tip of Two Part Damper Clip
358	No.5 Post Box Door	553	Stove Pipe Damper Clip
359	No.6 Post Box	560	'0' Ashtray w/ match holder
360	No.6 Post Box Flap	562	'0' Toy Skillet
361	Mailbox Lid	565	'0' Toy Regular Griddle
363	Classic No.7 Lemon Squeezer	568	'0' Toy Tite-Top Dutch Oven
363	No.11 Square Waffle Iron, male ball hinge	569	'0' Cover for Toy Tite-Top Dutch Oven
364	No.11 Square Waffle Iron, female ball hinge	570	'00' Ashtray with matchbook holder
366	Waffle Iron, rectangular, three section	573	Trivet for Toy Tite-Top Dutch Oven
367	Waffle Iron, rectangular, three section	575	Service Kettle
367	No.6 Lemon Squeezer	576	'0' Colonial Design Toy Tea Kettle
368	No.6 Lemon Squeezer	578	Serving Kettle with 3 short legs
371	Nut Cracker Base and Jaw	579	Serving Kettle with 3 long legs
371	No.10 Wood Handled Skillet	580	Service Kettle
372	Nut Cracker Base	581	Service Kettle Cover
372	No.11 Wood Handled Skillet	589	Stove Pipe Damper, 18 inch
373	Nut Cracker Jaw	603	3 Pt. Casserole
373	No.12 Wood Handled Skillet	606	No.6 Regular Griddle

No.	Description	No.	Description
607	No.7 Regular Griddle	720	No.13 Skillet
608	No.8 Regular Griddle	721	No.7 Victor Skillet
609	No.9 Regular Griddle	722	No.8 Victor Skillet
610	No.10 Regular Griddle	723	No.9 Victor Skillet
611	No.6 Wood Handle Griddle	724	No.5 Skillet
612	No.7 Wood Handle Griddle	724A	No.5 Skillet, aluminum
613	No.8 Wood Handle Griddle	725	No.7 Wood Handle Skillet
614	No.9 Wood Handle Griddle	726	No.8 Wood Handle Skillet
615	No.10 Wood Handle Griddle	727	No.9 Wood Handle Skillet
616	No.10 Bail Griddle	728	No.20 Hotel Skillet
616	Parlor Stove	728	No.7 Shallow Skillet with three hole handle
617	No.12 Bail Griddle	729	No.8 Shallow Skillet with three hole handle
618	No.14 Bail Griddle	730	No.9 Shallow Skillet
619	No.16 Bail Griddle	731	No.10 Shallow Skillet with three hole handle
620	No. {?}Good Health Handle Griddle	732	No.8 Deep Skillet
625	No.262 Corn or Wheat Stick Pan	733	No.9 Deep Skillet
629	No.272 Corn or Wheat Stick Pan	734	No.10 Deep Skillet
630	No.282 Corn or Wheat Stick Pan	735	No.2 Wood Handle Skillet
631	No.240 Turk Head Pan	736	No.6 Regular Griddle
632	No.2700 Wheat & Corn Stick Pan	737	No.7 Regular Griddle
633	No.2800 Wheat & Corn Stick Pan	738	No.8 Regular Griddle
634	No.130 Turk Head Pan	739	No.9 Regular Griddle
635	No.140 Turk Head Pan	740	No.10 Regular Griddle
636	No.270 Corn or Wheat Stick Pan	741	No.12 Bail Griddle
637	No.280 Corn or Wheat Stick Pan	742	No.14 Bail Griddle
638	No.27 Wheat & Corn Stick Pan	743	No.16 Bail Griddle
639	No.28 Wheat & Corn stick Pan	744	No.12 Gas or Vapor Griddle Base
640	No.13 Turk Head Pan	744	No.7 Long Griddle
641	No.14 Turk Head Pan	745	No.8 Long Griddle
643	No.3 Oval Roaster	746	No.9 Long Griddle
644	No.3 Oval Roaster Cover	749	No.8 Deep Long Pan
645	No 5 Oval Roaster	752	No.8 Shallow Long Pan
646	No.5 Oval Roaster Cover	753	No.3 Wood Handle Skillet
647	No.7 Oval Roaster	754	No.7 Skillet, unmarked
648	No.7 Oval Roaster Cover	755	No.8 Skillet, unmarked
649	No.9 Oval Roaster	758	No.4 Wood Handle Skillet
650	No.9 Oval Roaster Cover	763	Side Handled Griddle, 11 inch, (export ware)
651	Flat Bottom Griddle w/ wood handle	764	No.12 Handled Griddle
653	No.3 Good Health Skillet	768	Center Hinge Parts for early Flop Griddle
656	No.6 Good Health Skillet	768	No. 8 Chicken Pan, block logo, with heat ring
658	No.8 Good Health Skillet	768	Square Fry Skillet
659	No.9 Good Health Skillet	769	Square Fry Skillet Cover
664	No.14 Good Health Skillet	769	Center Hinge Parts for early Flop Griddle
665	Breakfast Skillet	769	No. 18 Long Griddle, trough around perimeter
666	Colonial Breakfast Skillet	770	Square Ashtray with matchbook holder
667	No.8 "50th Anniversary" Skillet, King HDW. Co.	771	No.10 Shallow Skillet
668	No.3 Skillet, unmarked, 3 hole handle	771	No. 8 Long Griddle
669	No.4 Skillet, unmarked, 3 hole handle	771	'0' Size Skillet Ashtray
674	Drilled burner for stoves	771	Folding Griddle, end section
677	Drilled Giant burner for series 700 & 800 stoves	772	Folding Griddle, end section
681	Simmering Burner for 700 & 800 stoves	772	'00' Size Handled Kettle (smoke set)
683	Stove Burner used on stoves No.s 150 & 160	773	'00' Size Bailed Kettle (smoke set)
689	Star Burner for stoves	773	Folding Griddle, center section
690	Star Burner for stoves	774	No.12 Erie Gas Griddle, btm. part
694	No.14 Bailed Handle Skillet	775	Square Toy Skillet
695	No.5 Victor Skillet	776	No.10 Bail Griddle
697	No.6 Victor Skillet	777	No.8 Extra Deep Skillet or Chicken Pan
698	No.6 Wood Handle Skillet	778	No.9 Extra Deep Skillet
699	No.6 Skillet	779	No.10 Extra Deep Skillet
700	No.5 Wood Handle Skillet	780	No.2 Scotch Bowl
700	No.6 Erie Skillet	781	No.3 Scotch Bowl
701	No.7 Skillet	782	No.4 Scotch Bowl
702	No.7 Erie Skillet	783	No.5 Scotch Bowl
702	No.4 Skillet	784	No.2 Yankee Bowl
703	No.2 Skillet	785	No.3 Yankee Bowl
703	Contemporary Mail Box	786	No.4 Yankee Bowl
703A	No.2 Rau Bros Skillet	787	No.5 Yankee Bowl
704	No.8 Skillet	788	No.6 Regular Kettle
705	Contemporary Mail Box	789	No.7 Regular Kettle
705	No.8 N.E. Griddle	790	No.7 Regular Kettle, Erie
706	No.9 N.E. Griddle	791	No.8 Regular Kettle
707	No.10 N.E. Griddle	792	No.9 Regular Kettle
707	No.8 Skillet, early style	794	No.7 Buldge Pot
708	No.8 Skillet, early style	795	No.8 Buldge Pot
709	No.3 Skillet	796	No.9 Buldge Pot
710	No.9 Skillet	797	No.7 Low Kettle
711	Erie Skillet	798	No.8 Low Kettle
711	No.7 Oval Griddle	803	No.7 Rimmed Pot
712	No.8 Oval Griddle	804	No.8 Rimmed Kettle
713	No.9 Oval Griddle	809	No.6 Flat Bottom Kettle
714	No.10 Oval Griddle	810	No.7 Flat Bottom Kettle
715	No.10 Erie Skillet	810	Electric Sandwich Grill
715	No.8 Skillet, smooth bottom with 3 inset rings	811	No.8 Flat Bottom Kettle
716	No.10 Skillet	812	No.9 Flat Bottom Kettle
717	No.11 Skillet	813	No.7 Flat Bottom Buldge Pot
718	Erie Skillet	814	No.8 Flat Bottom Buldge Pot
718	No.14 Skillet	815	No.9 Flat Bottom Buldge Pot
719	No.12 Skillet	816	No.7 Eccentric Kettle

Part #	Description
817	No.8 Eccentric Kettle
820	Barbecue Grill Coal Tray
821	Barbecue Grill
824	No.8 Low Eccentric Kettle
825	No.9 Low Eccentric Kettle
827	No.8 extra Large Eccentric Pot, style B
830	No.9 Safety Kettle
833	No.8 Dutch Oven
834	No.9 Dutch Oven
835	No.10 Dutch Oven
836	No.11 Dutch Oven
837	No.8 Dutch Oven Cover, early flat type
837	No.2 Scotch Bowl with flat bottom
838	No.3 Scotch bowl with flat bottom
838	No.9 Dutch Oven Cover, early flat type
839	No.10 Dutch Oven Cover
840	No.11 Dutch Oven Cover
841	No.8 Flanged Dutch Oven Cover
842	No.9 Flanged Dutch Oven Cover
843	No.10 Flanged Dutch Oven Cover
844	No.11 Flanged Dutch Oven Cover
845	Table Service Casserole
846	No.7 Erie Tea Kettle
847	No.12 Bail Griddle (part of ERIE Gas Griddle)
848	Steak Platter
849	Steak Platter
850	No.9 Hot Service Plate
851	Steak Platter
851	No.7 Flat Bottom Tea Kettle
853	Table Service Casserole
854	Cover for Table Service Casserole
855	No.7 1/2 Hot Service Plate
856	Steak Platter
856	Cover for Tea Kettle
858	No.8 Safety Cooker, flat bottom
859	Loaf Pan Cover for p/n 877
860	No.10 Flat Bottom Kettle
861	No.9 Safety Kettle, three legs, round bottom
862	No.10 Safety Kettle (Skinner)
862	Rabbit Cake Mold, front
863	Rabbit Cake Mold, back
863	Safety Kettle, round bottom
864	No.9 Safety Kettle
865	Lamb Cake Mold (early)
866	Lamb Cake Mold (early)
867	No.6 Flat Bottom Kettle Cover
868	No.7 Flat Bottom Kettle Cover
869	Odorless Skillet
870	Junior Patty Bowl
871	Patty Bowl
872	Hinge part of Wafer Iron p/n 895
873	Nut Cracker
875	No.7 Long Broiler
875	Double Broiler, bottom
876	No.8 Long Broiler
876	Double Broiler, top grate
877	Loaf Pan
878	Erie Double Broiler, bottom
880	Erie Double Broiler, top
881	No 8 Flat Bottom Kettle Cover
882	No.9 Flat Bottom Kettle Cover
883	No.10 Flat Bottom Kettle
883	No.7 Waffle Iron Base, low with side handle
884	No.8 Waffle Iron Base, low with side handle
885	Wafer Iron
885	No.8 Waffle Iron, female joint
886	No.8 Waffle Iron, male joint
888	No.7&8 Waffle Iron with finger hinge
889 1893	No.8 Waffle Iron, 1880 & patents
889	No.7 Waffle Iron half
890 1893	No.8 Waffle Iron, 1880 & patents
890	No.7 Waffle Iron half
891	Waffle Iron Paddles, rectangular, two section
892	Waffle Iron Paddles, rectangular, two section
893	Hollands Broiler
894	Wafer Iron Base
895	Wafer Iron half
897	Santa Cake Mold, front
898	Santa Cake Mold, back
899	French Waffle Iron
900	No.2 Waffle Iron Base
901	No.1 Waffle Iron Base
902	No.0 Waffle Iron Base
903	No.00 Waffle Iron Base
904	No.2 Waffle Iron, 3 cakes
905	No.2 Waffle Iron, 3 cakes
906	No.1 Waffle Iron, 3 cakes
907	No.1 Waffle Iron, 3 cakes
907	No.7 Long Griddle
908	No.8 Long Griddle, small logo
908	No.0 Waffle Iron, 4 cakes
909	No.0 Waffle Iron, 4 cakes
909	No.9 Long Griddle, small logo
910	No.00 Waffle Iron, 6 cakes
911	No.00 Waffle Iron, 6 cakes
911	No.11 Long Griddle
913	No.8 Waffle Iron Base, low with bail handle
914	No.8 Waffle Iron Paddles
915	No.8 Waffle Iron Base, high with bail handle
916	No.7 Oval Waffle Iron Base
917	No.8 Oval Waffle Iron Base
918	Flat Bottom Kettle with side handles
919	No.18 Heart Star Waffle Iron,
920	patent, size 8
920	No.19 Heart Star Waffle Iron, patent, size 9
921	No.7 Oval Waffle Iron
921	No.866 Lamb Cake Mold, back
922	No.866 Lamb Cake Mold, front
922	No.7 Oval Waffle Iron
923	No.8 Oval Waffle Iron
924	No.8 Oval Waffle Iron
925	No.9 Oval Waffle Iron
926	No.9 Oval Waffle Iron
928	No.18 Heart Star Waffle Iron,
1922	patent, size 8
929	No.19 Heart Star Waffle Iron,
1922	patent, size 9
930	No.273 Corn Stick Pan
931	No.283 Corn stick Pan
932	No.19 Heart Star Waffle Iron, size 9
933	No.19 Heart Star Waffle Iron, size 9
934	French Waffle Iron with three waffles
935	French Waffle Iron with three waffles
936	4 qt. Maslin Kettle
937	6 qt. Maslin Kettle
938	8 qt. Maslin Kettle
939	12 qt. Maslin Kettle
940	No.1 Muffin Pan, 11 cups
941	No.2 Muffin Pan, 11 cups
942	No.3 Muffin Pan, 11 cups
943	No.5 Muffin Pan, 8 cups
944	No.6 Muffin Pan, 11 cups
945	No.7 Muffin Pan, 8 cups
946	No.8 Muffin Pan, 8 cups
947	No.9 Golf Ball or Brownie Cake Pan, 10 or 12 cups
947	Lamb Cake Mold, early, large with legs out front
948	Lamb Cake Mold, early, large with legs out front
948	No.10 Popover Pan, several variations
949	No.10 Popover Pan
950	No.11 Muffin Pan, 12 cups
951	No.12 Muffin Pan, 11 cups
952	No.14 Erie era Muffin Pan, 12 rectangular cups
953	No.20 Turk Head or Queen Cake Pan, 11 cups
954	No.22 Corn Bread Pan (bread stick pan)
955	No.23 Bread Stick Pan, 22 half sticks
956	No.2 Vienna Roll Bread Pan, loaves
957	No.4 Vienna Roll Bread Pan, sections
957	No.24 Corn Bread Pan (identical to p/n 961 but unmarked)
958	No.26 Vienna Bread Roll Pan
959	No.24 Bread Pan, 6 section
959	No.50 Hearts Star Gem Pan
960	No.26 Bread Pan, 2 section
960	No.100 Hearts Star Gem Pan
961	No.21 Corn Bread Pan (bread stick pan), 7 sticks
962	No.32 Apple Cake Pan or Egg Poacher
963	No.31 Danish Cake Pan
964	Erie Wax Ladle
965	Cake Mold or Bundt Pan
966	No.19 Golfball Pan, 6 cups
967	No.6 Waffle Iron
968	No.7 Waffle Iron
969	Plett Pan (marked GRI SW OLD on bottom)
970	No.6 Waffle Iron Base, low with side handle
971	No.6 Waffle Iron
972	No.7 Waffle Iron Base, low with side handle
973	No.7 Waffle Iron
975	No.8 Waffle Iron Base, low with side handle
976	No.8 Waffle Iron
977	No.8 Waffle Iron
978	No.9 Waffle Iron Base, low with side handle
979	No.9 Waffle Iron
980	No.9 Waffle Iron

Part #	Description	Part #	Description
981	Alfred Andresen Heart Design Waffle Iron	1173	Legs for Gas Hot Plate No.s 501 & 502
981	Western Importing Co. Heart Design Waffle Iron	1178	No.501 Single Gas Hot Plate
982	No.8 Victor Waffle Iron Base, low, early	1180	Loose Cap Burner for Gas Hot Plate
983	No.8 Victor Waffle Iron	1181	No.502 Gas Hot Plate
984	No.8 Victor Waffle Iron	1182	No.503 Triple Gas Hot Plate
985	No.8 Waffle Iron Base, high with side handles	1183	Legs for Gas Hot Plate No. 503, wishbone style
986	No.11 Square Waffle Iron Base, low with side handle	1224	No.101 Electric Hot Plate
987	No.11 Square Waffle Iron Base, high with bail handle	1226	No.101 Electric Hot Plate
988	No.11 Square Waffle Iron,	1233	No.3 Skillet, Best Made S.R. and Co. (for Sears)
1901	patent	1235	No.5 Skillet, Best Made S.R. and Co. (for Sears)
989	No.11 Square Waffle Iron,	1236	No.6 Skillet, Best Made S.R. and Co. (for Sears)
1901	patent	1238	No.8 Skillet, Best Made S.R. and Co. (for Sears)
990	No.12 Square Waffle Iron Base, for two rectangular irons	1239	No.9 Skillet, Best Made S.R. and Co. (for Sears)
991	No.13 Rectangular Waffle Base, for three rectangular irons	1240	No.10 Skillet, Best Made S.R. and Co. (for Sears)
992	No.14 Rectangular Waffle Base, for four rectangular irons	1243	No.9 Self Basting Skillet Cover, Best Made S.R. and Co.
993	Waffle Iron Paddle, rectangular, 3 section	1245	No.9 Regular Griddle, Best (Sears)
994	Waffle Iron Paddle, rectangular, 3 section	1246	No.10 Regular Griddle, Best Made
995	Wafer Iron	1250	Waffle Iron, Best Made S.R. and Co.
999	Alfred Andresen Heart Shaped Design Waffle Iron	1251	Waffle Iron Base, low w/ side handle
999	Western Importing Co. Heart Shaped Waffle Iron	1253	No.10 Popover Pan, Best Made S.R. and Co.
1000	Burner for Hot Plate	1257	Bacon and Egg Fryer, Best Made S.R. and Co.; variation of p/n 666
1002	Deep Fat Fryer with medium logo	1258	No.8 Dutch Oven, Best Made S.R. and Co.
1003	Deep Fat Fryer	1259	No.9 Dutch Oven, Best Made S.R. and Co.
1004	Deep Fat Fryer Cover	1261	No.8 Dutch Oven Cover for p/n1258
1008	Grate from Wizzard Hot Plate	1262	No.9 Dutch Oven Cover for p.n 1259
1008	All-In-One Dinner Skillet, size 8	1265	No.9 Dutch Oven Trivet
1012	No.13 Oval Skillet	1270	Wheat & Corn Stick Pan, Best Made S.R. and Co.
1013	No.15 Oval Skillet	1277	No.7 Tite-Top Dutch Oven
1015	No.16 1/2 Oval Skillet	1278	No.8 Tite-Top Dutch Oven
1018	Skillet Divider Insert; for No.8 Skillet	1279	No.9 Tite-Top Dutch Oven
1021	No.90 Double Skillet Bottom	1288	No.8 Cover for Dutch Oven
1022	No.90 Double Skillet Top	1289	No.9 Cover for Dutch Oven
1029	No.4 Skillet, unmarked (Iron Mountain)	1295	No.8 Dutch Oven, no bail handle, small holes in handles
1030	No.5 Skillet, unmarked (Iron Mountain)	1298	No.8 Deep Tite-Top Dutch Oven
1031	No.3 Skillet, unmarked (Iron Mountain)	1305	Griddle for Hotel/Restaurant Gas Stove (p/n 260)
1032	No.7 Skillet, unmarked (Iron Mountain)	1308	Size 3 Sad Iron
1033	No.8 Skillet, unmarked (Iron Mountain)	1310	Sad Iron Handle
1034	No.8 Deep Skillet, unmarked (Iron Mountain)	1313	Classic Sad Iron Heater, round
1035	No.8 Skillet Cover, unmarked	1314	Dome Sad Iron Heater
1036	Burner for Hot Plate	1329	No.1001 Single Gas Hot Plate
1036	No.8 Dutch Oven, unmarked	1332	Loose Cap Burner for Gas Hot Plate
1037	No.8 Dutch Oven Cover, unmarked	1335	Food Chopper Stand
1038	No.9 Dutch Oven, unmarked	1402	Grease Receptacle
1039	No.9 Dutch Oven Cover, unmarked	1423	3 inch Damper
1040	No.10 Dutch Oven, unmarked	1424	4 inch Damper
1041	No.10 Dutch Oven Cover, unmarked	1425	5 inch Damper
1046	No.6 High Dome Cover, raised ltr.	1426	6 inch Damper
1047	No.7 Self Basting Skillet Cover, high	1428	8 inch Damper
1048	No.8 Self Basting Skillet Cover, high	1437	4 1/2 inch New American Damper
1049	No.9 Self Basting Skillet Cover, high	1457	Stove Burner for Stoves No.s 130 &140
1050	No.10 Self Basting Skillet Cover, high	1462	Stove Burner for Stoves No.s 230, 250, 260, and 270
1056	8 inch Steak Plate	1482	Lard or grease Pot, square with wire bail handle
1064	"Griswold" name plate for display stands	1487	7 inch Oval New American Damper
1065	Dutch Oven Display Stand, top castings	1501	No.3 Merit Skillet
1066	Name Plate for Wood Skillet Display Stand	1502	No.5 Merit Skillet
1068	Name Plate for Skillet Display Stand	1503	No.7 Merit Skillet
1069	5-Tier Dutch Oven Display Stand, top casting with Logo	1503	No.3 Mail Box Body
1077	No.7 Long Griddle	1504	No.8 Puritan Skillet
1078	No.8 Long Griddle, unmarked	1506	No.10 Merit Skillet
1081	No.6 Skillet, unmarked (Iron Mountain)	1507	No.8 Puritan Randle Griddle
1082	No.9 Skillet, unmarked (Iron Mountain)	1508	No.9 Puritan Regular Griddle
1083	No.10 Skillet, unmarked (Iron Mountain)	1511	No.9 Long Griddle, Puritan
1085	No.14 Skillet, unmarked (Iron Mountain)	1512	No.10 Popover Pan, Puritan
1088	No.8 Skillet Cover, low, unmarked	1513	No.1270 Wheat Stick Pan, Merit or Puritan
1093	No.3 Skillet Cover, high, smooth	1516	No.10 Puritan Skillet Cover
1094	No.4 Skillet Cover, high, smooth	1517	No.8 Puritan Waffle Iron
1095	No.5 Skillet Cover, high, smooth	1518	No.8 Puritan Waffle Iron
1096	No.6 Skillet Cover, high, smooth	1520	No.8 Puritan Dutch Oven Cover
1097	No.7 Skillet Cover, high, smooth	1521	No.9 Puritan Dutch Oven Cover
1098	No.8 Skillet Cover, high, smooth	1522	No.10 Merit Dutch Oven Cover
1099	No.9 Skillet Cover, high, smooth	1528	Rarebit Dish
1100	No.10 Skillet Cover, high, smooth	1529	Rarebit Dish
1102	No.80 Double Skillet, bottom	1556	No.2 Eldurado Charcoal Furnace
1102	No.8 Hinged Deep Skillet	1602	Classic Sad Iron Stand
1103	No.80 Double Skillet, top	1604	Classic Sad Iron Stand
1108	No.18 Cast Iron Grill	1605	No.702 Electric Hot Plate
1124	No.2020 Elevated Gas Hot Plate, 2 burner	1618	Removable grate for Gas Hot Plate No.703
1130	Burner for Hot Plate	1679	No.703 Three Burner Hot Plate
1131	Single Hot Plate	1688	Leg for Gas Hot Plate
1131	No.31 Single Gas Hot Plate	1689	Grate for Hotel/Restaurant Gas Stove (p/n 260)
1132	No.33 Gas Hot Plate, 3 Burner	1691	Drilled Twin Burner for Gas Hot Plate
1133	No.33 High Leg Frame for 3 Burner	1701	Leg for Gas Hot Plate
1160	Star Burner for Gas Hot Plate	1707	Clamp Screw for Food Chopper No.s1,2,3,4
1161	Drilled Burner for Gas Hot Plates	1708	Wing Nut for Food Choppers
1168	No.401 Single Gas Hot Plate	1711	Body for Food Chopper No.1
1169	No.402 Double Gas Hot Plate	1712	Body for Food Chopper No.2
1171	No.32 Double Gas Hot Plate	1713	Body for Food Chopper No.3
1172	Legs for Gas Hot Plate 502	1714	Body for Food Chopper No.4

1721	Ring for Food Chopper No.1	2469	Scroll for Puritan Food Chopper No.11
1722	Ring for Food Chopper No.s 2,3	2470	Crank for Food Chopper No.s 2,3, and Puritan No.11
1724	Ring for Food Chopper No.4	2474	Crank for Food Chopper No.4
1725	Decorative Flat Iron Trivet, large	2483	4 Pound Sad Iron
1726	Decorative Tree Trivet, large	2485	Square Sad Iron Heater
1727	Decorative Round Design Trivet	2488	Body for Puritan No.11 Food Chopper
1728	Decorative Tassel and Grain Design Trivet	2494	Tobacco Cutter Base
1729	Decorative Grape Design Trivet	2497	Tobacco Cutter Blade Clamp
1730	Decorative Eagle Design Trivet	2498	Tobacco Cutter Lever Arm
1731	Scroll for Food Chopper No.1	2500	Tobacco Cutter Handle
1732	Scroll for Food Chopper No.s 2,3	2503	No.3 Hinged Skillet
1733	Decorative Flat Iron Trivet, small	2505	No.5 Hinged Skillet
1734	Scroll for Food Chopper No.4	2506	No.6 Hinged Skillet
1735	Decorative Tree Trivet, small	2507	No.7 Hinged Skillet
1736	Decorative Wreath and Eagle Trivet, small	2508	No.8 Hinged Skillet
1737	Decorative Grape Design Trivet, small	2509	No.9 Hinged Skillet
1738	Coffee Pot Trivet, small	2528	No.8 Hinged Chicken Fryer
1739	Coffee Pot Trivet, large	2547	Wishbone Leg for Gas Hot Plate No.703
1740	Star Trivet	2551	Cover for No.8 Dutch Oven
1741	Crank for Food Chopper No.1	2552	Cover for No.9 Dutch Oven
1742	Crank for Food Chopper No.2,3	2553	Cover for No.10 Dutch Oven
1744	Crank for Food Chopper No.4	2554	Cover for No.11 Dutch Oven
1832	No.203 Double Gas Hot Plate	2568	No.8 Hinged Dutch Oven
1834	Legs for Gas Hot Plate No.s 201,202,203	2578	No.8 Hinged Dutch Oven
1837	Burner for Gas Hot Plate No.202	2585	Base for No.2511 Reflector Heater
1900	Decorative Flat Iron Trivet, large	2593	No.3 Self Basting Hinged Skillet Cover
1901	Decorative Tree Trivet, large	2595	No.5 Self Basting Hinged Skillet Cover
1902	Decorative Round Design Trivet	2598	No.8 Self Basting Hinged Skillet Cover
1903	Decorative Tassel and Grain Design Trivet, large	2603	No.7 Dutch Oven
1904	Decorative Grape Design Trivet, large	2604	No.7 Dutch Oven Cover
1905	Decorative Eagle Design Trivet, large	2605	No.6 Dutch Oven
1906	Decorative Flat Iron Trivet, small	2606	No.6 Dutch Oven Cover
1907	Decorative Tree Trivet, small	2608	No.12 Hotel Waffle Iron
1908	Decorative Wreath and Eagle Trivet, small	2609	No.12 Hotel Waffle Iron
1909	Decorative Grape Design Trivet, small	2611	No.2 Fruit & Lard Press & cross bar
1916	Burner for Gas Hot Plate No.502	2627	No.3 Oval Roaster
2003	No.3 Hammered Skillet	2628	No.3 Oval Roaster Cover
2005	No.5 Hammered Skillet	2629	No.5 Oval Roaster
2008	No.8 Hammered Skillet	2630	No.5 Oval Roaster Cover
2013	No.3 Hinged Skillet, Hammered	2631	No.7 Oval Roaster
2015	No.5 Hinged Skillet, Hammered	2632	No.7 Oval Roaster Cover
2020	Elevated Hot Plate	2634	No.12 Dutch Oven
2028	No.8 Hinged Deep Skillet, Hammered	2635	No.13 Dutch Oven
2039	No.9 Hinged Skillet, Hammered	2636	No.12 Dutch Oven Cover
2039	No.9 and No.8 Regular Griddle, Hammered	2637	No.13 Dutch Oven Cover
2040	No.8 Hinged Double Skillet Top, Hammered	2703	No.3 Chefs Skillet with bakelite handle
2058	No.8 Hinged Double Skillet Bottom, Hammered	2705	No.5 Chefs Skillet with bakelite handle
2070	No.10 Hammered Popover	2708	No.8 Chefs Skillet with bakelite handle
2073	No.273 Hammered Crispy Corn Stick Pan	2849	No.9 regular Griddle
2075	Pup Ashtray with Match Holder	2980	No.34 Plett Pan
2093	No.3 Hammered Self Basting Skillet Cover	2980A	No.34 Plett Pan, small logo
2095	No.5 Hammered Self Basting Skillet Cover	2992	No.33 Monk Pan
2098	No.8 Hammered Self Basting Skillet Cover	2992	Andresen Monk Pan
2103	No.3 Square Fry Skillet	2992	Western Importing Co. Munk Pan
2106	No.6 Square Fry Skillet	3269	No.11 Square Waffle Iron, male ball joint
2108	No.8 Square Fry Skillet	3270	No.11 Square Waffle Iron, female ball joint
2148	No.11 Square Waffle Iron	3348	No.5 Erie, inset HR
2149	No.11 Square Waffle Iron	6138	No.15 Muffin Pan, 12 cups
2165	No.8 Dutch Oven, Hammered	6139	No.16 Muffin Pan, 6 cups
2185	No.5 Oval Roaster	6140	No.17 Muffin Pan, 6 cups
2298	Scroll for Food Chopper No.s 2,3	6141	No.18 Popover Pan, 6 cups
2301	Scroll for Food Chopper No.1	6408	Stove Pipe Damper, 5 inch
2306	Scroll for Food Chopper No.4	6667	No.601 Gas Hot Plate
2352	Clamp Screw for Food Choppers	6669	No.603 Triple Hot Plate
2358	Crank for Food Choppers No.s 0,1,2,3	6806	5 qt Tea Kettle
2361	Clamp Screw for Food Chopper No.4	6797	Maslin Kettle, 12 qts.
2363	No.8 Ham Boiler	7032	Elevated Hot Plate
2367	Thumb Nut for Food Chopper No.0	7082	Elevated Hot Plate
2383	Ham Boiler		
2400	Folding Pancake Griddle, 3 cakes; both sides are solid		

Aluminum

2402	No.21 Waffle Iron, American French Pattern
2403	No.21 Waffle Iron, American French Pattern
2404	No.21 Waffle Iron Base
2405	Folding Pancake Griddle, 2 cakes, solid side
2406	Folding Pancake Griddle, 3 cakes, solid side
2408	Folding Pancake Griddle, separate pans for p/n 2405 & 2406
2423	Alfred Andresen Krum Cake Pan (wafer)
2424	Alfred Andresen Krum Cake Pan (wafer)
2428	No.77 Waffle Iron Base, high w/ side handles
2429	No.9 Waffle Iron Base, high w/side handles
2434	No.11 Long Griddle
2458	Food Chopper Crank
2459	Food Chopper Scroll
2460	No.10 Food Chopper body
2462	Top Casting for 6 lb. Sad Iron
2463	Top Casting for 4 lb. Sad Iron
2468	Puritan Food Chopper No.11

4-0	Toy Sauce Pan
16	Coffee Pot with Base
20	Toy Skillet
20C	No.20 Skillet Cover, aluminum
32	2 qt Sauce Pan
33	3 qt Sauce Pan
33C	Cover for 2 Qt. & 3 Qt. Sauce Pan
34	4 qt Sauce Pan
35	Round Tray
40	Sauce Pan
42	2 Qt Colonial Sauce Pan
42C	Cover for 2 qt Colonial Sauce Pan
43	Qt. Colonial Sauce Pan
44	4 Qt Colonial Sauce Pan
44C	Cover for 4 qt Colonial Sauce Pan
47	Diamond Plate on Food Cutter Stand
51	Tea Kettle

Number	Description	Number	Description
53L	Half of Omelet Pan	414	Sauce Pan, 4 qt.
53R	Half of Omelet Pan	414C	Sauce Pan Cover
54L	Half of Omelet Pan	422 1/2	Berlin Boiler, 2 1/2 qt.
54R	Half of Omelet Pan	424	Berlin Boiler, 4 qt
56	Shired Egg Dish	424C	Cover
84A	Sauce Pan, 2 qt.	425	Berlin Boiler, 5 qt.
91	1 1/2 qt Sauce Pan, Symbol Ware	425C	Cover
92	2 qt Sauce Pan, Symbol Ware	426	Berlin Boiler, 6 qt.
93	3 qt Sauce Pan, Symbol Ware	426C	Cover
95	No.8 Skillet	427	Berlin Boiler, 7 qt.
96	No.10 Skillet	427C	Cover
98	Dutch Oven	426C	Cover
99	Oval Roaster	430	No.8 Handle Griddle
101	Coffee Pot, 1 qt.	432 1/2	Berlin Sauce Pan, 2 1/2 qt.
102	Coffee Pot, 2 qt.	432 1/2C	Cover
103	Coffee Pot, 3 qt.	434	Berlin Sauce Pan, 4 qt.
104	Coffee Pot, 4 qt.	434C	Cover
105	Coffee Pot with Base	435	Berlin Sauce Pan, 5 qt.
109	Coffee Pot or Pitcher	435C	Cover
111	Tea Pot, 1 qt.	436	Berlin Sauce Pan, 6 qt.
112	Tea Pot, 2 qt.	436C	Cover
116	Coffee Pot or Pitcher 5 pt.	437	Berlin Sauce Pan, 7 qt.
118	Aristocraft All Purpose Grill	437C	Cover
123	Colonial Coffee Pot, 3 pt.	434	4 Qt. Sauce Pan with iron handle
124	Colonial Coffee Pot, 4 pt.	442 1/2	Berlin Pot, 2 1/2 qt.
126	Colonial Coffee Pot, 6 pt.	442 1/2C	Cover
128	Skillet with wood handle	444	Berlin Pot. 4 qt.
133	Colonial Percolator, 3 pt.	444C	Cover
134	Colonial Percolator, 4 pt.	445	Berlin Pot, 5 qt.
135	Colonial Percolator, 6 pt.	445C	Cover
152 1/2	Dble Casserole, outside pan	446	Berlin Pot, 6 qt.
152 1/2B	Dble Casserole, inside pan	446C	Cover
152 1/2C	Cover for Casserole, Outside Pan	447	Berlin Pot, 7 qt.
424C	Cover for Casserole, Inside Pan	447C	Cover
165	Water Pitcher, 2 1/2 qt.	454	Cooking & Preserving Kettle, 4 qt.
172	Bail Water Pitcher, 2 1/2 qt.	454C	Cover
176	6 cup Coffee Percolator	456	Cooking & Preserving Kettle, 6 qt.
180C	Insert for Lemon Squeezer	456C	Cover
182	Baking Dish, 2 pt.	458	Cooking & Preserving Kettle, 8 qt.
183	Baking Dish, 3 pt.	458C	Cover
184	Baking Dish, 4 pt.	462 1/2	Tite Top Dutch Oven, No.6
200	Toy Skillet	462 1/2C	Cover
202	No.2 Skillet, Wood Handle	462 1/2T	Trivet
203	No.3 Skillet, Wood Handle	463 1/2	Tite Top Dutch Oven, No.7
204	No.4 Skillet, Wood Handle	463 1/2C	Cover
205	No.4 Skillet, Wood Handle	463 1/2T	Triveta
206	No.5 Skillet, Wood Handle	465	Tite Top Dutch Oven, No.8
206	Steamer insert for No.8 Dutch Oven	465C	Cover
206C	No.5 Skillet Cover	465B	Steamer insert
207	No.7 Skillet Wood Handle	465T	Trivet
207C	No.7 Skillet Cover	466	Tite Top Dutch Oven, No.9
208	No.8 Skillet, Wood Handle	466C	Cover
208C	No.8 Skillet Cover	466T	Trivet
209	No.9 Skillet, Wood Handle	468	Tite Top Dutch Oven, No.10
209C	No.9 Skillet Cover	468	Cover
213	Hammered Tea Kettle, 5 qt.	468T	Trivet
217N	No.7 Skillet with Alaskan Handle	470	Toy Kettle with Bail
218	No.8 Skillet with Alaskan Handle	483	Oval Roaster, No.3
219	No.9 Skillet with Alaskan Handle	483C	Cover
236	Triplicate Sauce Pans	483T	Trivet
239	Triplicate Sauce Pans, 2 1/2 qt.	485	Oval Roaster, No.5
240C	Cover	485C	Cover
241 1/2	Oyster Bowl	485T	Trivet
241 1/2	Utility Bowl	487	Oval Roaster, No.7
246	Omelet Pan	487C	Cover
247	Omelet Pan	487T	Trivet
249	Omelet Pan	489	Oval Roaster, No.9
250	Skillet Grill	489C	Cover
266	No.6 Drip Coffee Pot	489T	Trivet
270	Toy Bail Handle Griddle	501 1/2	"The Rapid" Tea Kettle, 3 1/2 pts.
303	Toy Handle Griddle	502 1/2	"The Rapid" Tea Kettle, 5 pts.
309	Wood Handled Griddle	504	"The Rapid" Tea Kettle, 4 qt.
341 1/2	1 1/2 Qt. Candy Kettle	505	"The Rapid" Tea Kettle, 5 qt.
343	No.3 Utility Kettle	506	"The Rapid" Tea Kettle, 6 qt.
344	Utility Kettle	508	"The Rapid" Tea Kettle, 8 qt.
345	Utility Kettle	512	Flat Btm. Tea Kettle, 2 qt.
401	Double Boiler, 1 qt.	513	Flat Btm. Tea Kettle, 3 qt.
402	Double Boiler, 2 qt.	514	Flat Btm. Tea Kettle, 4 qt.
403	Double Boiler, 3 qt.	515	Flat Btm. Tea Kettle, 5 qt.
404	Double Boiler, 4 qt.	516	Flat Btm. Tea Kettle, 6 qt.
409	'2' size Miniature Skillet, aluminum	518	Flat Btm. Tea Kettle, 8 qt.
411	2 Pt. Aluminum Buffet Sauce Pan	525	Colonial Tea Kettle, 5 qt.
411 1/2	Sauce Pan with Lip, 1 1/2 qt.	532	Colonial Tea Kettle, 2 qt.
412	Sauce Pan with Lip, 2 qt.	533	Colonial Tea Kettle, 3 qt.
412 1/2	Sauce Pan with Lip, 2 1/2 qt.	534	Colonial Tea Kettle, 4 qt.
412 1/2C	Cover	535	Colonial Tea Kettle, 5 qt.
413	Sauce Pan with Lip, 3 qt.	536	Colonial Tea Kettle, 6 qt.
413C	Cover	538	Colonial Tea Kettle, 8 qt.

544	Safety Fill Tea Kettle, 4 qt.
545	Safety Fill Tea Kettle, 5 qt.
546	Safety Fill Tea Kettle, 6 qt.
565	round Beakfast Skillet
566	Colonial breadfast Skillet, Wood Handle
626	Waffle Iron Low Base, No.6
627	Waffle Iron Low Base, No.7
628	Waffle Iron Low Base, No.8
629	Waffle Iron Low Base, No.9
701	Colonial Double Boiler, 1 qt.
702	Colonial Double Boiler, 2 qt.
703	Colonial Double Boiler, 3 qt.
704	Colonial Double Boiler, 4 qt.
708F	Hearts Star Waffle Iron Paddles
708M	Hearts Star Waffle Iron Paddles
709	Ladle
710	Slotted Spoon
713	Serving Spoon, 13 inch
715	Serving Spoon, 15 inch
710A	No.9 Skillet, aluminum
801	Hearts Star Gem Pan (50)
802	Hearts Star Gem Pan (100)
808	No.8 Muffin Pan
809	No.9 Golf Ball Muffin Pan
903A	No.8 Long Griddle
980 L&R	Bread Slicer
1055	Steak Platter
1082	Oval Tree Platter
1206	Skillet with wood handle
1208	Skillet with wood handle
1309	Handle Griddle, Wood Handle
1458	Baking & Preserving Kettle, 8 qt.
1458r	Baking Rack
1458CX	Cover with Thermometer
1485	Aristocraft Oval Roaster
1485T	Trivet
1511	Sauce Pan with Sq. Wood Handle
1512	Sauce Pan with Sq. Wood Handle
1513	Sauce Pan with Sq. Wood Handle
1534	Aristocraft Tea Kettle
1602	Aristocraft Coffee Pot
2010	Skillet with Wood Handle, No.10
2010C	Skillet Cover
2011	Skillet with Wood Handle, No.11
2011C	Skillet Cover
2012	Skillet with Wood Handle, No.12
2012	Skillet Cover
2075	Alum. Ashtray with Two Pups
2082	Aristocraft Venison Platter
2083	Aristocraft Deep Platter
2092	Aristocraft Venison Platter Side Dishes
2103	Skillet with Wood Handle, No.3
2135	Tea Kettle, 5 qt.
2141	Sauce Pan, Hammered, 1 qt.
2143	Sauce Pan, Hammered, 3 qt.
2190	Small Family Tree Platter
2191	Family Tree Platter
2192	Large Family Tree Platter
2210	Skillet Griddle, Wood Handle, No.10
2410	10 inch Omelet Pan
2411	11 inch Omelet Pan
2510	Jelly Cake Pan
2553A	No.10 Tite-Top Dutch Oven, aluminum
2637	No.13 Dutch Oven Cover
3010	Popover Pan, single hanging hole
3110	Bailed Griddle, No.10
3112	Bailed Griddle, No.12
3114	Bailed Griddle, No.14
3127	Tea Kettle, hammered, 5 qt.
3210	Long Griddle, No.10
3349	No.6 Wood Handle Skillet
3365	No.8 Handle Griddle, aluminum
3514	Griddle Broiler, No.12
4210	Berlin Boiler, No.10
4210C	Cover
4310	Berlin Sauce Pan, No.10
4310C	Cover
4410	Berlin Pot, No.10
4410C	Cover
4512	Cooking Kettle, No.12
4512C	Cover
4516	Cooking Kettle, No.16
4516C	Cover
4520	Cooking Kettle, No.20
4520C	Cover
4524	Cooking Kettle, No.24
4524C	Cover
4612	Tite Top Dutch Oven, No.11
4612C	Cover
4650	Combination Cooker, 5 qt.
6139	No.16 Gem Pan
8010	No.10 Popover Pan
8011	No.11 Muffin Pan
8017	No.17 Muffin Pan
8018	No.18 Pop-Over
8022	No.22 Corn & Bread Stick
8027	Wheatstick Pan (27)
8028	Wheatstick Pan (28)
8022	No.22 Bread Stick Pan
8030	Wheat & Cornstick (2700)
8040	Wheat & Cornstick (2800)
8262	Tea Size Cornstick Pan
8272	Corn & Wheatstick Pan
8273	Corn Stick Pan, (273)
8280	Wheat Stick Pan, (280)
8282	Large Cornstick Pan
A2	Alum. Oval Roaster, Extra Heavy
A2C	Alum. Oval Roaster Cover, Extra Heavy
A2E	Plate for Electric Waffle Iron
A4-0	Toy Sauce Pan, aluminum
A16	Coffee Pot with base
A20	Miniature Skillet
A28	Deep Skillet or Chicken Pan
A40	Sauce Pan
A42	7 qt. Berlin Kettle
A51	Tea Kettle, aluminum
A53L	Omelet Pan
A53R	Omelet Pan
A54L	Omelet Pan
A54R	Omelet Pan
A56	Tea Kettle
A65	Bundt Pan, aluminum
A105	Coffee Pot with base
A113	Coffee Pot
A116	Coffee Pot or Pitcher, 5 pt.
A118A	Aristocraft All Purpose Grill
123	3 pt. Coffee Pot
A124	4 pt. Colonial Coffee Pot
A128	Deep Skillet, aluminum
A134	4 pt. Colonial Percolator
A136	6 pt. Colonial Percolator
A142	2 pt. Gooseneck Tea Pot
A152 1/2	2 1/2 qt. Double Casserole or Baking Dish
A152 1/2C	Cover for 2 1/2 qt. Casserole Dish
A172	Bailed Water Pitcher
A184	4 pt. Casserole Dish
A200	Miniature Aluminum Skillet
A202	No.2 Wood Handle Skillet
A203	No.3 Wood Handle Skillet
A208C	No.8 Skillet Cover, aluminum
A213	5 qt. Hammered Aluminum Tea Kettle
A236	Triplecate Sauce Pans
A240C	Cover(s) for Triplicate Sauce Pans
241 1/2	Oyster Bowl
A250	Skillet Grill
A266 6	Cup Drip Coffee Pot
A270	Miniature Bail Handle Kettle
A303	Miniature Handle Griddle
A308	No.8 Griddle with wood handle
A327	No.7 Long Griddle
A339	No.9 Flat Bottom Griddle
A411	Sauce Pan Cover
A412	No.426 6 qt. pot
A412C	Cover
A414C	Sauce Pan Cover
A424C	Cover for 4 qt. Sauce Pan
A456	No.6 Flat Bottom Kettle
A458	No.8 Maslin Kettle
A458C	No.8 Maslin Kettle Cover
A565	Round Breakfast Skillet
A470	Toy Kettle with bail
A483	No.3 Oval Roaster
A485	No.5 Oval Roaster
A485C	Oval Roaster Trivet
A487	No.7 Oval Roaster
A487C	No.7 Oval Roaster Cover
A489	No.9 Oval Roaster
A498	zAristocraft Roaster
A498C	Aristocraft Roaster Cover
A498T	Trivet
A502	No.5 Tea Kettle
A508	No.8 Flat bottom Tea Kettle
AA516	2 qt. Tea Kettle
A544	4 qt. Safety Fill Tea Kettle
A545	5 qt. Safety Fill Tea Kettle
A566A	Colonial Breakfast Skillet with wood handle

Code	Description
A702	2 qt. Double Boiler
A709	Ladle
A710	Slotted Spoon
A713	13 inch Serving Spoon
A715	15 inch Serving Spoon
A765	Trivet for Combination Cooker
A801	No.50 Hearts Star Gem Pan
A802	No.100 Hearts Star Gem Pan
A923	Plates for Electric Waffle Iron
A932	Shield for Electric Cord
A967	Hot Plate Griddle
A980L&R	Bread Slicer
A1055	7 inch Steak Platter
A1082	Oval Tree Platter
A1208C	Deep Skillet Cover
A1309	No. Handle Griddle with wood handle
A1411	Waterless Cooking Kettle, No.11
A1411C	Cover for Waterless Cooking Kettle
A1411T	Trivet for Waterless Cooking Kettle
A1458	No.8 Baking Kettle
A1485	No.5 Aristocraft Oval Roaster
A1485T	Trivet for No.5 Aristocraft Oval Roaster
A1511	Sauce Pan with square wood handle
A1512	Sauce Pan with square wood handle
A1513	Sauce Pan with square wood handle
A1534	Aristocraft Tea Kettle
A1602	Aristocraft Coffee Pot
A2082	Aristocraft Venison Platter with wood holder
A2083	Aristocraft Deer Platter
A2092	Aristocraft Venison Platter with side dishes
A2108	No.8 Hammered Skillet Cover
A2103	No.3 Skillet with wood handle, hammered aluminum
A2135	5 qt. Tea Kettle
A2141	1 qt. Sauce Pan, hammered finish
A2142	2 qt Sauce Pan
A2143	3 qt. Sauce Pan, hammered finish
A2159	No.9 Wood Handle Griddle, hammered finish
A2165	No.8 Hammered Dutch Oven
A2185	Hammered No.5 Oval Roaster
A2185C	No.5 Oval Roaster Cover
A2190	Small Family Tree Platter
A2191	Family Tree Platter
A2192	Large Tree Platter
A2510	Jelly Cake Pan
A3210	No.10 Long Griddle
A3514	Griddle/Broiler
A4524	Maslin Kettle, 24 qt
A8011	No.11 French Roll Pan
A8018	Popover Pan, 6 section
A8027	No.27 Whole Wheat Stick Pan
A8030 (2700)	Wheat and Corn Stick Pan
A8040 (2800)	Wheat and Corn Stick Pan
A8262	Tea Size Cornstick Pan
A8272	Corn or Wheat Stick Pan
A8273	No.273 Corn Stick Pan
A8280	No.280 Wheat Stick Pan, aluminum
A8282	Large Corn Stick Pan

THE KING STOVE & RANGE COMPANY & THE MARTIN STOVE & RANGE COMPANY

Much of the early history of the King Stove & Range Company and the Martin Stove and Range Company has been lost to the ravages of time. Typical of the industry, old records, catalogs, etc. were lost or destroyed. Consequently, compiling these companies histories, is based on sketchy records and a bit of speculation. Although this may not be completely accurate, it does create a historical perspective.

W.H and Charles Martin were salesmen for the King Hardware Company of Atlanta, Georgia. While traveling as salesmen, they learned that the Lizzie Loman Stove Works in Sheffield, Alabama was for sale. In 1905 the Martin brothers convinced King Hardware to purchase the small foundry resulting in the Martin brothers taking over management of the foundry for King Hardware. The foundry was renamed, King Stove & Range Company. The Martin brothers joined together in the production of coal & wood heaters, stoves, and ranges.

In 1917, the Martin brothers purchased the King Stove & Range Co. from King Hardware. Shortly there after, the Martins purchased a bankrupt foundry known as the Florence Stove Foundry, in Florence, Alabama. Florence is across the Tennessee River from Sheffield. The Florence Stove Foundry was then renamed the Martin Stove & Range Company. With the new addition came expansion of Martins line to include hollow ware and sad irons. This explains why both the King Stove & Range Co. and the early Martin Stove & Range marks, and the style of hollow ware pieces, were identical. They were apparently made from the same patterns with only the mark being changed. It is generally believed that King Stove & Range hollow ware pieces were produced in the Martin Foundry. It also appears that the King trademark began to disappear except for a few pieces, such as ashtrays, trivets, etc. Although confusing, it shows how entwined these companies were; eventually becoming one in the same. It is also known that Martin Stove & Range marked pieces were sold through the King Hardware.

The Martin Stove & Range company produced an extensive line of hollow ware; including skillets, griddles, Dutch ovens, sauce pans, kettles, long pans, shallow skillets, ham boilers, country skillets, country ovens, charcoal sad iron heaters, sad irons, and at least eight different styles of gem pans. A few toys are also known to exist.

Unlike many of the large foundries, only five different logos are known for Martin and four for King. While this does not leave much variation in collecting, several of the logos are difficult to find so it is not easy to complete a set. Skillets are known to have been produced in two finishes, plain and polished; three styles: complete heat ring, broken heat ring, and smooth bottom; and three logos: fancy or early, block, or late of which there are two styles. There is also one skillet, a No.3 known with the logo inverted. This was nicknamed the Monday Morning Skillet.

Other finishes are known on Martin pieces. Several skillets are known with a porcelain finish, apparently added by another company. Also, at least one piece is known to be nickel-plated.

Many Martin pieces were unmarked. These are often easy to recognize however, because of unique features. The covers for Dutch ovens, skillets, flat bottom kettles, and sauce pans, have handles with points projecting upwards at both ends. The handles on the cover of both the country ovens and the country skillets are also unique; a straight bar between the end supports. A collector who recognizes these traits certainly has the advantage in adding these pieces to their collection.

The Martin Stove & Range Company discontinued producing hollow ware in 1953. However, some pieces were sporadically produced; one example is in 1963 when a No.12 Dutch oven was combined with a charcoal stove and marketed as a Fish Cooker.

The Martins continued expanding, and in 1939, purchased a bankrupt manufacturing plant in Huntsville. The company made magazine heaters for the Army and stamped bomb crates and other material during World War II. Production began in Huntsville on a line of electric heaters in the late 1950s, and a plant was opened in Athens in 1966 to keep up. All three companies merged in 1973 to become Martin Industries, being known for wood, coal, and electric heaters, and for producing decorative and other castings. Even today, Martin Industries continues to have a strong influence throughout the South.

Early markings of the Martin Stove & Range Company (left) and The King Stove & Range Company (right).

SKILLETS

REGULAR SKILLET-Size: 8; **Markings**: KS&R CO, SHEF-FIELD ALA, 8 (top of handle); **Circa**: 1905-1917; **VALUE: $30-$50**.

REGULAR SKILLET-Size: No.8; **Markings**: PERFECTION, and what appears to be a molders mark; **Finish**: iron; **Circa**: 1910; **VALUE: $30-$50**.

REGULAR SKILLET-Size: No.8; **Markings**: standard logo; **Finish**: iron; **Circa**: 1920-1950; **VALUE: $25**; No.3, $15-$20; No.5, $20-$25; No.7, $35; No.9 $40; No.10, $45, No.12, $55; No.14, $75.

REGULAR SKILLET-Size: No.8; **Markings**: standard logo, 8 (top of handle); **Finish**: iron; **Circa**: 1930; **VALUE: $30-$40**. Note drop in handle.

REGULAR SKILLET-Size: No.3; **Markings**: standard logo; **Finish**: iron; **Circa**: 1920-1950; **VALUE: $15-$20**.

REGULAR SKILLET-Size: No.7; **Markings**: KS&R Co logo, 7; **Finish**: iron; **Circa**: 1905-1917; **VALUE: $45-$60**.

MONDAY MORNING SKILLET-Size: No.3; **Markings**: standard logo (upside down); **Finish**: iron; **Circa**: unknown; **VALUE: $35**. The story told by Charles Martin, Chairman of the Board of the Martin Stove & Range Co. is that a worker came to work on Monday morning, hung over from the weekend, and applied the logo plate upside down on this pattern.

REGULAR SKILLET-Size: No.3; **Markings**: 3, MARTIN, 2, STOVE & RANGE CO., FLORENCE ALA.; **Finish**: iron; **Circa**: 1940s-1953; **VALUE: $15-$20; No.5, $25; No.8, $30**. Notice broken heat ring. This skillet is also found with a "1" instead of a "2."

SAFETY SKILLET-Size: No.8; **Markings**: standard logo; **Finish**: iron; **Circa**: 1930; **VALUE: $75-$100 with cover**. The tabs on the skillet keep the cover from sliding off.

SMOOTH BOTTOM REGULAR SKILLET-Size: No.7; **Markings**: standard logo; **Finish**: iron; **Circa**: unknown; **VALUE: $30-$35; No.3 $20-$25; No.5 $30-$35**.

BROILER SKILLET-Size: 10 1/8' dia.; **Markings**: standard logo, PERFECTION; **Finish**: iron; **Circa**: 1940s-1953; **VALUE: $45-$65**.

DEEP SKILLET-Size: No.8; **Markings**: standard logo; **Finish**: iron; **Circa**: 1930s-1940s; **VALUE: $65; No.9, $85**.

DOUBLE SKILLET-Size: No.8, 10 1/4" dia. x 3" d., (top) 1 1/2" d.; **Markings**: standard logo, 8 on top of handles; **Finish**: iron; **Circa**: 1930s-1940s; **VALUE: $65-$75**. Neither top nor bottom section has a heat ring.

SAUCE PAN-Size: No.5, 7 1/4" dia. x 3 1/4" d.; **Markings**: standard logo, MARTIN (top of handle), (cover) No. 5; **Finish**: iron; **Circa**: 1920-1940s; **VALUE: $75-$85**. The handle is removable.

DOUBLE SKILLET-Size: No.8, 10 1/4" dia. x 3 1/4" d., (top) 1 3/4" d.; **Markings**: standard logo; **Finish**: iron; **Circa**: 1920s-1930s; **VALUE: $100-$125**. This double skillet with the safety bottom is unusual

SAUCE PAN-Size: No.6; **Markings**: standard logo, MARTIN (top of handle), (cover) No 6; **Finish**: iron; **Circa**: 1920s-1940s; **VALUE: $75-$85**. Note different slant of handle.

COUNTRY SKILLET-Size: No.10; **Markings**: 10 on handle, (cover) 10, KS&R; **Finish**: iron; **Circa**: 1910-1940s; **VALUE:** $70; No.7, $45; No.8, $50, No.9, $60, No.12, $80, No.14, $100.

SKILLET COVER STYLES-(clockwise) Perfection, Low Dome, High Dome; **Sizes**: 7, 8, 9, 10; **Finish**: iron; **Circa**: 1920s-1940s; **VALUE: Perfection:** No.7, $30-$35; No.8, $30-$35; No.9, $40-$45; No.10, $45-$50. **High Dome:** No.7, $20-$25; No.8, $20-$25; No.9, $30-$35; No.10, $35-$40. **Low Dome:** No.7, $20-$25; No.8, $20-$25; No.9, $30-$35; No.10, $35-$40.

ADVERTISING SKILLET COVER-Size: 11" dia.; **Markings**: Wesson - Snodrift, No.8, the Wesson Oil & Snodrift People, New Orleans, La; **Finish**: iron; **Circa**: 1930s; **VALUE:** $200-$225.

Basting Ring design for, (left) Low Dome cover, and (right) Perfection cover.

BACON FRYER (Shallow Skillet)-Size: No.7; **Markings**: 7 (top of handle), KS&R CO, SHEFFIELD, ALA; **Finish**: iron; **Circa**: 1910; **VALUE: $30-$45.** Position of marking is unusual.

ADVERTISING SKILLET COVER-Size: No.8; **Markings**: MAZOLA, No.8, CORN PRODUCTS REFINING CO, NEW YORK CITY; **Finish**: iron; **Circa**: 1930s-1940s; **VALUE: $200-$225.**

BACON FRYER (Shallow Skillet)-Size: No.8; **Markings**: KS&R CO, SHEFFIELD ALA, 8 (top of handle); **Finish**: iron; **Circa**: 1910-1920s; **VALUE: $35-$40; No.7, $35-$45.**

BACON FRYER (Shallow Skillet)-Size: No.7; **Markings**: 7 (top of handle), standard logo; **Finish**: iron; **Circa**: 1940s; **VALUE: $30; No.8, $30**. Later style handle.

BACON FRYER (Shallow Skillet)-Size: No.8; **Markings**: MARTIN STOVE & RANGE CO. FLORENCE ALA.; **Finish**: iron; **Circa**: 1940s; **VALUE: $15-$25; No.7, $15-$25**. This marking is considered the late logo.

GRIDDLES

LONG GRIDDLE-Size: No.10, 12" x 20"; **Markings**: standard logo, 10 (top of handle); **Finish**: iron; **Circa**: 1920s-1940s; **VALUE: $65; No.8, $45; No.9, $55, No.11, $85**.

ROUND GRIDDLE-Size: No.9, 10 1/4" dia.; **Markings**: 9 (top of handle), standard logo; **Finish**: iron; **Circa**: 1920s-1940s **VALUE: $55**; No.7, $35; No.8, $25; No.10, $65.

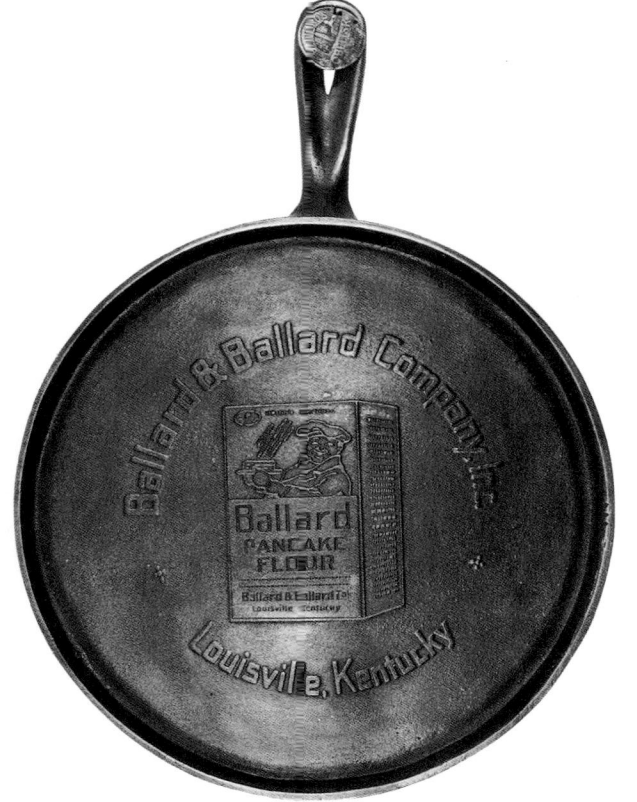

ADVERTISING GRIDDLE-Size: No.10 dia.; **Markings**: 10, Ballard & Ballard advertisement; **Finish**: iron; **Circa**: 1940s; **VALUE: $150**; No.8, $150; No.9, $150. The No.9 and No.10 are the same size.

Ballard & Ballard Brass Tag - VALUE: $50.

DUTCH OVENS & KETTLES

COUNTRY DUTCH OVENS-Size: (left) No.16, 16" dia.; (right) No.8, 8" dia.; **Markings**: (cover) No.16, (cover) 8; **Finish**: iron; **Circa**: 1920s-1940s; **VALUE: No.7 $50; No.8, $35, No.9, $50; No.10, $60, No.11, $65, No.12, $80; No.14, $100; No. 16, $250**. Note distinctive handle on cover. It is also interesting that these two Dutch ovens have different style kettle ears.

COUNTRY DUTCH OVEN COVER-Size: No.12; **Markings**: 1910; **Finish**: iron; **Circa**: 1910; **VALUE: $30-$40**. Although this marking is unfamiliar, it has the Martin style handle. It is also an earlier style.

DUTCH OVEN WITH PERFECTION COVER-Size: No.7, MARTIN'S PERFECTION, No7, FLORENCE ALA; **Markings**: standard logo, (cover) No7; **Finish**: iron; **Circa**: 1920s-1930s; **VALUE: $75; No.8, $55; No.9, $70; No.10, $100**.

DUTCH OVEN WITH LOW COVER-Size: No.7; **Markings**: standard logo, (cover) No7; **Finish**: iron; **Circa**: 1930s-1940s; **VALUE: $75; No.8, $55; No.9, $70; No.10, $100**.

LOW DUTCH OVEN COVER-Markings: No8, 8 D (underside); **Finish**: iron; **VALUE: $15; No.7, $10; No.9, $20, No.10, $25**. Notice design of drip rings. The Perfection cover has larger drip rings as illustrated in the Skillet section.

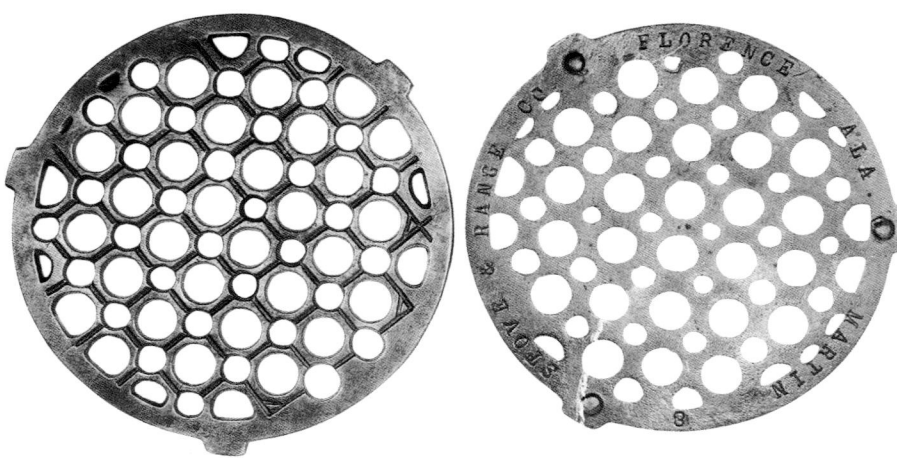

DUTCH OVEN TRIVETS-Size: No.8, & No.9; **Markings**: 8 or 9, MARTIN STOVE & RANGE, FLORENCE ALA; **Finish**: iron; **Circa**: 1920s-1940s; **VALUE: $50; No.7, $50-$60, No.10, $50-60**.

FLAT BOTTOM KETTLE-Size: No.8; **Markings**: standard logo, 8; **Finish**: iron; **Circa**: 1920-1940s; **VALUE: $60; No.7, $50**.

GEM PANS

CORN STICK PAN-Size: 12 3/8" 6 7/8" not including handles; **Markings**: MARTIN STOVE & RANGE CO. FLORENCE ALA; **Finish**: iron; **Circa**: 1920s-1940s; **VALUE: $30-$40**. It is interesting that markings are aligned left rather than centered.

PERFECTION No.6 HEARTS GEM PAN-Size: 9 3/8" x 5 3/8"; **Markings**: none; **Finish**: iron; **Circa**: 1920s-1930s; **VALUE: $50-$60**.

CORN COB PAN-Size: 12 1/4" x 5 1/2"; **Markings**: none; **Finish**: iron; **Circa**: 1920s-1940s; **VALUE: $25-$30**. Identifiable by the distinct handles.

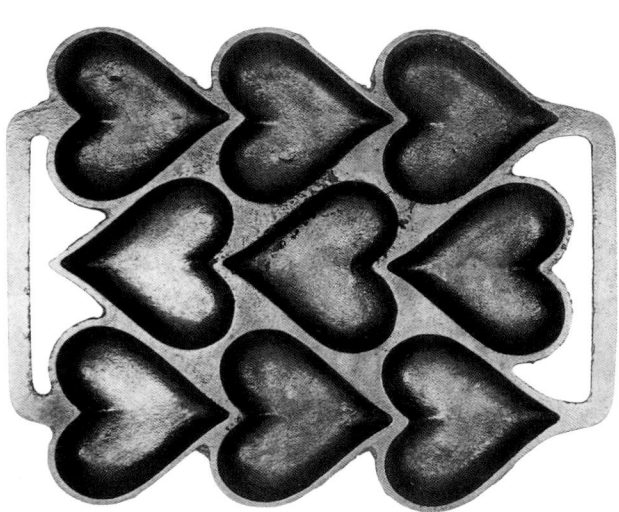

PERFECTION No.9 HEART GEM PAN-Size: 10" x 8 1/4"; **Markings**: none; **Finish**: iron; **Circa**: 1920s-1930s; **VALUE: $40-$60**. The piece is being REPRODUCED.

PERFECTION No.12 HEART GEM PAN-Size: 12 3/4" x 8 1/4"; **Markings**: none; **Finish**: iron; **Circa**: 1920s-1930s; **VALUE: $60-$75**.

TOYS & MINIATURES

COMMEMORATIVE MINI COUNTRY DUTCH OVEN-Size: 3 3/8" dia. x 2 1/2"h; **Markings**: PILOT INTERNATIONAL, APRIL 1928, SHEFFIELD ALA, (bottom) KING STOVE & RANGE CO; **Finish**: iron; **Circa**: 1928; **VALUE: $100-$200**. Pilot is an international fraternal organization whose 1928 convention was held in Mobile, Alabama.

TOY WITH DEEP SKILLET-Size: (left) 10 1/4" dia. x 3" d., (toy) 4 1/2" dia. x 1 3/8" d.; **Markings**: standard logo; **Finish**: iron; **Circa**: 1920s-1940s; **VALUE: (Skillet) $80; toy, $70**. Note reinforced edge of both pieces.

TOY DUTCH OVEN OR HOT POT-Size: 4 1/4" dia. x 2" s.; **Markings**: standard logo, (cover) not marked; **Finish**: iron; **Circa**: unknown; **VALUE: $75**.

TOY SAFETY SKILLET (shown with full size for comparison)-Size: 4 3/16" dia. x 3/4" d.; **Markings**: standard logo; **Finish**: iron; **Circa**: 1920s-1940s; **VALUE: $150**.

TOY FLAT BOTTOM KETTLE & BANK-Size: 4 1/4" dia. x 2 3/4" h.; **Markings**: standard logo; **Finish**: iron; **Circa**: unknown; **VALUE: (Kettle) $50-$75; (Bank) $100**. Bank was made by removing bail handle and adding slot to cover.

STOVES & MISCELLANEOUS

No. 30C HEATER-Size: 26" high; **Markings**: No. S 30 C, KING STOVE & RANGE, SHEFFIELD; **Finish**: iron; **Circa**: unknown; **VALUE**: $150-$200.

TOY KITCHEN RANGE-Size: 10" h x 9" w.; **Markings**: PERFECTION; **Finish**: iron; **Circa**: unknown; **VALUE**: Rare.

CHARCOAL FURNACE-Size: No.3, 10" dia. x 8" high x; **Markings**: 3, (no other markings); **Finish**: iron; **Circa**: 1920s-1960s; **VALUE**: $100; No.2, $150; No.1, $200.

No.8 LAUNDRY STOVE-Size: 19" h. x 18 1/2" w.; **Markings**: MARTIN STOVE & RANGE CO. FLORENCE ALA, No8; **Finish**: iron; **Circa**: unknown; **VALUE**: $200-$250.

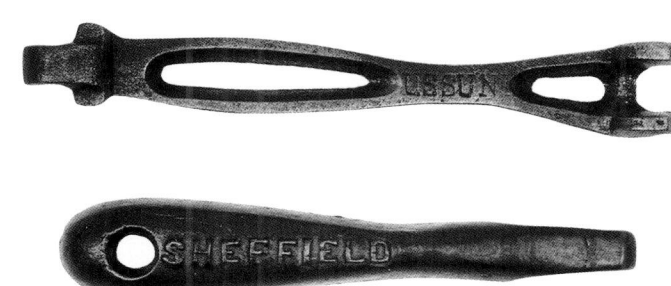

STOVE LID LIFTERS-Size: (top) 7 1/2", (btm.) 6 3/4"; **Markings**: (top) US SUN, (btm) SHEFFIELD; **Finish**: iron; **Circa**: unknown; **VALUE: $15-$25**. Martin Stove & Range manufactured a line of stoves called the Sun Line.

COVER TRIVETS-Size: (left) 6 3/16" dia., (right) 7 1/8"; **Markings**: KS&R Co; **Finish**: iron; **Circa**: 1912-1930; **VALUE: $35-$50 each**. These trivets hung on the side of the kitchen range to rest covers on.

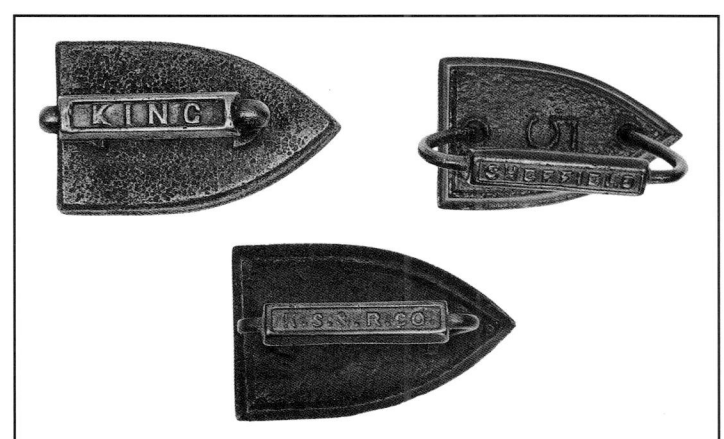

SAD IRONS-Markings: (top, left) KING, (top right) SHEF-FIELD, (btm.) KS & R Co; **Finish**: iron; **Circa**: 1910-1920s; **VALUE: $30-$40 each**.

DUTCH OVEN COVER-Size: No.8; **Markings**: No8; **Finish**: yellow porcelain with white speckles; **Circa**: 1940s-1950s; **VALUE: $40-$50**.

ASHTRAYS-Markings & Finish: (center) KING, orange porcelain; (clockwise from bottom left): KING, (black iron); Fire Places by Martin, (black iron); Martin STOVES, (gray porcelain with orange porcelain exterior); Martin STOVES, (nickel exterior); Martin HEATERS, (black iron); MARTIN STOVE & RANGE CO, FLORENCE ALA, (black iron); KING STOVE & RANGE CO, SHEFFIELD ALA, (nickeled exterior); (center); **Circa**: 1930s-1960s; **VALUE: $10-$35**.

REGULAR SKILLET-Size: No.8; **Markings**: standard logo; **Finish**: wine porcelain with black iron interior; **Circa**: 1950s; **VALUE: $60-$75**.

REGULAR SKILLET-Size: No.5; **Markings**: standard logo; **Finish**: orange porcelain exterior with gray porcelain interior; **Circa**: 1950s; **VALUE: $30**.

REGULAR SKILLET-Size: No.14; **Markings**: standard logo; **Finish**: Yellow porcelain with white speckles; **Circa**: 1940s-1950s; **VALUE: $150-$200**.

REGULAR SKILLET-Size: No.8; **Markings**: standard logo; **Finish**: reddish brown porcelain with black iron interior; **Circa**: 1950s; **VALUE: $40-$60**.

REGULAR SKILLET-**Size**: No.8; **Markings**: 8, MARTIN STOVE & RANGE CO., FLORENCE ALA (late logo); **Finish**: iron; **Circa**: 1950s-1969s; **VALUE: $30-$40**. The late logo is block letters. Note breaks in heat ring.

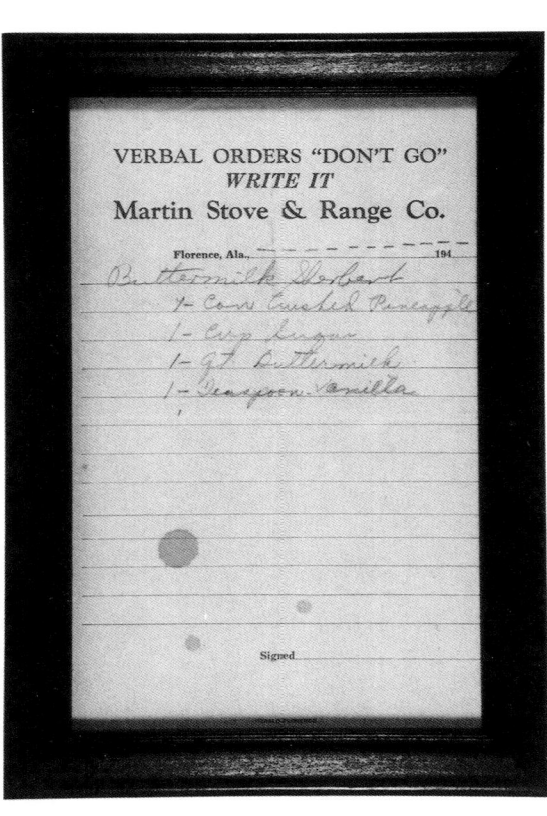

NOTE PAPER (framed)-**Circa**: 1940s; **VALUE: $50-$60**.

KNIVES-**Circa**: 1950s-1960s; **VALUE: $45-$65**.

THE LODGE MANUFACTURING COMPANY
South Pittsburg, Tennessee

Joseph Lodge
March 29, 1848-January 4, 1931

Joseph Lodge, the son of Richard and Susan Catherine Maison Lodge, was born March 29, 1848 in Thornbury, Pennsylvania.

Subsequent to his fathers death in 1863, Joseph, at the age of 15, became an apprentice in a machine shop in Wilmington, Delaware. It was the year in which the Battle of Gettysburg was fought just 100 miles from his birthplace of Thornbury. A year after the Civil War ended, Joseph went west to earn money to send to his mother. He walked from Indiana to Wisconsin to Iowa to Missouri. During his travel by foot, he often earned his supper and nights lodging by chopping wood.

In west Tennessee, Joseph joined with a crew that was drilling wells with an auger. He also worked in a foundry in Meridan and at a railroad shop in Mobile. From New Orleans he sailed to Cuba. Joseph worked at his trade for a year and a half, making money which he sent home to his mother.

In the fall of 1869, after a brief visit home in Thornbury, Joseph sailed from New York to Rio de Janeiro, and on to Peru as an oiler on a vessel of the Peruvian Navy. Landing in Peru, he began a six year stay during which he was employed as a Master Mechanic and later a General Superintendent of the Arequipa Mollendo Railroad.

While in Peru, Joseph began writing to Anna Elizabeth Harvey of Philadelphia; a young lady who once had been his teacher. A courtship developed by letter until,

Lodge Mfg. Co. Workers, c.1910

in the summer of 1876, Joseph very suddenly left Peru and traveled home. He couldn't find employment in Pennsylvania so he traveled to Tennessee. Returning to Pennsylvania, he married Elizabeth Harvey and took her back to South Pittsburg where he built her a new home. Two and a half years later a daughter, Edith, was born, followed two years later by a son, Richard.

The Southern States Coal & Iron Company employed Joseph as manager of their saw mill. He was promoted to master mechanic and later to general superintendent of their blast furnace and coal mines. A few years later when the company was absorbed by the Tennessee Coal, Iron and Railroad Company, he continued in the same position. In 1892, Joseph organized the Shuster Foundry for the manufacture of soil pipe. When the Schuster Foundry had been in operation for seven years, Joseph sold it to the Central Foundry. At that time, he was named president of the Central Coal & Iron Company, and moved his family to Tuscaloosa, Alabama. He gave one of the coal miner communities the name of Kellermann, after a business associate who was soon to become his son-in-law.

Prior to his departure from South Pittsburg, Joseph founded a company for the manufacture of cast iron hollow ware named the Blacklock Foundry, after Henry Blacklock, an associate of Joseph Lodge. The officers were: C.H. Blacklock, President, Joseph Lodge, Vice President and Treasurer, and Henry Blacklock, Secretary and Superintendent. Unfortunately, Henry Blacklock lacked the ability to perform the responsibility entrusted to him and involved the foundry in financial stress. Consequently, Joseph Lodge returned with his family to South Pittsburg and began to supervise the operations of the Blacklock Foundry. The building and its contents went up in flames in a dramatic night time fire in 1910. Joseph Lodge rebuilt the foundry the same year at the south end of South Pittsburg. The new corporation was named Lodge Manufacturing Company. The company was incorporated and a charter was issued August 17, 1910.

Joseph Lodge, company president was aided by his brother Will Lodge, who was in charge of purchasing; his son Richard Leslie Lodge, vice president, his son-in-law Charles Richard Kellermann, who worked with the engineering aspects of the foundry and was plant manager, and Jeptha Bright, a South Pittsburg attorney who served as Lodge's legal council for many years.

Upon the death of Joseph Lodge in 1931, his son Richard Leslie Lodge took over as president. In the later years of his life, the board elected the three sons of his sister, Edith Lodge Kellermann as officers of the company. They were: Charles Richard Kellermann Jo, Francis Kellermann, and Leslie Kellermann.

The company has had three presidents which succeeded Joseph Lodge: Charles Richard Kellermann Jr., who served from 1948 until his retirement in 1973, his brother William Leslie Kellermann, from 1973 until his death in 1987, and the current President and Chief Executive Officer Robert Finch Kellermann, a great grandson of the founder. Two other great grandsons, Bill Kellermann and Henry Lodge also provide leadership in Lodge today.

In earlier years, in addition to hollow ware, the Lodge line of products included foundation vents, sad irons, decorative fireplace fenders, and an extensive line of Andirons and fireplace grates. It also included a vast line of Sugar Kettles and large English Pots.

During the Great Depression of 1930, the Lodge Manufacturing Company was one of the few businesses that continued to work at least three days a week. During this time, Lodge manufactured ornamental castings such as dogs, cats, horses and trivets. A separate building was built to spray these ornamental castings and to this day it is known as the "dog house."

Work at Lodge was done manually until the late 1960s when a Disa-matic was installed. This automatic molding machine which was made in Denmark, was among the first used in the United States. In 1992, an additional Disa-Matic was added in a 6.5 million dollar upgrade to the Lodge factory. In 1998, an additional 4 million dollar upgrade was completed.

Between 1979 and 1986 the original building frame was demolished and replaced by a steel building. The Lodge complex now consists of four buildings: a main building which houses the foundry, the cleaning, grinding and shipping departments; the "dog house;" a building which houses the machine shop, pattern shop and job shop, and a separate office building.

Lodge now offers a 140 item product line. In addition to traditional cookware such as skillets, griddles, and Dutch ovens, they also produce trendy and seasonal items for baking such as perch, cactus, and chili pepper pattern baking pans as well as snowman and other holiday pieces.

The original few pieces of camp ware have been expanded to over 56 items, including the Boy Scouts of America official Dutch oven, a reversible griddle (smooth on side and ribbed on reverse). Lodge also produces custom imprinted products. These pieces could very well become the collectibles of the future. The current Lodge product line can be seen on their web site at http://www.lodgemfg.com.

Lodge boasts that it is the family pride and determination that has developed the insignificant foundry in this Tennessee village to the most modern cast iron cookware foundry in the world, processing over 85 tons of iron daily.

Even today, working at Lodge is a family affair. Many of Lodges 220 employees work alongside their brothers, fathers, sisters, sons, and daughters.

SKILLETS & SKILLET COVERS

REGULAR SKILLET-Size: No.8, 10 1/2" x 7/8" d.; **Markings**: 8 raised on top of handle, LODGE, D molders mark; **Circa**: 1910-1920; **VALUE: $25-$30; No.6, $30-$335; No.7, $25-$30; No.9, $30-$35; No.10; $35-$40**. No break in heat ring.

REGULAR SKILLET-Size: No.8, 9 7/8" dia. x 1 3/4" d.; **Markings**: raised 8 (top of handle), raised W (on bottom); **Circa**: 1900-1910; **VALUE: $25-$30; No.6, $25-$30; No.7, $25-$30; No.9, $30-$35; No.10, $35-$40; No.12, $50-$60**. The raised letter on the bottom is a molders mark, very typical of Lodge. The raised 8 on top of the handle is also typical of earlier Lodge skillets. This skillet may date back to the Blacklock Foundry.

REGULAR SKILLET-Size: No.5, 8" dia. x 1 7/8" d.; **Markings**: LODGE, 5, L molders mark; **Circa**: 1925-1930; **VALUE: $10-$15; No.3, $15-$20; No.4, $40-$50; No.6. $15-$20; No.7, $15-$20; No.8 $15-$20, No.9, $20-$25; No.10, $30-$35; No.12, $35-$45**. No break in heat ring.

SKILLET STICKER- Markings: circa: 1950s-1970; Used for the Chefs Choice line of cookware.

REGULAR SKILLET-Size: No.5, 8 1/8" x 1 3/4" d.; **Markings**: 5; **Circa**: 1940s-1960s; **VALUE: $5-$10; No.3, $5-$10; No.4, $15-$20; No's.6, 7,8, $5-$10; No.9, $10-$15; No.10, $15-$20; No.12, $30-$40; No.14, $45-$65**. Three breaks in the heat ring.

REGULAR SKILLET-Size: No.4; **Markings**: LODGE, A molders mark; **Circa**: 1925-1930s; **VALUE: $45-$60; No.3, $20-$25; No.5, $20-$25; No.6, $20-$25; No.7 $25-$30; No.8, $20-$25; No.9, $25-$30; No.10 $35-$40; No.12, $45-$60**. One break in heat ring. This seems to be the most desirable series for collectors.

REGULAR SKILLET-Size: No.5, 8 1/2" dia.; **Markings**: 5, raised 8 molders mark; **Circa**: 1930s; **VALUE: $15-$20; No.3, $10-$15; No.4, $35-$40; No.6, $15-$20; No.7, $15-$20; No.8, $15-$20; No.9, $20-$30; No.10, $25-$30; No.12, $35-$45; No.14, $65-$85**. One break in the heat ring.

SKILLET STICKER- Circa: 1950s-1970; Used for the Plantation Ware line of cookware.

COMMEMORATIVE SKILLET-Size: 5 1/8" dia.; **Markings**: anniversary logo, 100 YEARS & STILL COOKING; **Circa**: 1996; **VALUE: $35-$45**. Limited production - given to retail outlets, distributors, and special customers.

REGULAR SKILLET-Size: No.7; **Markings**: 7, AJ; **Circa**: 1960s, 1990s; **VALUE: $5-$10; No.3, $5; No.4, $15; No's 6,7,8, $5-$10; No.9, $10; No.10, $10-$15; No.12, $25-$35; No.14, $25-$35**. Three very shallow breaks in the heat ring.

SKILLET-Size: No.9; **Markings**: LODGE, 9 (raised on handle); **Circa**: unknown; **VALUE: $150-$200**. Note the three pour spouts which are very unusual. Also early markings and single break in heat ring.

REGULAR SKILLET-Size: 10, 12 1/8" dia. X 2 1/4" d.; **Markings**: egg in skillet logo; **Circa**: 1993-present; **VALUE: $10-$15**. This is the first regular skillet without a heat ring, produced on a regular basis by Lodge.

AXFORD TOP-O' STOVE BROILER-Size: (No.9), 11" dia.; **Markings:** PAT PEND (on handle), AXFORD; **Circa:** 1931; **VALUE: $50-$60**. Note ghost mark of LODGE under AX-FORD. Also notice no break in the heat ring.

REGULAR SKILLET-Size: No.3; **Markings:** Maid of Honor; **Circa:** 1950s; **VALUE: $20-$25;** No.5, $20-$25; No.8, $20-$25. Made for Sears Roebuck & Co. Note four breaks in the heat ring.

Skillet Sticker for Maid of Honor Skillet; circa: 1950s.

AXFORD TOP-0' STOVE BROILER-Size: (No.9),11" dia; **Markings:** PAT PEND (on handle), AXFORD BROILER; **Circa:** 1931; **VALUE: $50-$60;** No.8, $50-$60; No.12, $125-$150. Note tab opposite handle. Also notice one break in heat ring. There is a ghost mark of LODGE at the top below the break of the heat ring.

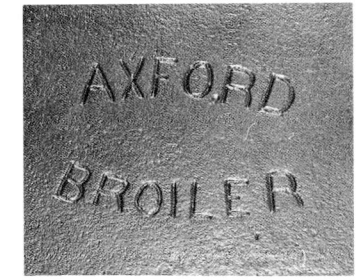

AXFORD TOP-O'STOVE BROILER-
Size: (No.9); **Markings**: PAT 1931 (top of handle), AXFORD BROILER; **Circa**: 1931- ?; **VALUE**: $50-$60; No.6, $60-$75; No.8, $50-$60; No.12; $125-$150. Again, notice the ghost mark of LODGE. The No.6 was added to the line in the 1940s or '50s and the No.12 was deleted. The Grill Pan, as it is now called in Lodge advertising, is currently available in a size nine.

AXFORD BROILER JUNIOR-
Size: (no.6) 9 3/4" dia. x 1 7/8" d.; **Markings**: (handle) AXFORD JR, (bottom) PAT PEND, AXFORD JUNIOR BROILER; **Circa**: 1930; **VALUE**: $90-$110.

AXFORD BROILER-
Size: 11" dia.; **Markings**: BROIL-RITE, AXFORD BROILER, (top of handle) AXFORD; **Circa**: 1930s; **VALUE**: $50-$60. Until recently, it was believed that this piece may not have been made by Lodge. However, recent information leads to the probability that this piece was made by Lodge for a California distributor.

AXFORD COMBINATION SKILLET COVER-Size: 11" dia.; **Markings**: AXFORD COMBINATION COVER AND SKILLET, USE ON AXFORD BROILER FOR CHICKEN AND POT ROAST, PATENT PENDING; **Circa**: unknown; **VALUE: $75**. Was this Lodge's answer to the double skillet?

CORN BREAD SKILLET-Size: 9" dia.; **Markings**: D, 8 CB; **Circa**: 1930s - present; **VALUE: $30-$35 (early glossy finish)**. Note vent hole in the center. Unmarked Wagners are solid.

SQUARE SKILLET-Size: 9 5/8" x 9 1/2" x 1 58" d.; **Markings**: none; **Circa**: 1940s-present; **VALUE: $40-$50 (early, glossy finish)**.

STIR FRY PAN- Size: 12 7/8" dia. x 3 1/2" d.; **Markings**: skillet logo; **Circa**: 1990s- present; **VALUE: $35-$40**.

DUTCH OVEN SKILLET with HIGH BASTING COVER-Size: No.8, 10 1/2" dia. x 3 1/2" d.; **Markings**: raised 8 on handle, 1 molders mark on the bottom, (cover) LODGE NO8, SKILLET LID, II molders mark inside cover; **Circa**: 1930s; **VALUE: $45-$55; No.7, $45-$65; No.9, $65-$75; No.10, $75-$80**. Cover has later style handle.

DUTCH OVEN SKILLET WITH LOW COVER-Size: (No.9) 11 1/2" dia.; **Markings:** P (inside cover), F on (bottom of skillet tab); **Circa:** 1920s-1930s; **VALUE: $30-$45**. Both letters are molders marks.

DEEP SKILLET-HAMMERED FINISH-Size: 10 9/16" dia. X 3" d.; **Markings:** (bottom) 8, F, (cover) 8, raised T; **Circa:** 1940s; **VALUE: $75-$85**.

4-IN-1 DOUBLE SKILLET-Size: 9 3/4" dia. x 3" d., (cover) 10" dia, x 15/16" d.; **Markings:** 5-IN-1 inside star on cover skillet, no other markings; **Circa:** 1940s-1950s; **VALUE: $60-$75**.

HIGH SELF BASTING LID-Size: No.7, 10" dia. 2" h. plus handle; **Markings:** LODGE NO 7, SKILLET LID; **Circa:** 1920s-1930s; **VALUE: $35-$45; No.8, $35-$45; No.9, $45-$50; No.10, $65-$70**.

LOW SKILLET LID-Size: No.8, 10 5/8" dia.; **Markings:** 8, (underside) raised F molders mark; **Circa:** 1930s; **VALUE: $25-$30**; No.4, $30-$35; No's.5, 6, 7, $25-$30; No.9, $30-$35; No.10, $35-$40; No.12, $50-$65. No.14, $75-$100.

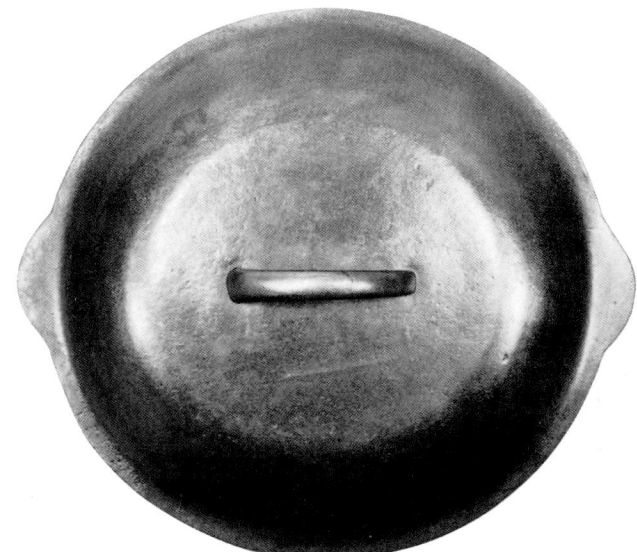

LOW SKILLET LID-Size: No.8; **Markings:** (underside) 8, T molders mark; **Circa:** 1940s-1950s; **VALUE: $20-$25**; No.3, $30-$40; No.4, $25-$30; No's.5, 6, 7, $20-$25; No.9, $25-$30; No.10, $35-$40; no.12, $45-$65; No.14, $75-$100.

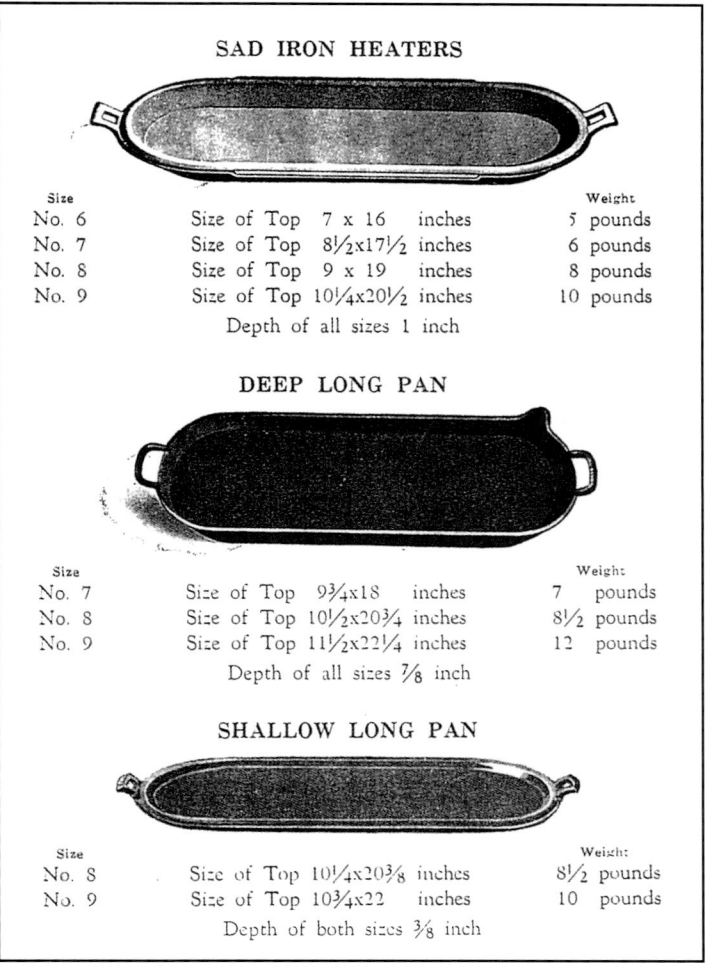

OLD STYLE GRIDDLE-Size: No.8, 9 5/8" dia.; **Markings:** (raised top of handle) 8, (bottom) 8; **Circa:** 1916-1930s; **VALUE: $30-$40; No.6, $50-$60; No.7, $30-$40; No.9, $40-$50; No.10, $45-$50**. The values are based on the raised 8 on the handle. This item was continued into the 1950s but without the raised 8 on the handle.

SAD IRON HEATER- Markings: unknown; **Circa:** 1915-1930s; **VALUE: No.6, $50-$75; No.7, $30-$40; No.8, $40-$50; No.9, $50-$60**.

DEEP LONG PAN- Markings: unknown; **Circa:** 1906-1930s; **VALUE: No.7, $30-$40; No.8, $40-$50; No.9, $45-$55**. This was in the line of the Blacklock Foundry.

SHALLOW LONG PAN- Markings: unknown; **Circa:** 1915-1930s; **VALUE: No.8, $10-$15; No.9, $15-$25**.

NEW STYLE GRIDDLE-Size: No.9, 11" dia.; **Markings:** (raised on handle) 9, (bottom) BELKNAP, 9 (raised molders mark); **Circa:** unknown; **VALUE: $25-$35**.

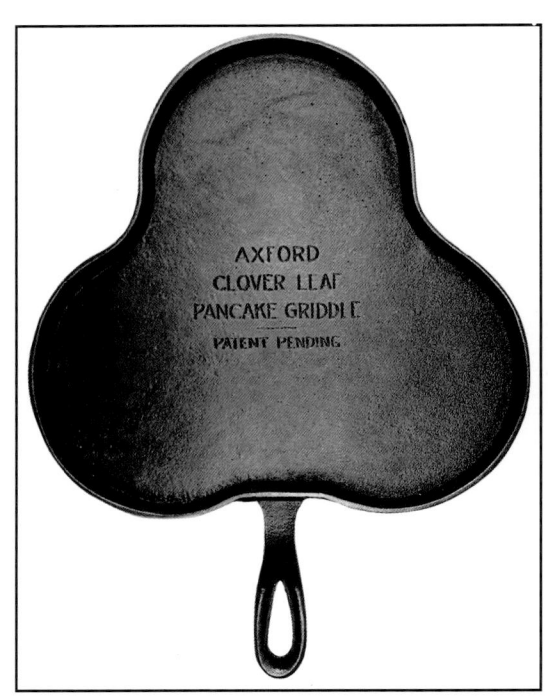

CLOVER LEAF GRIDDLE-Size: 11 1/2" w. x 15" l. including handle; **Markings:** AXFORD CLOVER LEAF PANCAKE GRID-DLE, PATENT PENDING; **Circa:** 1935; **VALUE: $150**.

BACON & EGG GRIDDLE-Size: 10/1/4" x 8 1/2" x 3/4"d; **Markings:** none; **Circa:** 1930s-1840s; **VALUE: $65-$80**.

DUTCH OVENS, OVAL ROASTERS & WAFFLE IRONS

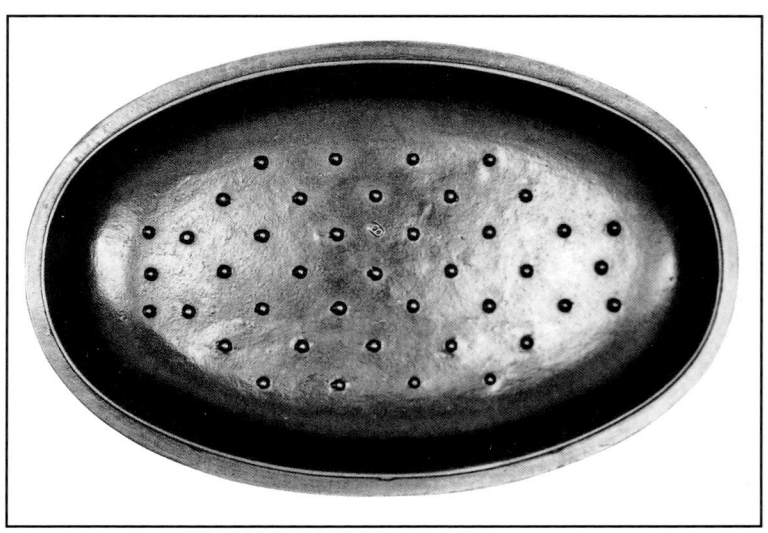

OVAL ROASTER-Size: No.4, 13 1/4" l. x 8 1/2" w. x 3 3/8" d.; **Markings:** none, (cover) B molders mark; **Circa:** 1930s-1940s; **VALUE: $125-$150; No.7, $150-$175; No.9, $175-$185**.

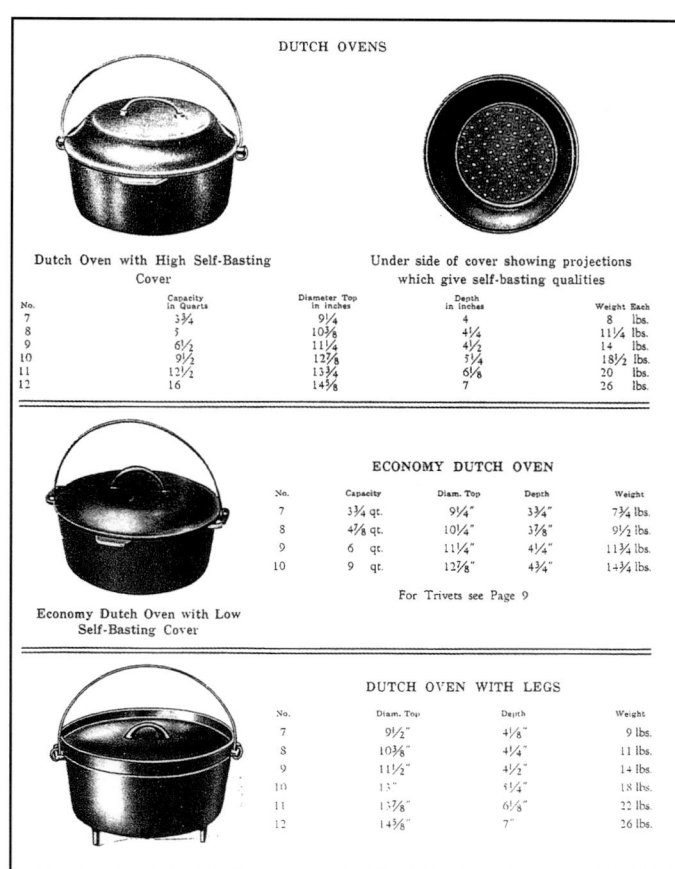

DUTCH OVENS

Dutch Oven with High Self-Basting Cover

Under side of cover showing projections which give self-basting qualities

No.	Capacity in Quarts	Diameter Top in inches	Depth in inches	Weight Each
7	3¾	9¼	4	8 lbs.
8	5	10⅜	4¼	11¼ lbs.
9	6½	11¼	4½	14 lbs.
10	9½	12⅞	5¼	18½ lbs.
11	12½	13¾	6⅛	20 lbs.
12	16	14⅝	7	26 lbs.

ECONOMY DUTCH OVEN

Economy Dutch Oven with Low Self-Basting Cover

No.	Capacity	Diam. Top	Depth	Weight
7	3¾ qt.	9¼"	3¾"	7¾ lbs.
8	4⅞ qt.	10¼"	3⅞"	9½ lbs.
9	6 qt.	11¼"	4¼"	11¾ lbs.
10	9 qt.	12⅞"	4¾"	14¾ lbs.

For Trivets see Page 9

DUTCH OVEN WITH LEGS

No.	Diam. Top	Depth	Weight
7	9½"	4⅛"	9 lbs.
8	10⅜"	4¼"	11 lbs.
9	11½"	4½"	14 lbs.
10	13"	5¼"	18 lbs.
11	13⅞"	6⅛"	22 lbs.
12	14⅝"	7"	26 lbs.

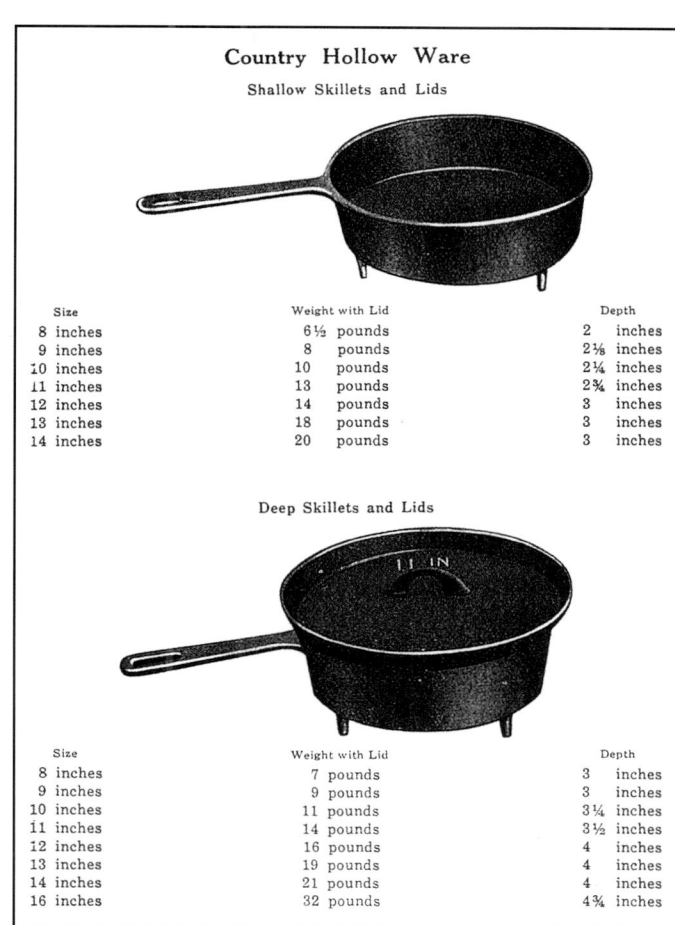

Country Hollow Ware
Shallow Skillets and Lids

Size	Weight with Lid	Depth
8 inches	6½ pounds	2 inches
9 inches	8 pounds	2⅛ inches
10 inches	10 pounds	2¼ inches
11 inches	13 pounds	2¾ inches
12 inches	14 pounds	3 inches
13 inches	18 pounds	3 inches
14 inches	20 pounds	3 inches

Deep Skillets and Lids

Size	Weight with Lid	Depth
8 inches	7 pounds	3 inches
9 inches	9 pounds	3 inches
10 inches	11 pounds	3¼ inches
11 inches	14 pounds	3½ inches
12 inches	16 pounds	4 inches
13 inches	19 pounds	4 inches
14 inches	21 pounds	4 inches
16 inches	32 pounds	4¾ inches

Above: **DUTCH OVEN WITH HIGH COVER**-Circa: 1920-1940s; **VALUE: No.7, $30-$35; No.8, $30-$35; No.9, $35-$40; No.10, $45-$60; No.11, $60-$70; No.12, $75-$85**.

ECONOMY DUTCH OVEN-Circa: 1925-present; **VALUE: No.7, $30-$35; No.8, $30-$35; No.9, $45-$50; No.10, $50-$60**. Values refer to Dutch ovens prior to 1960s which were polished.

DUTCH OVEN WITH LEGS (BAIL HANDLE)-Circa: 1915-present; **VALUE: No.7, $50; No.8, $50; No.9, $60; No.10, $70; No.11, $85; No.12, $175**.

Top right: **SHALLOW COUNTRY SKILLETS**-Markings: number on cover; Circa:1915-1940s; **VALUE: 8 IN, $20-$25; 9 IN, $25-$30; 10 IN, $30-$40; 11 IN, $40-$50; 12 IN, $50-$60; 13 IN, $75-$85; 14 IN, $100-$150**. Values based with covers.

DEEP COUNTRY SKILLETS-Markings: number on cover; Circa: 1915-1940s; **VALUE: 8 IN, $30-$40; 9 IN, $30-$45; 10 IN, $35-$45; 11 IN, $50-$60; 12 IN, $65-$85; 13 IN, $85-$100; 14 IN, $125-$155; 16 IN, $150-$200**.

Bottom right: **DEEP COUNTRY OVENS**-Size; Markings: number on cover; Circa: 1915-1940S; **VALUE: 8 IN, $45; 9 IN, $50; 10 IN, $60; 11 IN, $75; 12 IN, $75-$100; 13 IN, $100-$150; 14 IN, $150-$175; 16 IN, $200-$250**.

SHALLOW COUNTRY OVENS- Markings: number on cover; Circa: 1915-1940s; **VALUE: 8 IN, $40; 9 IN, $45; 10 IN, $55; 11 IN, $60; 12 IN, $60-$85; 13 IN, $85-$135; 14 IN, $135-$160**.

Country Hollow Ware
Deep Ovens and Lids

Size	Weight with Lid	Depth
8 inches	7 pounds	3 inches
9 inches	9 pounds	3 inches
10 inches	12 pounds	3¼ inches
11 inches	14 pounds	3½ inches
12 inches	17 pounds	4 inches
13 inches	19 pounds	4 inches
14 inches	23 pounds	4 inches
16 inches	30 pounds	4¾ inches

Shallow Ovens and Lids

Size	Weight with Lid	Depth
8 inches	7½ pounds	2 inches
9 inches	8½ pounds	2 inches
10 inches	11½ pounds	2¼ inches
11 inches	13 pounds	2⅞ inches
12 inches	14 pounds	3 inches
13 inches	18 pounds	3⅛ inches
14 inches	22 pounds	3⅝ inches

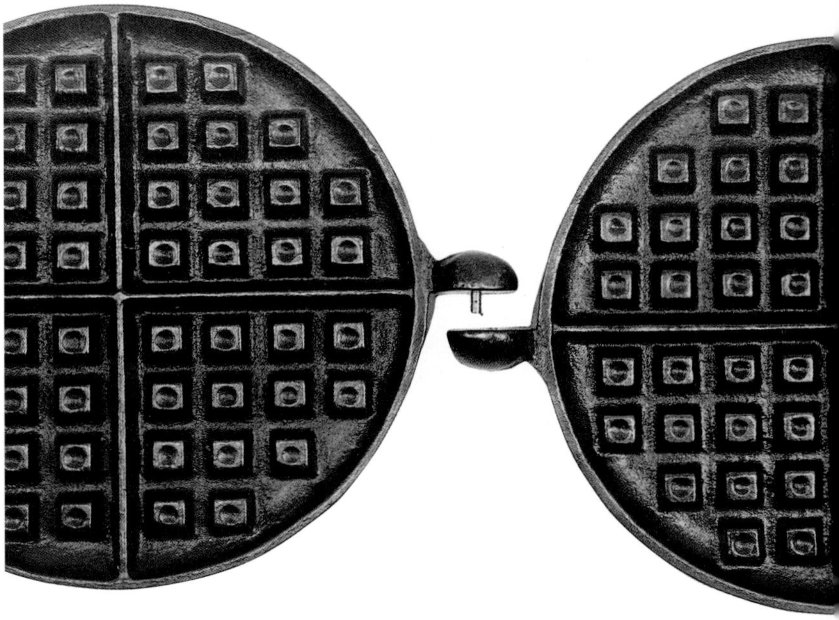

WAFFLE IRON-Size: No.8, (paddles) 7 3/8" dia.; **Markings:** LODGE, 8 (on both sides), B (under both handles), 8 (on base); **Circa:** 1920s-1940s; **VALUE:** $50-$65 No.7, $60-$75; No.9, $60-$75. Value $10 less with wire handles.

GEM PANS, MUFFIN PANS, CAKE MOLDS

No.18 GEM PAN-Size: 6 1/4" x 11 5/8"; **Markings:** none; **Circa:** 1915-1940s; **VALUE:** $45-$65. Commonly referred to as a Vienna roll pan.

No.20 MUFFIN PAN-Size: 11" x 13 7/8"; **Markings:** 20; **Circa:** 1916-1950; **VALUE:** $50-$60. This piece is commonly referred to as a Turks Head pan.

No.19 MUFFIN PAN-Size: 7 5/16" x 11 3/8"; **Markings:** 19; **Circa:** 1916-1950; **VALUE:** $30-$40.

No.19 Muffin Pan-Size: 7 5/16" x 11 3/8"; **Markings:** 19; **Circa:** unknown; **VALUE:** $45-$50. Center marking is unusual, and appears to be early.

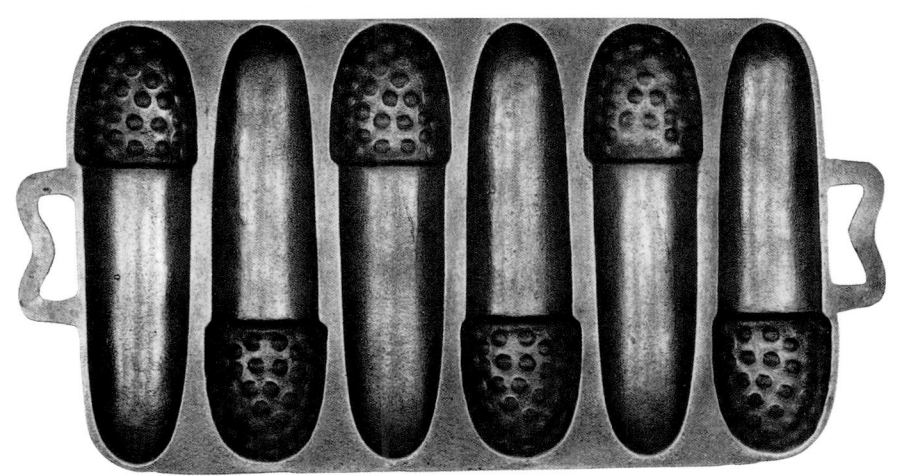

ACORN STICK PAN-Size: 6 1/2" x 11 7/8"; **Markings:** none; **Circa:** 1925-1940; **VALUE:** $200-$300. Design was patterned after a California Oak Acorn. Very smooth finish.

NO.29 MUFFIN PAN-Size: 6 1/8" x 11 7/8"; **Markings:** none; **Circa:** 1930s; **VALUE:** $35-$40. This piece is sometimes found marked CAHILL.s

NO TRUMP PAN-Size: 8 5/16" x 9 7/8"; **Markings:** D (raised molders mark); **Circa:** 1930s-1940s; **VALUE: $75-$100**. Very smooth finish. A later issue is slightly smaller and not polished, and is still in production.

CORN STICK PANS-Size: (left to right) 5 3/8" x 9", 5 1/2" x 12 1/2", 5 1/2" x 15 5/8"; **Markings:** none; **Circa:** 1935-1970s; **VALUE: $15-$25**. The seven section pan is still in the Lodge line.

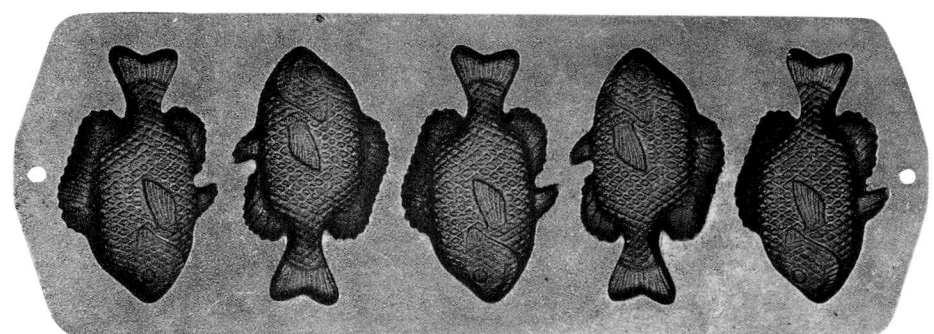

PERCH PAN-Size: 15 1/4" x 5 5/8"; **Markings:** LODGE, 5PP2; **Circa:** 1990s-present; **VALUE: $15-$20**.

CACTUS PAN-Size: 15 1/2" x 5 5/8"; **Markings:** LODGE, 5CP2; **Circa:** 1990s-present; **VALUE: $15-$20**.

MICKEY MUFFIN PAN-Size: 9 1/2" w. x 9 3/4" h. x 1 1/4" d.; **Markings:** DISNEY, USA; **Circa:** 1998-1999; **VALUE:** $30-$40. Limited production for Disney; number produced is unknown.

PINEAPPLE CAKE PAN-Size: 12 5/8" l. x 9 7/8" w. x 2" deep; **Markings:** LODGE, USA, 2P2; **Circa:** 1995-present; **VALUE:** $30-$35.

LAMB CAKE MOLD-Size: 6 3/4" h. x 10 1/4" h.; **Markings:** none; **Circa:** 1930s-1950s; **VALUE:** $150-$200. Smaller than Griswold or Wagner. Strong muscle features but no nose detail; round leveling supports.

KETTLES & TEA KETTLES

TEA KETTLES

With Wooden Handle on Bail
Painted Black
Pit Bottom or Flat Bottom

With Wire Cooled Handle
Not Painted, Tumbled Polished
Flat Bottom

\	Pit Bottom			Flat Bottom	
Size	Capacity	Weight	Size	Capacity	Weight
No. 7	4½ qt.	8½ lbs.	No. 7	5 qt.	8½ lbs.
No. 8	5 qt.	10 lbs.	No. 8	5½ qt.	10 lbs.
No. 9	7 qt.	12 lbs.	No. 9	7½ qt.	12 lbs.

TEA KETTLES-Markings: star on cover; **Circa:** 1915-1940s; **VALUE: Flat Bottom:** No.7, $40-$60; No.8, $60-$70; No.9, $65-$75; **Pit Bottom:** No.7, $30-$35; No.8, $45-$50; No.9, $45-$60.

SUGAR KETTLES-Markings: unknown; **Circa:** 1910-1940s; **VALUE:** No's. 8-10, $40-$60; No's. 15-25, $60-$100; No's. 30-40, $150-$250.

ENGLISH POTS- Markings: unknown; **Circa:** 1910-1940s; **VALUE:** No's. 1/2-2, $25-$35; No's. 3-6, $45-$60; No's. 8-15, $65-$80; No's. 18 & 20, $85-$100; No.25, $100-$150.

IRON HAM BOILERS-Markings: unknown; **Circa:** 1910-1940s; **VALUE:** No.6, $30-$40; No.7, $40-$50; No.8, $50-$60; No.9, $60-$75.

FLAT BOTTOM HAM BOILER WITH IRON COVER-Markings; **Circa:** 1920s-1930s; **VALUE:** $100-$120.

SUGAR KETTLES

Size	Weight	Diameter	Depth
No. 8	24 pounds	16¾ inches	10⅜ inches
No. 10	26 pounds	17¼ inches	10⅞ inches
No. 12	34 pounds	18⅜ inches	11¾ inches
No. 15	42 pounds	19⅜ inches	13⅛ inches
No. 20	50 pounds	20¾ inches	13½ inches
No. 25	70 pounds	23⅜ inches	14½ inches
No. 30	75 pounds	24½ inches	15¼ inches
No. 35	90 pounds	26⅛ inches	16½ inches
No. 40	100 pounds	27¾ inches	18⅛ inches

ENGLISH POTS

Size	Weight	Size	Weight
No. ½	4 pounds	No. 8	28 pounds
No. ¾	4 pounds	No. 10	31 pounds
No. 1	6 pounds	No. 12	35 pounds
No. 1½	7 pounds	No. 15	40 pounds
No. 2	9 pounds	No. 18	48 pounds
No. 3	11 pounds	No. 20	55 pounds
No. 4	14 pounds	No. 25	78 pounds
No. 6	23 pounds		

IRON HAM BOILERS

No.	Weight	Size Top in inches	Depth inches
6	13 lbs.	9¼x16	7¼
7	21 lbs.	10½x19	8½
8	25 lbs.	11½x21	9½
9	30 lbs.	13 x 23	10

FLAT BOTTOM HAM BOILER
With Cast Iron Cover

The cover is made in two parts so that it can be more easily handled.

Made in Size 8 Only

	Weight	Size of Top	Depth
No. 8	25 lbs.	11⅜"x21⅛"	8"

Weight of Cover, 9 Pounds

SAD IRONS

Irons

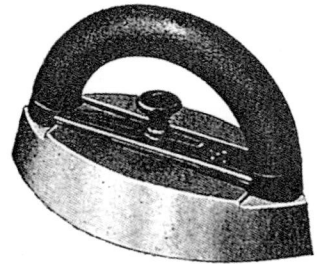

Mrs. Potts' Irons
Each Set consists of 3 Irons, 1 Handle and 1 Stand. Set No. 55 High Polish

MRS. POTTS SAD IRON-Markings: unknown; **Circa:** 1910-1930s; **VALUE: $15-$20 with handle**.

BLACKLOCK SAD IRON-Markings: BLACKLOCK; **Circa:** 1906-1930s; **VALUE: $10-$15**.

The Blacklock Sad Iron
Unsurpassed in style of finish and shape. Made in all weights from 4 to 9 pounds, inclusive. Finished in black japan or aluminum.

PRESSING IRONS-Markings: weight number; **Circa:** 1910-1920s; **VALUE: $20-$75**.

TAYLORS GOOSE-Markings: weight number; **Circa:** 1910-1920s; **VALUE: $20-$50**.

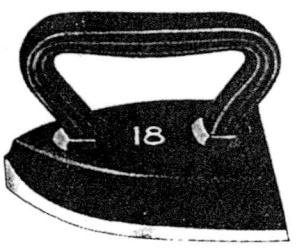

Pressing Irons
Made in even numbers from 10 to 26 pounds. Finished in black japan or aluminum.

Tailor's Goose
Made in Twelve Sizes, 10, 12, 13, 14, 15, 16, 18, 20, 21, 22, 24, and 26 pounds. Finished in black japan or aluminum.

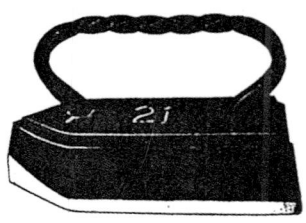

Sad Irons and Pressing Irons are 10 per cent light of marked weight. Tailor's Goose are made full weight.

MISCELLANEOUS

LUCKY DOG PAPER WEIGHT-
Size: 1 3/4" h.; **Markings:** none; **Circa:** 1990s; **VALUE: $35-$50**.

THE VOLLRATH MANUFACTURING CO.
Sheboygan, Wisconsin

Jacob Johann Vollrath
Sept. 19, 1824 - May 15, 1898

In the 1830s, in America, Wisconsin was still a territory, not a state. In Germany, a half a world away, Jacob J. Vollrath, age 19, was finishing his apprenticeship as an iron molder. Jacob Vollrath was born in Dorrebach, Germany in 1824. His father died when he was two years old and, his mother married Johann Meyer in 1828.

In the spring of 1844, after finishing his apprenticeship, Jacob Vollrath crossed the border into Belgium and secured passage aboard a British sailing vessel. He arrived in Albany, New York where he settled near his aunt and uncle, Susanna and Philip Weimer who had preceded him there. In 1846 he was followed by his mother, stepfather, and their three children. Plans were already in progress to move to Wisconsin via the Erie Canal, which had just opened to travel.

The two families settled in Rockfield, about 30 miles northwest of Milwaukee, however, Jacob returned to Milwaukee to find employment. There he met Elisabetha Fuchs, who had immigrated from Germany with her father in 1843. On May 2, 1847 they were married. In the spring of 1853, after starting several industrial partnerships, Jacob, his wife, and their three children moved to Sheboygan, Wisconsin.

More partnerships led Jacob to starting a business of manufacturing plows and cast iron kitchen ranges in 1861. Ten years later, John Michael Kohler married Jacob Vollrath's oldest daughter Lillie, and went to work for Jacob at his Union Steel & Foundry Factory. In 1873 Jacob Vollrath, with another task in mind, sold the well established Union Steel & Foundry factory to his son-in-law John Michael Kohler.

In those days, in Germany, porcelain enameling, pots, pans, pitchers, etc.; coating cast iron shapes with a fired-on ceramic glaze, was common. In the United States, however, such utensils were hard to come by. Jacob Vollrath was determined to bring the porcelain enamel process to the United States. His plan was simple. His 23 year old eldest son, Andrew, a knowledgeable foundry man who was fluent in German, was to be dispatched to Europe. Andrew's mission was to make himself an expert in porcelain enamel and to bring its secrets back to Sheboygan. By 1874 Jacob had constructed the new plant and set it up as the Sheboygan Cast Steel Company, an all purpose foundry for doing general foundry work while the porcelain enamel operation was being developed.

Andrew returned from Germany in 1874, and father and son tested the secret formula. They repeated the testing time after time without success and finally concluded that some vital part of the process had been overlooked. There was nothing to do but send Andrew back to Germany. When Andrew returned the second time,

Vollrath Factory Workers 884

in 1976, the process was theirs. The samples they produced were of excellent quality.

After making a few enameled cast iron utensils, Jacob went from one community to another selling his limited stock. Then he would make another supply and sell it. In the beginning, he operated what was practically a one man business. The enamel ware business flourished.

Because Vollrath enamel ware became so much in demand, it became evident that new facilities and greater production capacity was needed. In 1884, the company was reorganized and Jacob incorporated under the name of Jacob J. Vollrath Manufacturing Company with himself as President, son Andrew as Vice President, son Carl A. W. as Superintendent, and son-in-law John Riess as Secretary/treasurer. By the turn of the century, enamel ware formed of either cast iron or stamped steel made by Vollrath spread throughout the country and the factory had expanded to cover a whole city block. They introduced two lines of cast iron enamel ware; one named "X ware" which was black iron outside with a gray or pure white porcelain interior. This line included sizes 6 through 9; spiders (skillets), regular kettles and pots, tea kettles, long griddles and, handled griddles. This line also included Maslin kettles, sizes 2 through 24, Yankee bowls, sizes 1 through 6, Ham boilers, sizes 7 through 9, bailed griddles sizes 10 through 16, Basting pans, sizes 1 through 6, and Baking pans, sizes 1 & 2 which were gray porcelain inside and out (XX ware). They also introduced another line named "Imperial" Stove Hollow Ware which had a white porcelain interior and either blue or chocolate exterior. The exterior pattern was rippled, and very attractive. The items available in this finish included spiders, pots, regular kettles, lipped preserving kettles, and tea kettles, all sized in 6 through 9. Vollrath also introduced an iron cuspidor with a white interior and a speckled exterior, a Striped Cuspidor with white porcelain interior and brightly painted exterior, and an Octagon Cuspidor with similar finish.

Jacob J. Vollrath died on May 15, 1898, naming his wife Elisabetha as sole heir. Andrew Vollrath became President. Elisabetha Vollrath died in 1906. Because of the terms of Jacobs will, the business was divided into six equal parts, one to each of his children, and one to the children of his deceased daughter Lillie who died when she was 35. Exercising their rights of Jacobs will, the heirs bought out then President Andrew Vollrath. Carl A.W. Vollrath replaced Andrew as president. Andrew, now out of the company, established his own business in direct competition, called the Porcelain Enameling Association of America. The company name was changed to Polar Ware in 1923. This company remains a competitor today.

By 1912 the Jacob J. Vollrath Manufacturing Company name had been changed to the Vollrath Company, and had moved to a new plant. In addition to the familiar steel enamel ware of white, trimmed in red or black, and bisque, trimmed with green, vibrant colors of Apple green, tangerine, bisque and blue, blue and pink, yellow, and mandarin red were added to the Vollrath line. In 1932, decorated child's set consisting of a cup, plate, and bowl, in bisque with a choice of green, red or yellow trim was added. Decorations included an elephant ("Green Jumbo"), rabbit ("Red Bunny"), and duck ("Yellow Duckling"). Their cast iron porcelain line had been modified and a "New Idea" line was added. These pieces were white inside and a grayish blue outside. These pieces were produced in seven sizes of kettles, and three sizes of Dutch ovens. Ever planning for the future however, stainless steel items were being introduced into the product line.

Also during the 1930s and 1940s, a considerable line of ground-polished Cast iron cookware was being produced. It consisted of skillets, sizes 3-12 (minus No. 11), Dutch ovens, sizes 7-9, round griddles, long griddles, and a Chicken Fryer. Although the bottom was unmarked, the inside of the cover was marked with a bold, protruding VOLLRATH, which was apparently designed to act as basting points. The polished line also included a Deep Fat Fryer, Double Skillet, Waffle Iron, and Corn Stick Pans. The Vollrath marking was unique from other makers in that the marking was done from the side rather than from the handle. Some of these pieces were marked with only a number but the same characteristic held true. The number, usually underlined, was from the side. Vollrath skillets can also be identified by the underside of the handle which are recessed with a distinct reinforcement ridge down the center.

When World War Two arrived, Vollrath joined the war effort, converting production to the military. The company turned out immense quantities of mess-hall gear, hospital equipment, and more than 12 million G.I. Canteens.

During the 1950s, enamel was phased out, being replaced with stainless steel. The remaining cast iron production was phased out in the 1960s.

Vollrath's customer makeup has changed dramatically since Jacob Vollrath traveled from one community to another selling his enameled cookware. Vollrath still sells cookware and food service products today, but now sells its products globally. The firm now markets primarily to commercial customers, such as restaurants, hotels, schools, nursing homes and hospitals. Even in this modern era of technology, the Vollrath history remains alive, as collectors are now seeking the early goods of Jacob J. Vollrath.

This huge tea kettle was a familiar landmark that graced the southeast end of the Vollrath Company property from about 1927 to sometime after World War Two.

Built by pattern maker Henry Williams at Falls Machine Co. in Sheboygan Falls, Wisconsin, the 2,256 gallon capacity tea kettle was made of layers of wood placed one over the other, covered with canvas and many coats of paint. An impressive sight, it measured ten feet in diameter, was eight feet high to the top of the kettle (ten and a half feet to the top of the handle), and sported a cover five feet in diameter and two feet high. Prior to finding a permanent home atop its loft perch, the "Largest Tea Kettle in the World" won a blue ribbon at the 1904 Louisiana Purchase Exposition. It also appeared, pulled by a team of horses, in area parades for several years. In the 1940s the tea kettle was taken down. It was decided that since styles of tea kettles had changed from the version depicted, that the old display no longer represented Vollrath products adequately. The final destination of the tea kettle remains a mystery.

SKILLETS & GRIDDLES

REGULAR SKILLET-Size: No.5, 8 1/4" dia. x 1 3/4" d.; **Markings**: VOLLRATH WARE, 5, also 5 on top of the handle; **Circa**: 1920s-1940s; **VALUE: $15-$20**; No.3, $15-$20; No.4, $60-$75; No.6, $20-$25; No.7, $15-$20; No.8, $20-$25; No.9, $30-$40; No.10, $40-$50; No.11, $75-$100; No.12, $60-$75. The No.4, No.6, & No.11 were not listed by 1940. Vollrath skillet markings were unique in that they were positioned on the side. Also note the recessed design of the bottom of the handle.

REGULAR SKILLET-Size: No.5; **Markings**: 5, with sticker; **Circa**: 1950s-1960s; **VALUE: $35-$50**. Skillet is marked from the side; also notice sticker is applied from the side.

REGULAR SKILLET-Size: No.6; **Markings**: <u>6</u> (underlined); **Circa**: 1950s-1960s; **VALUE: $15**; No.3, $10; No.7, $15; No.8, $15-$20; No.9, $20-$25; No.10, $30-$40; No.12, $45-$55. The number underlined, sideways, is the most commonly seen mark for Vollrath.

REGULAR SKILLET-Size: No.8; **Markings**: -8; **Circa**: 1950s-1960s; **VALUE: $15-$20**. This marking is unusual because the dash is next to the number, rather than below it. A ghost of the Vollrath marking can be seen above the 8 on this skillet.

COLONY CHICKEN FRYER-Size: 11 dia. x 3 1/8" d.; **Markings**: 8 on top of handle, and bottom of skillet (cover) VOLLRATH WARE U.S.A.; **Circa**: 1940s; **VALUE: $60-$75**. This excellent quality skillet is popular with cooks and collectors alike. The raised letters inside the cover functions as drip rings.

REGULAR SKILLET-Size: No.7; **Markings**: 7; **Circa**: 1950s-1960s; **VALUE: $15-$20**. The number 7 with a dot under it instead of the underline is unusual. The 7 sideways and the unique hollowed handle design identify it as Vollrath.

ROUND GRIDDLE-Size: No.8, 9 3/4" dia.; **Markings**: 8, VOLLRATH WARE; **Circa**: 1930s-1950s; **VALUE: $35-$45; No.9, $35-$45; No.10, $45-$60**. The NO.10 was discontinued in the 1950s.

DUTCH OVENS & KETTLES

DUTCH OVEN-Size: No.45 (No.8), 4 3/4 qts, 10 3/4" dia. x 4 1/4" d.; **Markings**: 45, VOLLRATH WARE (both cover and bottom); **Circa**: 1930s-1950s; **VALUE: $65; No.35 (6), $85; No.65 (9), $65; No.85 (10), $75**. These sizes were also made porcelainized, blue gray exterior, white interior. Note off-set bail attachment.

DUTCH OVEN TRIVET-Size: No. 65 (9); **Markings**: 65; **Circa**: 1930s-1940s; **VALUE**: $25-$35, No.35, $50-$60; No.45, $25-$35; No.85, $50-$60.

MASLIN KETTLE-Size: 24 quarts, 16 1/4" dia. x 9 1/4" d.; **Markings**: 24 on top of handle; **Finish**: "X-Ware" (white enamel inside only); **Circa**: 1890-1920s; **VALUE**: $150-$175; No.2, $45-$50; No's.3,4,5,6,7, $25-$35; No's. 8, 10, 12, $45-$65; No's. 14, 16; $75-$85; No.20, $85-$120. Values based on porcelain being in excellent condition.

MASLIN KETTLE-Size: 4, 9 1/2" dia x 4 5/8" d.; **Markings**: 4, VOLLRATH WARE; **Circa**: 1920s-1930s; **VALUE**: $65-$85; No.6, $45-$65; No.8, $45-$65. Wire basket most likely not original to this kettle.

"IMPERIAL" KETTLE-Size; **Markings**: VMFG CO; **Circa**: 1900; **VALUE**: $95-$125. "Imperial" is the finish, and was available in either blue or chocolate.

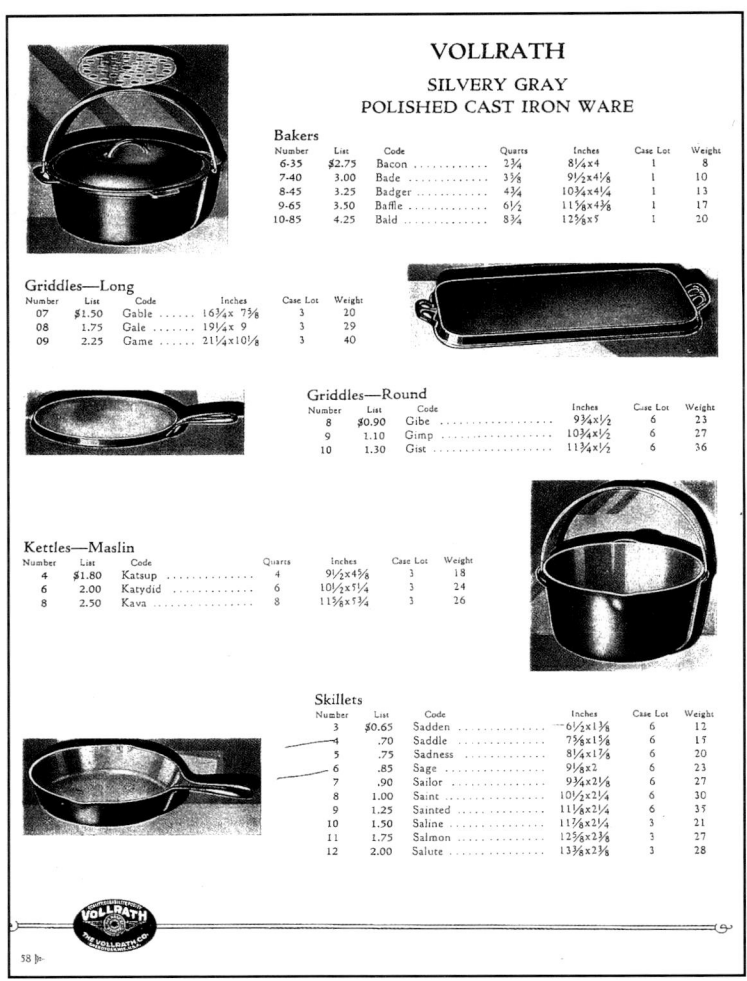

Page from a 1932 Catalog.

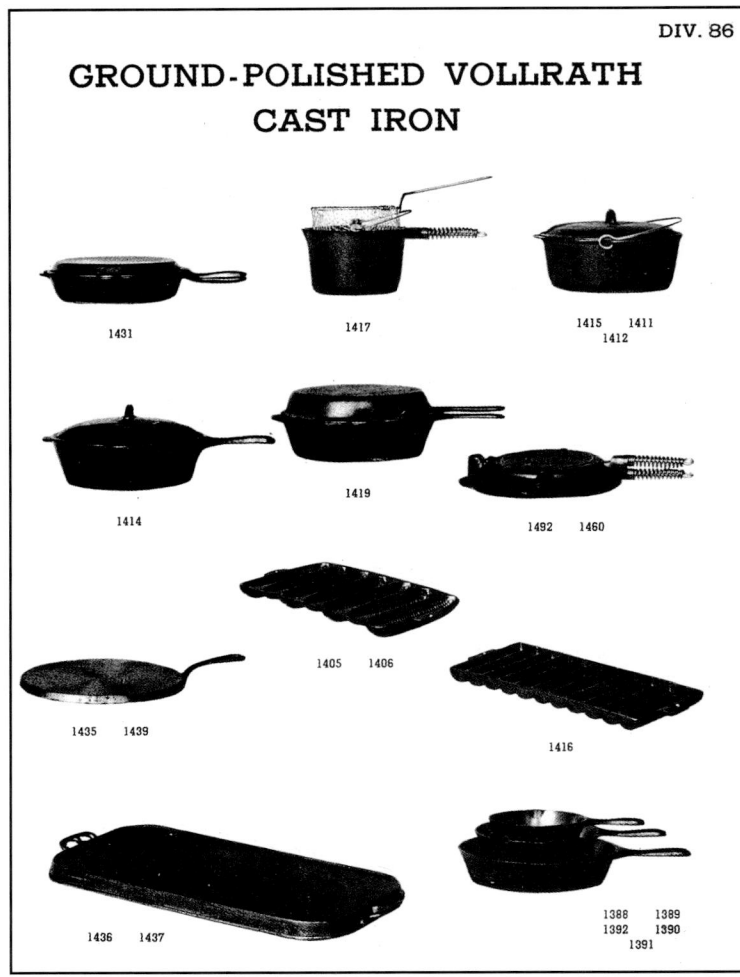

Product Flyer, circa: 1940s-1950s.

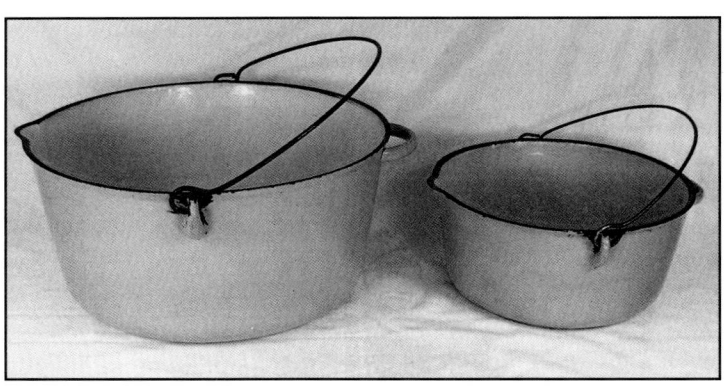

MASLIN KETTLES-Size: (left) No.8, 11 5/8" dia. x 5 1/2' d., (right) No.3, 8 5/8" dia; **Markings**: (left) 8, VOLLRATH WARE, (right) 3 (with gate mark); **Finish;** porcelain, light blue outside, white inside; **Circa**: 1910-1920s; **VALUE: $65-$75**.

THE EXCELSIOR MANUFACTURING CO.
G. F. FILLEY, PRESIDENT
St. Louis, Missouri

Collectors searching for information about the origin and maker of cast iron cookware marked "G.F. Filley" may be foiled if they pursue that marking alone. Typically, most hollow ware pieces were made by a stove company as accessories to their stoves. G.F. Filley pieces were manufactured by the Excelsior Stove Works and subsequently by Excelsior Manufacturing Company of St. Louis, Missouri, makers of the famous Charter Oak Cooking Stoves. The hollow ware was marked G.F. Filley after the president and founder Giles F. Filley.

Giles F. Filley was born, the son of Oliver and Annis (Humphrey) Filley, February 15, 1815 in Simsbury, near Hartford, Connecticut. His father was both a manufacturer and a farmer and belonged to a family whose existence in New England dated back to the landing of the "Mayflower." At the age of 19, after completing his schooling in New England, Giles Filley ventured to St. Louis, Missouri to join his older brother, Oliver, in his tin shop. Under his brothers supervision he learned the tinner's trade, and after completing his apprenticeship, became a partner in the business of manufacturing tin ware. In 1841 he sold his share in the tin business to his brother Oliver and opened a crockery store. The abundance of potters clay in Missouri attracted his attention and, believing that the manufacture of earthenware of a high grade might be profitable, he went to England in 1844 to investigate the different processes of manufacturing such wares. When he returned to St. Louis, he brought with him a number of skilled workmen, who

Giles F. Filley, 1815-1900

established, under his direction, a pottery plant. Filley Pottery is sought by collectors today. Also in 1844, Giles F. Filley married, in Hartford, Connecticut, Miss Maria M. Farrington, and nine sons were born of their union.

In 1849 Giles Filley sold out his crockery business and established what was long known as the Excelsior Stove Works for the manufacture of stoves and related accessories and products. Starting with a relatively small factory, employing about twenty molders and twenty men in other departments, these works were expanded

Sketch of the Excelsior Stove Works, c. 1858.

until several hundred men were employed and the factory encompassed two city blocks. It was here that Giles Filley invented and introduced the Charter Oak Cooking Stove. By the end of three years of operation they had finished 20,000 stoves. They had given the stove manufacturing center of the country, Albany, New York, it's fatal shock.

The Excelsior Stove Works was incorporated in 1865 as The Excelsior Manufacturing Company. In 1895 Giles F. Filley retired because of his age and the business was reorganized under the name of the Charter Oak Stove & Range Company; the name being prompted by the widespread fame of the Charter Oak cooking stove. Charter Oak stoves were manufactured until 1949.

While engaged in building a great manufacturing enterprise, Giles Filley also contributed in many other ways to the progress and prosperity of St. Louis, and to the development of the resources of his adopted city and state. He furnished the stone for the great Eads Bridge which spans the Mississippi River in St. Louis, and was one of the builders of the Kansas Pacific Railroad. In all things, he was a moving, active force in St. Louis for more than fifty years.

Although Giles Filley had no political interest, he found forceful convictions and expression in numerous ways on many occasions. He was an uncompromising opponent of human slavery, and was one of the organizers of the "Free Soil" or Liberty Party in Missouri in 1848. At that time he was one of the founders of the "Union" newspaper, which was succeeded by the "Dispatch" in which Mr. Filley was a stockholder, and this paper was in turn succeeded by the "Post Dispatch." Giles Filley was the staunch champion of President Lincoln's administration during the Civil War. During the War he was one of the most ardent Unionists in St. Louis, and one of the most able and most influential supporters of the efforts of the national administration to suppress the secession movement. He armed a company of his employees to assist General Lyon in the defense of the United States Arsenal, these troops being among the first in the whole country to be armed and equipped for the defense of the Union. Giles F. Filley died in the year 1900.

It appears from historical information about the Stove Works, that cast iron cookware was probably made shortly after establishing the Excelsior Stove Works in 1849. However, the earliest written record found in this writing was an invoice from The Excelsior Manufacturing Company dated 1867. Items on this invoice included: Tea kettles, No's. 1,2,3,&4, Biscuit Ovens with lids, No's. 1,2,3,4, & 5, Skillets with lids, odd lids, Sugar Kettles, Waffle Irons & "Waterman Bakers." It is interesting that the gem pans, later called Excelsior Gem Pans, were identified as "Waterman Bakers." Nathaniel Waterman of Boston, Massachusetts patented eleven styles of "Roll Pans" in 1859, setting the standard of designs for most manufacturers. G.F. Filley gem pans did not conform to those standard designs except for the number 5 which was the only pan in their series which did conform. The #3 Filley pan was, however, similar to the Waterman #7 in design, and the Filley #6 was a variation of the Waterman #8. Is it possible that the G.F. Filley unique designs had not been introduced in 1867, or was it that the company had simply not designated their line as "Excelsior" gem pans? It was probably the latter, however, only a catalog or advertisement can establish that fact.

It is the uniqueness of the Excelsior Gem Pans that makes them so interesting to collectors. They are a combination of unique design and finish, contrasting with quite grotesque casting marks, characteristic of early casting methods. Most gem pans have very crude "gate" marks on the bottom and a few have "sprue" marks which indicate an earlier casting method used up to the early 1800's. An exception to these often gross casting marks is the No. 7 which was cast from an "in gate," the molten iron entering the mold form the edge of the pan. This technique was used from about 1860 by large, more advanced manufacturers such as Griswold and Wagner. The No. 7 Filley is the nicest quality casting of all eleven Filley Gem Pans, Nos. 1 through 12. One exception to this progression however, is the No. 9. No number 9 was listed and apparently a No. 9 was never made; no one seems to know why. Also, a No. 15 is listed in the 1884 & 1885 catalog but not illustrated. Based on the price (about double compared to the others), it appears it must have been a commercial size.

The Excelsior Manufacturing Company produced an extensive line of cookware. An 1883 catalog lists: Hotel gridirons, forks, skimmers, sauce pans, fry pans (French style), hotel colanders, Chinese strainers, scoops, ladles, hotel beating bowl, and a Hotel Kneading Machine. It appears all but the grid iron and kneading machine were tin or steel.

The 1884 Catalog lists several other items of cast iron cookware such as: square cake griddles, waffle irons, English pots, cast tea kettles, deep (Dutch) ovens with lids, biscuit ovens with lids, skillets with lids, odd lids, and sugar kettles from 4 to 20 gallons. It lists separately "Excelsior Hollowware": pots, kettles, spiders, griddles, and "St. Louis Hollowware" which was apparently larger and unfinished. Also, most Excelsior skillets were marked only "G.F.F." An 1885 catalog illustrates small charcoal furnaces. Most Waffle Irons had the standard grid pattern, however, some had Giles F. Filley as part of the pattern. A 1909 Charter Oak Catalog lists smooth cast wash pots or sugar kettles, numbers 1 through 9, from six to thirty five gallons. It lists and illustrates only a No. 6 Gem Pan.

In addition to their regular line, Excelsior produced toy size tea kettles marked G.F. Filley. There is also a toy size skillet, pot, and griddle which are of similar design, and believed by some collectors to be Filley, but which are not marked. They do fit into the openings of the Excelsior/Filley toy stoves.

It is unfortunate that information about The Excelsior Manufacturing Companies hollow ware line is so difficult to find. That leaves many questions unanswered.

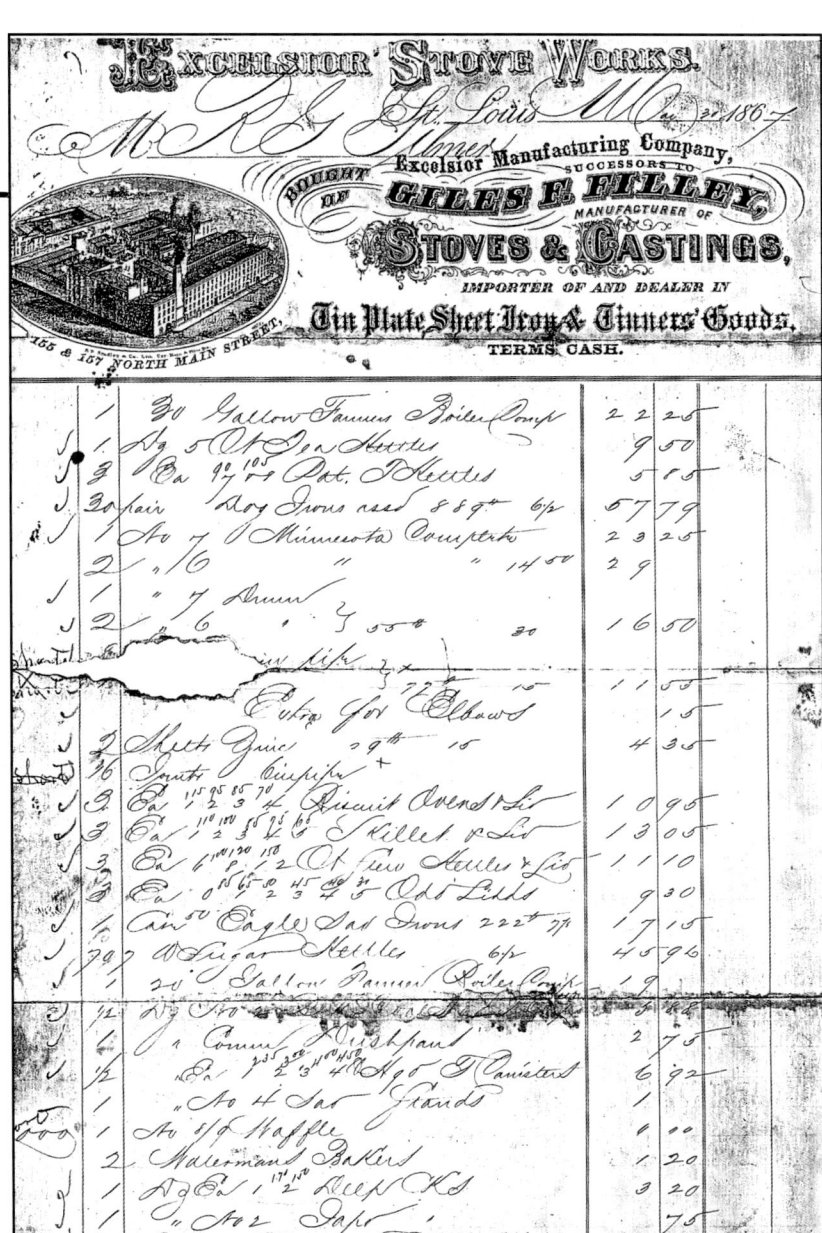

Excelsior Stove Works Invoice, c.1867. Notice Waterman Bakers fourth from the bottom.

GEM PANS

No.1 GEM PAN-Size: 13" x 6 5/8"; **Markings**: G.F. FILLEY, NO 1; **Circa**: 1865-1900; **VALUE: $325-$375**.

No.2 GEM PAN-Size: 12 3/8" x 7"; **Markings**: G.F.FILLEY, NO 2; **Circa**: 1865-1900; **VALUE: $300-$325**.

No.3 GEM PAN-Size: 11 3/4" x 7 3/4"; **Markings**: G.F. FILLEY, NO 3; **Circa**: 1865-1900; **VALUE: $100-$150**.

No.6 GEM PAN-Size: 12 1/2" x 6 1/2"; **Markings**: G.F. FILLEY, No 6; **Circa**: 1860-1906; **VALUE: $125-$150**.

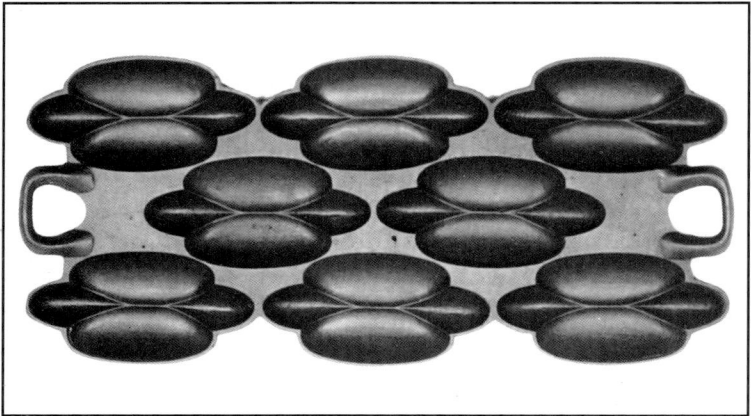

No.4 GEM PAN-Size: 14" x 6 1/2"; **Markings**: G.F.FILLEY, NO 4; **Circa**: 1865-1900; **VALUE: $250-$300**.

No.7 GEM PAN-Size: 12 1/2" x 6 3/8"; **Markings**: G.F. FILLEY, No.7; **Circa**: 1865-1900; **VALUE: $350-$400**. This pan has the finest finish of all the Filley gem pans. It is also very difficult to find.

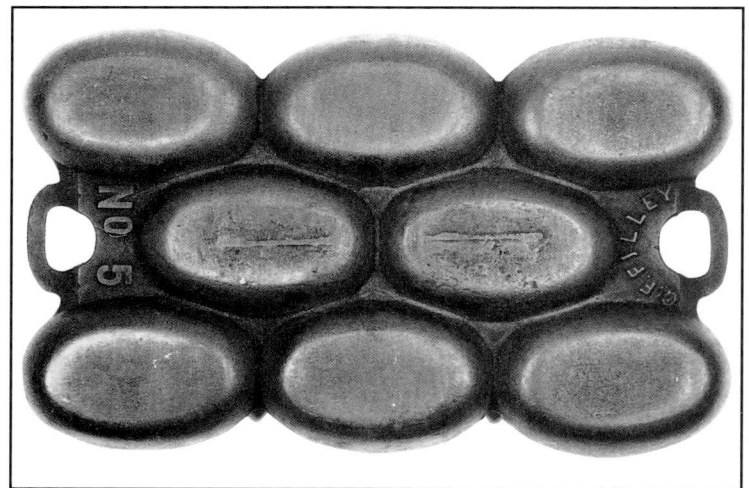

No.5 GEM PAN-Size: 11 1/2" x 7"; **Markings**: G.F. FILLEY, NO 5; **Circa**: 1865-1900; **VALUE: $100-$125**.

No.8 GEM PAN-Size: 13" x 6 1/8"; **Markings**: G.F. FILLEY, NO 8; **Circa**: 1865-1900; **VALUE: $200-$250**.

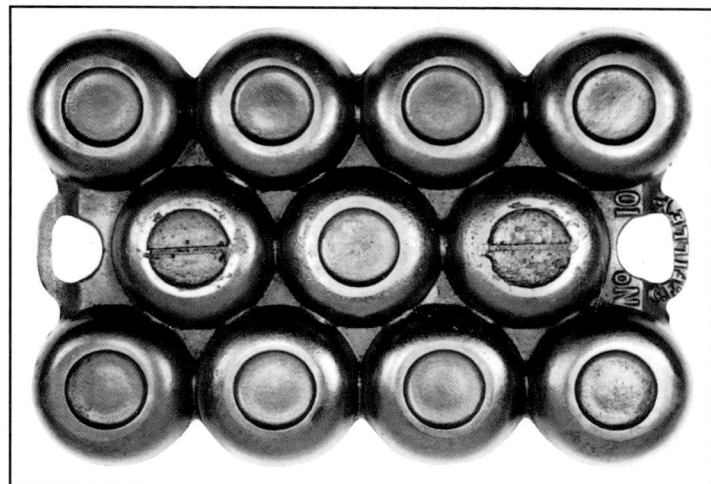

No.10 GEM PAN-Size: 12 3/8" x 8 1/2"; **Markings**: G.F. FILLEY, No 10; **Circa**: 1865-1900; **VALUE: $100-$150**.

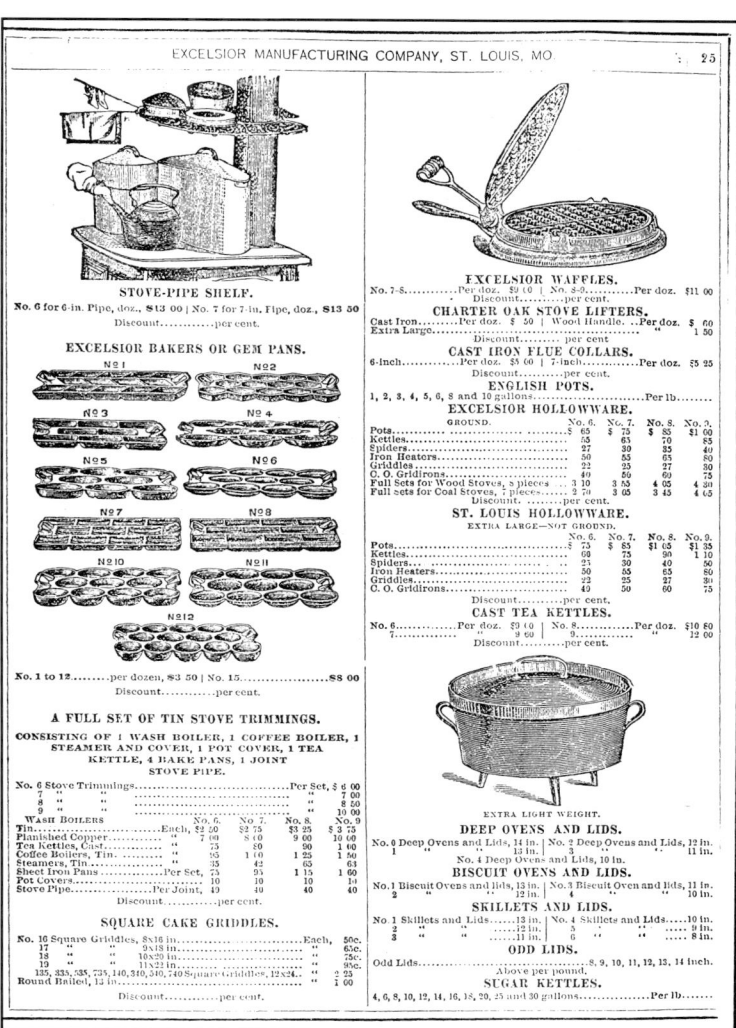

Page from 1884 catalog.

No.11 GEM PAN-Size: 12 1/4" x 8 1/2"; **Markings**: G.F. FILLEY, No 11; **Circa**: 1865-1900; **VALUE: $150-$200**.

No.12 GEM PAN-Size: 12 1/8" x 6 3/4"; **Markings**: G.F. FILLEY, NO 12; **Circa**: 1865-1900; **VALUE: $200-$225**.

SKILLETS

REGULAR SKILLET-Size: 9" dia. x 2" d.; **Markings**: G F F, ST LOUIS; **Circa**: 1850-1900; **VALUE: $60-$75**.

REGULAR SKILLET-Size: No.7, 9 5/8" dia x 2 1/4" d.; **Markings**: (raised) B, EXCELSIOR MFG CO, ST LOUIS MO; **Circa**: 1865-1900; **VALUE: $50-$60**.

SHALLOW SKILLET OR GRIDDLE-Size: No.7, 9 1/2" dia.; **Markings**: 7 (top of handle), EXCELSIOR MFG CO, ST LOUIS MO; **Circa**: 1865-1900; **VALUE: $60-$75**.

DUTCH OVENS

No.2 DUTCH OVEN-Size: 11 3/8" x 4 5/8"; **Markings**: (cover) G. F. FILLEY, 2, ST. LOUIS MO; **Circa**: 1850-1900; **VALUE: $100-$125**. Also made numbers 0, the largest at 14", No.1 & No.3.

No.3 DUTCH OVEN COVER-Size: 12" dia.; **Markings**: G. F. FILLEY, 3, ST. LOUIS MO'; **Circa**: 1850-1900; **VALUE: $25-$35**.

WAFFLE IRONS

WAFFLE IRON-Size: No.8 & 9; **Markings**: G. F. FILLEY, ST LOUIS, 8 & 9, (inside pattern) GILES F. FILLEY; **Circa**: unknown; **VALUE: $100-$125**.

STOVES

No.1 PARLOR STOVE-Size: 36" h. plus finial; **Markings**: NO 1, G.F.FILLEY, ST LOUIS; **Circa**: unknown; **VALUE: $1,000-$1,200**.

PARLOR HEATER-Size: 36: h. plus heat exchanger; **Markings**: INVINCIBLE NO. 5, G. F. FILLEY; **Circa**; **VALUE: $1,500-$1,800**.

STOVE TOP OVEN-Size: 17 3/4" h. x 13" w. x 19 1/2" l.; **Markings**: CHARTER OAK, (PLAQUE) CHARTER OAK OVEN, PATENTED BY GILES F. FILLEY, JAN 11, 1881; **Circa**: 1880s-1920; **VALUE: $**. The construction is tin. This oven sat on a kitchen range and was used for baking. It is frequently referred to as a Bolo oven.

TOYS

TOY TEA KETTLE-Size: 3 1/2" h. x 4" dia.; **Markings**: G.F. FILLEY, ST LOUIS; **Circa**: early 1900s; **VALUE: $200-$250**.

No.103 TOY STOVE-Size: 13 1/2" h. x 19 1/8" l. x 12" w.; **Markings**: CHARTER OAK, G. F. FILLEY, ST LOUIS, No 103; **Circa**; **VALUE: $2,500**.

BIBLIOGRAPHY

Blacklock Foundry, Catalog c. 1898
Cronan, Charles, *Florence Times Daily*, May 10, 1989
Cobum, Barry, *Florence Times Daily*, Feb. 24, 1989
Encyclopedia of the History of St. Louis, Hyde-Conrad, 1899
Excelsior Stove Works, Catalog c.1860
Excelsior Manufacturing Company, Catalog c.1883, Catalog c. 1884-85, Catalog c. 1885, Catalog c.1886-87, Charter Oaks Catalog, c. 1883
Franklin, Linda Campbell, *300 Years of Kitchen Collectibles* (4th edition), books Americana, 1997
Goulds St. Louis Directory, Leson-Gould Co., St. Louis, 1905
Griswold Manufacturing Company, Catalog No. 40, Catalog No. 45, Catalog No. 47, Catalog No. 49, Catalog No. 50, Catalog E-9, Catalog c.1890-91, Catalog c. 1899, Catalog c. 1901, Catalog c. 1905, Catalog c. 1942, Catalog c. 1945, Bulletin E-11, Bulletin E-39
Haussler, Jon, *Griswold Muffin Pans*, Schiffer Pub. Ltd., 1997
Hildebrand, et al, *Sheboygan County, 150 Years of Progress*, Windsor Publications Inc., 1988
History of Sheboygan County Wisconsin, S.J. Publishing Co., Chicago, 1912
Kelly, Martelia Cameron, *A History of South Pittsburg Tennessee, The First Hundred Years*, Hustler Printing Company Inc. 1973
Lodge, John, "The Story of Marion County," Marion Historical Society, Curtis Publishing Corp., 1990
Lodge Manufacturing Company, Catalog No. 4, Catalog No. 5, Catalog No. 7, Catalog No. 8, Catalog No. 9, Catalog c. 1935, Catalog c. 1940, Catalog c.1960
Martin Stove & Range Company, Catalog c. 1940, Catalog c. 1950
Stevens, Walter B., *St. Louis, the Fourth City 1764-1911*, S.J. Clarke Publishing Co., 1911
Sketchbook of St. Louis, Taylor & Crooks, c. 1858
Todsen, Thomas A., *Kettles 'n Cookware*, Vol. 3, No. 3, David G. Smith, 1994
The Vollrath Story, Celebrating 125 Years, n.p., 1999
The Vollrath Company, Catalog No. 58, Catalog c. 1900, Catalog, c. 1940
"Vollrath, Das Alte Geschlect," author unknown, n.p., c. 1980
Wagner Manufacturing Company, Catalog No.10, Catalog No. 20, Catalog No. 30, Catalog No. 48, Catalog No. 50, Catalog No. 58, Catalog c. 1894, Catalog, c. 1897, Hotel Ware Catalog, c. 1930
Webb, Nonie Hlobil, *Marion County Tennessee*, n.p., 1987

INDEX

For ease of use, this index is divided by manufacturer, in the order of their appearance in this book.

WAGNER

ABC Plate	90, 117
Ashtray	116
Bacon & Egg	25
Bacon Press	25
Banner	113
Bread Pans	84
Breakfast	25
Brochure	
see Paper	
Broiler Grid	111
Bun Warmer	100
Bundt Pan	84
Butter Dish	105
Butter Slicer	109
Calculator	114
Candy Tray	104
Carders	102, 103
Casseroles	98, 100
Catalog	
see Paper	
Chicken Fryer	
see Skillets, Deep	
see Bacon & Egg	
Childs Warm Plate	90, 117
Cigarette Lighter	112
Coffee Pot	67, 71
Corn Bread Pans	23, 83
Crep-ette	49
Cup	105
Custard Cup	101
Deep Fat Fryer	40
Dippers	96, 97
Display Stands	
Skillet	77
Skillet Cover	78
Dutch Oven	78
Utensil	78
Door, Boiler	112
Check	113
Double Mark	23
Dutch Oven	50, 51
Fat Free Fryer	48, 115
Flop Griddle	44
Fondue Pot	110
Fruit Press	110
Funnels	110
Gem Pans	
see Muffin Pans	
Gourmet Pan	
see Sauce Pans	
Glass Covers	34
Griddle	
Bail	46, 47
Fat Free	48
Flop	44
Handled	45, 46
Long	42, 43
Revolving	47, 48
Toy	88, 89
Wood handled	45
Heat Regulator	21, 111
Ice Cream	
Form	107
Spade	95
Jelly Cake Pan	85
Jelly Mold	106
Juice Extractors	109, 110
Juice Squeezer	110
Kettles	59, 61, 62, 88
Kook All	37, 63
Ladles	95-98, 111
Lamb Cake Mold	86
Lard Spade	98
Lid Lifter	112
Loaf Pan	84, 117
Long Pan	44
Mailbox	113
Magnalite	39-41, 52, 58, 70, 85, 102-104, 117
Measures	72, 73
Miniatures	
see Toys	
Molds	
Jelly	106
Patty	107
Ice Cream	107
Muffin Pans	79-84
National	15-17, 32
Nursery Sauce Pan	35
Omelet Pans	35
Oval Roaster	52-58
Pail	112
Paper	48, 66, 73, 117-119
Pattern	
Skillet	113
Bean Pot	115
Percolator	
see Coffee Pot	

Picnic Grill	108	
Pie Pan	85, 86, 104	
Pitcher		
also see Measures		
Platter	102-104	
Pot	59	
Press, Bacon	25	
Pressure Cooker	64	
Prison Pan	105	
Protective Plate	111	
Ramequins	101	
Rice Boiler	36	
Roll Pans		
see Muffin Pans		
Round Roaster		
see Dutch Oven		
Sad iron Heater	44, 111	
Sauce Pans	35, 37-41	
Scotch Bowl	60	
Shirred Egg	100	
Scoops	91-94	
Skillets		
Bacon & Egg	25	
Chef	22, 23	
Chicken Fryer	27	
Commemorative	27, 87	
Cornbread	23	
Deep	27, 28	
Double	29	
Grill	25	
Half	30	
Hotel	25	
Kitchen Kook-All	36	
National	15-17, 32	
Oven	20	
Regular	10-21, 116	
Shallow	30, 31	
Square	23, 24	
Toy	86	
Wood Handle	17-20, 27	
Frying Pan	19	
Wards	21	
Skillet Covers	18, 31-34	
Skillet Display Stand	77	
Skillet Cover Display Stand	7	
Slicer		
Butter	109	
Cheese	109	
Spoons	94, 95	
Steam Pressure Cooker	64	
Stove Lid Lifter	112	
Tea Kettles	65-67, 88, 89	
Tea Pots	70, 71	
Toy		
Griddles	88-90	
Skillets	86, 87, 90	
Set	89	
Kettle	88, 90	
Tea Kettle	88, 89	
Waffle Iron	90	
Tray		
Candy	104	
Round	104	
Triplicate Sauce Pans	41	
Trivets	52, 64, 112, 116	
Tumbler		
see Cup		
Vienna Roll	82	
Waffle Irons	73-76, 90	
Wardway		
Oval Roaster	57	
Wax Ladle	111	
Yankee Bowl	61	

GRISWOLD

Andressen	158
Aristocraft	138, 146, 151
Ashtrays	181
Best Made	143, 161
Brochure	
see Paper	
Casseroles	167, 168, 186
Chicken Pan	
see Skillets	
Choppers	170, 189
Cigar Trimmer	187
Coffee Pots	157
Coffee Roaster	182
Dampers	
see Stove Pipe	
Dutch Ovens	147-149, 186
Electric	161,162,174-176,189
Fakes	
see Reproductions	
Fluter	182
Gem Pans	
see Muffin Pans	
Good Health	143
Grease Receptacle	179
Grinders	
see Choppers	
Griddles	
Bail handle	141
Best Made	143
Electric	175
Good Health	143
Handle	141
Hot Plate	144
Long	145, 146
Merit	142
Puritan	145
Vapor	142
Wood Handle	142
Grill	146
Hammer	182
Heaters	171, 172
Hot Plates	
see Stoves	
Kettles	152-156, 157, 164
Krum Kake	159
Long Pan	188
Mailbox	183
Master Patterns	153, 188
Miniatures	
see Toys	
Muffin Pans	162, 163, 185
Nursery Hot Plate	173
Nursery Sauce Pan	139
Oval Roasters	149, 150
Paper	137, 152, 156, 171, 190-192
Patty Bowls	169
Percolator Plate	180
Pitchers	158
Plett Pan	144
Polishing Stars	182
Porcelain	184-186
Puritan	137, 145, 171
Quaker Ware	184, 185
Rarebit Dishes	166, 167
Reproductions	165, 189
Sad Iron	180, 181
Sauce Pans	138-140
Service Kettles	169
Scotch Bowl	153, 154, 189
Skillets	
Aristocraft	138
Breakfast	134, 185
Deep	135, 137, 138
Iron Mountain	134
Loth's	135
Odorless	132, 164
Merit	134
Milled Bottom	135
Regular	128-130, 134, 135, 184, 186
Shallow	133
Square	136, 185
Snack	136
Steel	132
Toy	165
Wood handle	130-132, 134
Skillet Covers	137
Skillet Divider	136
Skinner	153
Skillet Grill	179
Stars, polishing	182
Steak Platter	166
Stoves	171-174
Stove	
Pipe Installer	178
Pipe Dampers	176-178
Lid Lifters	179
Stove Ware Adjuster	180
Symbol Ware	151
Tamper	183
Tea Kettles	157
Thimble, Stove Pipe	176
Tray	166
Trivet	152, 155, 180, 181
Waffle Irons	158-162

Martin Stove & Range

Ashtrays	217
Bacon Fryers	209, 210
Bank	215
Dutch Ovens	212, 215, 217
Oven Covers	208, 212, 213
Oven Trivets	213
Gem Pans	214
Griddles	210, 211
Kettles	213
Knives	219
Sad Irons	217
Sauce Pan	207
Skillets	
Regular	203-206, 218
Deep	206
Double	206
Country	208
Shallow	209, 210
Skillet Covers	208, 209
Stoves	216
Lid Lifters	217
Cover Trivets	217
Toys	215

LODGE

Axford Broilers	225-227
Bacon & Egg	232
Country Ovens	233
Country Skillets	233
Dutch Oven	228
Griddles	231, 232
Ham boiler	238
Lamb Cake Mold	237
Kettles	238
Long Pans	231
Muffin Pans	234-237
Oval Roaster	232
Paper Weight	239
Sad Irons	239
Sad Iron Heater	231
Skillets	
Broiler	225, 226
Corn Bread	227
Deep	228, 229
Regular	222-224
Stir Fry	
Skillet Lids	229, 230
Tea Kettles	238
Waffle Iron	234

VOLLRATH CO.

Dutch Oven	244
Griddles	244
Kettles	245, 246
Skillets	243

EXCELSIOR MFG. CO.

Dutch Ovens	252, 253
Gem Pans	249-251
Skillets	252
Stoves	253
Waffle Irons	254
Toys	